William J Fay   235
#749

ISRAEL'S WISDOM
LITERATURE

ISRAEL'S WISDOM LITERATURE

Its Bearing on Theology
and the History of Religion

O. S. RANKIN

SCHOCKEN BOOKS • NEW YORK

First published 1936

First SCHOCKEN PAPERBACK edition 1969

By arrangement with T. & T. Clark, Edinburgh

Israel's Wisdom Literature forms part of the Kerr Lectures
delivered in Trinity College, Glasgow, 1933–36

Library of Congress Catalog Card No. 69–19260

Manufactured in the United States of America

TO

MY MOTHER

PREFACE

THE Wisdom literature of Israel is here treated from the point
of view of the influence it has had upon the growth and content
of theological and religious thought. The topics with which
the several chapters deal appear to the writer to be those which
are central to the teaching of the Wisdom-school, or which
emerge from that teaching, or which can be fully considered
only in the light of the contribution which that teaching made.

The study of the Wisdom literature may be described as
being of major importance, since in these writings can be traced
more clearly than in any other single line of study the development of theological and religious conceptions which Judaism
bequeathed to the Gospels and to later Christian thought.
Here also can be followed more closely than elsewhere those
cross-currents of thought within Judaism itself upon issues of
supreme consequence.

Appreciation of the Wisdom-writings cannot be said to be
general. This is in large part due to the circumstance that so
much of this literature lies outside the canon of the Old Testament. Also the character of those Wisdom-writings which lie
within the Old Testament is partly responsible. The several
collections of maxims contained in the Book of Proverbs must
seem, apart from one or two striking passages, to be mundane
and pedestrian in the eyes of the ordinary reader, and to the
teacher of religion they offer no suitable foundation for instruction. The Book of Ecclesiastes (Qoheleth) is one of the most
readable writings in the Old Testament, but, because of its
spirit of pessimism, pays the penalty of its own genius. On
the other hand, the Book of Job, on account of its narrative,
its prologue, its dialogue, its high poetic merit, its presentation

of a personal struggle of faith with the problem of suffering, occupies a position of splendid isolation. For this very reason, doubtless, the high merit of the other products of the Wisdom-school which reflect the progress of thought throughout succeeding generations has tended to be overlooked.

The debt which Judaism and Christianity owe to the Wisdom-school is extremely large. It was through the teachers of Wisdom that the ethical postulates and religious problems were clarified in the crucible of rational reflection. It was through them that deductions were drawn from the belief in God as Creator and world-Governor, His justice and holiness, in regard to divine providence, divine and human responsibility, the problem of evil, human nature and free-will. In the Christian Gospels the view of God's providence, His interest in the individual, the strain of religious pessimism in regard to the world and man's ambitions, the regard for the poor and humble (the trace of Ebionitism), the contrast of material and spiritual values and of the way of life and the way of death, the spirit of humanism and universalism, have the mark of the teaching of the Wisdom-school of thought.

From the prophets Judaism and Christianity inherited a purified and spiritual conception of deity, a zeal for social justice, an eschatological outlook and a belief in God as revealing Himself in history. It is a prophetic writing which presents that most poignant but attractive of all pictures of one who was " despised and rejected of men." The predictive element in the prophetic message, the heroic character of those who witnessed in God's name against the nation and its rulers, against their day and generation, make the prophet a more impressive figure than the teacher of Wisdom with his sober dialectic. But in the post-exilic period the voice of prophecy became feebler, and at length altogether ceased. Apocalyptic succeeds prophecy and brings to birth the doctrine of a future life. Political and religious expectations were fanned into flame through those visionaries who forecast a new age and

final events. Nevertheless, the Apocalyptist had little otherwise to add to what the prophets had given. There remained
the teacher of Wisdom whose ancestry in Israel, if Gressmann
and Humbert judge aright, is older than even the first of the
writing prophets.

The outstanding exponents of religious thought from the
beginning of the second century B.C. to the dawn of Christianity
are the Wisdom-teachers, chief among whom are Jesus the son
of Sirach and the author (or authors) of the Wisdom of Solomon.
Besides these and other writers of books, and perhaps more
influential in the aggregate, were those engaged in the study and
interpretation of the Law, whose ethical sentences were afterwards collected in the " Sayings of the Fathers." In the time
of Sirach, Wisdom in a mystical manner had become identified
with the Law, and apparently as early as the second century
B.C. at least certain teachers of the Law had received the name
of the Wise.

In addition to the literary features which have led to the
writings called Wisdom literature being grouped under that
name as a class by themselves, there are certain characteristics
which justify the use of the expression Wisdom-school of
teachers. Though interest in morality and religion is common
to prophetic, apocalyptic, and other forms of composition,
there is in the Wisdom writings a quite distinctive quality of
mind, method, and outlook in respect of ethics and religious
belief. Here we see growing stronger and more apparent as
time advances a searching for first principles, the application
of these principles, a wrestling with the problems of faith, a
criticism applied to the subjects of character and conduct, an
observation of human nature, even an analysis of human nature,
the atmosphere of discussion, the reliance upon reason along
with the recognition of reason's limits. Here was prepared that
deeper approach to the subject of ethics and religion which we
observe in the Sermon on the Mount.

Jesus affirmed that He came not to destroy the Law but

to fulfil it. He claimed that He was fulfilling the prophetic ideal. In New Testament theology He is represented as performing the office of priest. In the Gospels there is an apocalyptic element. Cardinal to the preaching of the Early Church were His death and resurrection. But that upon which all estimates of His work and Person found, or from which they proceed, is the realization that " it is not as a mere factor that He is connected with the Gospel " (Harnack), and that it was a Gospel— namely, teaching—which He brought. In the Synoptic Gospels no sentence characterizes so well this dual aspect, the Teacher and His teaching, as that which describes Jesus as saying : " Come unto me, all ye that labour and are heavy laden, and I will give you rest. Take my yoke upon you, and learn of me ; for I am meek and lowly of heart : and ye shall find rest unto your souls. For my yoke is easy, and my burden is light " (St. Matt. 11^{28}). The consideration of what was " new " in the teaching of Jesus is within the scope of the subject-matter of this book. Sufficient here to say that the sentence of St. Matthew, whether it be an authentic utterance of Jesus or not, is supremely relevant to the question. There was a new element in Jesus' teaching. It is, however, of the greatest significance, in light of the important concepts which the Gospel inherited from the Wisdom-school, that the sentence which so distinctively characterizes His message is an adaptation and transformation of words of the Wisdom-teacher, Jesus ben Sirach (51$^{23.\ 26}$), who invites the unlearned to bear the burden and yoke of divine Wisdom.

Nor is it accidental that in the formation of the Christological doctrine of the Church the influence of the Wisdom-school continued. Already, in St. Matthew's Gospel, Jesus is regarded as the divine Wisdom in person (J. Weiss, *Schr. d. N.T.*, p. 375). At length in the Fourth Gospel, in the homilies of which some of the deeper notes of Wisdom-teaching may be heard, the theme of the prologue, the doctrine of the divine Word (Logos) by whom all things were made, moves boldly in the stream of thought which descended from Jewish speculation regarding pre-existent personified Wisdom. The appearance of this figure of Wisdom in Judaism thus presents a subject of inquiry which is of great interest and importance to the history of religion.

As visiting lecturer in the College of the United Church of Canada in Montreal, in the winter of 1931, the present writer gave a course of studies in the Wisdom literature ; and as Kerr lecturer, 1933–1936, delivered, in Trinity College, Glasgow, the content of most of the chapters which follow. He is thus glad to believe that, for some, this work will have an additional personal interest.

My thanks are due to my sister, Dr. Mary Theresa Rankin, and to Dr. W. W. D. Gardiner for their kindness in reading over the proofs.

The reader's attention is directed to the list of the Wisdom-books which appears in the first note at the foot of the first page.

O. S. R.

MANSE OF SORBIE,
WIGTOWNSHIRE, 31st *January* 1936.

CONTENTS

CHAPTER I

THE WISDOM LITERATURE, THE DOCUMENTS OF HEBREW HUMANISM. GOD AS CREATOR AND THE EMERGENT PROBLEMS

CHAPTER II

THE IDEAS OF INDIVIDUAL RESPONSIBILITY AND OF REWARD AND RETRIBUTION IN THE OLD TESTAMENT

xiv CONTENTS

CHAPTER III

THEORIES OF REWARD AND RETRIBUTION IN THE OLD TESTAMENT AND IN LATER JUDAISM

CHAPTER IV

THE DEVELOPMENT OF THE DEUTERONOMIST THEORY IN LATER JUDAISM

CHAPTER V

THE BELIEF IN A FUTURE LIFE—ITS GROWTH AND DEVELOPMENT
IN ISRAEL

CHAPTER VI

THE BELIEF IN A FUTURE LIFE—THE QUESTION OF ITS APPEARANCE
IN JOB AND THE "JOB-PSALMS" (PS. 73 and 49)

CHAPTER VII

AN INQUIRY INTO THE REASON OF THE LATENESS OF THE
DEVELOPMENT IN ISRAEL OF A BELIEF IN A FUTURE LIFE.
(RESISTANCE TO THE IDEA IN PRE-EXILIC ISRAEL)

ISRAEL'S
WISDOM LITERATURE

CHAPTER I

The Wisdom Literature,[1] The Documents of Hebrew Humanism.
God as Creator and the Emergent Problems

HUMANISM is a term that may be applied to a philosophy that is based upon the principle of Protagoras, that "Man is the measure of all things." It may also be applied to a scheme of thought, such as that of J. M. E. McTaggart, which, affirming the absolute worth of the human personality as immortal *in its own right*, and concluding that it is improbable that there should be two absolutes—Man and God—denies the existence of God. With these two types of humanism, Hebrew thought offers perhaps the deepest possible contrast—a contrast which may provide a

---

[1] *The Wisdom literature consists of* the Book of Proverbs, originally separate collections of maxims of various dates (cf. references below, *The Introductions to the Old Testament*, Oesterley's *Commentary on Proverbs*, Gressmann, *Z.A.W.*, 1924, p. 286 f., etc.); the Book of Job (*c.* 450 B.C.); Qoheleth, *i.e.* Ecclesiastes (250–200 B.C.); the Wisdom Psalms (1, 19b., 32[8-11], 34[12-23], 37, 49, 73, 94[8f.], 111, 112, 119, 127, 128, 133); the Wisdom of Jesus Sirach (200–*c.* 180 B.C.); the Book of Tobit (*c.* 170 B.C.) in 4[13f.], 12[6-11], 14[9f.]; 1 Esdras, 3[1]–4[63] (*c.* 100 B.C.); The Letter of Aristeas, paras. 187–294 (*c.* 40 B.C.); The Wisdom of Solomon (*c.* 30 B.C.); 4 Maccabees (*c.* A.D. 30); The Book of Baruch, 3[9]–4[4] (after A.D. 70); Pirqe Aboth (Sayings of the Fathers, from 150 B.C. to A.D. 250); the didactic poem of 250 hexameters of Pseudo-Phocylides (150 B.C.–A.D. 70).

Whether the maxims of Menander that are extant in Syriac (Land : Anecdota Syriaca I. 1862, p. 64 f.) belong to the Jewish Wisdom literature

caveat against a too light appreciation of the Old Testament and Judaism which are the historical background and source of the religious values of Christian belief with which those positions conflict. Characteristic of Hebrew thought, arrived at the stage of explicit monotheism, is the belief that man is created by God after His image and likeness (P. Gen. 1[26f.], 5[1], 9[6]). As the estimate of human personality rises in course of time to the idea of immortality, it is still from God that man derives all he is or will be. Characteristic, too, is the notion that God's command, word and will is the only standard of truth and right. Dr. J. Baillie, in arguing against modern humanistic tendencies, says that Christianity, " while attributing true being and immortality to the souls of men no less than to God, insists at the same time that the being of man is a *derived* being and immortality—the being and immortality of a creature rather than that of a creator." [1] Now, if Christianity appears bound to this position, it is as clear that the historical and religious factors which have so conditioned Christian thought upon the nature and relationship of God and man are those which connect it with its antecedents in Judaism.

(cf. Fichtner, below; Hempel, *Althebräische Literatur*, p. 49; Schulthess, *Z.A.W.*, 1912, p. 199 f.) as Falkenberg (*Z.A.W.*, 1895, p. 226 f.) supposed, is doubtful.

The story (and maxims) of Ahikar, which has a place in Charles's *Pseudepigrapha of the Old Testament*, is an Assyro-Babylonian wisdom-book extant only in secondary versions. The oldest of these is the imperfectly preserved Aramaic fragment of the fifth century B.C. found among the ruins of Elephantiné, the home of a Jewish military colony, in Egypt cf. Cowley, *Aramaic Papyri of the Fifth Century B.C.*; Gressmann, *North Semitic Texts* in *Altorientalische Texte zum A.T.*, p. 454 f. For the wide influence of Ahikar on Hebrew literature see Charles (*Pseudepigrapha of the Old Testament*, Intro. to Ahikar), and Oesterley (Proverbs, *op. cit.*).

In regard to the dates, contents, etc., of the wisdom-writings, see in particular the editions of the Apocrypha and Pseudepigrapha by Kautzsch (German) and Charles, and *Die altorientalische Weisheit in ihrer israelitisch-jüdischen Ausprägung*, 1933, p. 7 f., by Johannes Fichtner.

---

[1] *And The Life Everlasting*, p. 276 f.

The Wisdom literature may be called the documents of Israel's humanism, not in the sense of a rejection of the supernatural, or even as intending a concern chiefly with man's welfare, but because its general characteristic is the recognition of man's moral responsibility, his religious individuality and of God's interest in the individual life. What Professor F. James says of the maxims of the Book of Proverbs,[1] namely, that the interest here is in the ordinary individual, is true of all the wisdom-writings. Even when Wisdom becomes the subject of theological reflection akin to that upon the Word or *Logos* in Christian dogma, and is personified as an intermediary being between God and the world, her function is to attract and appeal to men (cf. Pr. 8[4f.]). In one hymn Wisdom declares :

When He (God) set the heavens up, I was there: . . .
When He laid the foundations of the earth,
I was with Him then: . . .
Playing here and there over His world,
Finding my delight in humankind (Prov. 8 [27. 29. 30. 31], Moffatt's trans.).

Because the interest of the Wisdom books is of this nature, they yield not merely a vast body of moral teaching but complete the foundation of thought upon which a theology could be built. If the authors, with certain exceptions, as compared with the prophets of the eighth and seventh centuries and with second Isaiah, appear to have lost the gift and fire of genius, they do not represent a period of religious decadence.   They are not Israel's lesser men. They are the rationalists of Hebrew thought and religion. With the decline of prophecy and the rise of Apocalyptic, the wisdom-schools preserved the sound sense and soul of Judaism. They deepened its thought upon man and God. For the prophets, apart from the implications of their social message, it was the community which counted, and counted only in so far as it obeyed Jahve's will.   For the Lawgivers, even when the personal " thou shalt " or " thou shalt not " is subject of the divine

[1] " Some Aspects of the Religion of Proverbs," *Journal of Bib. Lit.*, vol. li, part i., 1932.

commandment, it is primarily the community [1] which is exhorted
to obedience. But " the wise " took into account the individual's
peace, welfare and happiness in the family and in the community.
They study particularly all the great human motives of conduct—
gratitude, friendship, love, hate, wealth, reputation. Wisdom
is the ability to assess truly the values of life. It is in the
Wisdom literature where reflection is made upon the chief good
(cf. Arist. 195, Ps. 73[25]) ; upon man in relation to the universe
(Job 38 f.) ; upon the possibility of religious faith over against
the circumstances, facts, and experiences of life ; upon the higher
and lower nature of man (4 Macc.) ; upon the problem of evil
and the subject of the divine providence. Here, too, the idea of
a future life is seen in the toils of Hebrew orthodox belief and
opposition (Qoh. Sir), and at length reaching development through
contact with Greek thought (Sap. Sol., 4 Macc.). When we
have considered the humanism of the wisdom-writers in light of
the evidence of their contact with, and enrichment from, the
Wisdom literature of the surrounding peoples, it is our purpose
to show the importance of Israel's humanism in the history of
religious thought in its development of the implications of the
idea of God as Creator and in its treatment of the emergent
problems of evil and the scope of the divine providence.

Light has been cast upon the origin of what we have described
as the humanism of Israel's Wisdom literature by those scholars
who have compared this literature in its forms and content with
the wisdom-writings of Babylonia and Egypt. The Assyro-
Babylonian Book of Ahikar,[2] a story of benevolence and in-

---

[1] Even in the fifth commandment (Honour thy father and thy mother),
the promise is made as context shows to the people as a whole. Cf. Lorenz
Dürr, *Die Wertung des Lebens im Alten Testament*, etc.   *Ein Beitrag zur
Erklärung des Segens des Vierten* [*i.e.* our fifth] *Gebotes*, 1926, p. 22 f.

[2] Cf. Bruno Meissner, *Babylonien und Assyrien*, vol. ii. (1920), p. 430.
" The story of the wise Ahikar with its accompanying maxims, which is known
to us from the Aramaic Papyrus of the 5th cent. B.C., must originally have
arisen in Assyria, since all the persons mentioned in it have Assyrian names
and the whole milieu is Assyrian. Besides, a by no means small portion of the
maxims is represented in the cuneiform literature." The *bon mot* of the

gratitude, was known to the Jews in Elephantiné in Egypt who possessed it in an Aramaic version. The story is referred to in the Book of Tobit (cf. 14[10]), and this book, Proverbs (especially 23[12f.]) and Sirach all show that the maxims of Ahikar had currency in Israel.[1] In Babylonia, as in Israel, the suffering of the pious was a religious problem that set the question how one " whose thought was entreaty and prayer, and whose delight was the day of the worship of God could seem as if he had not called upon his God ? " (I.V.R., 10 B 12 f.) ; and the Wisdom literature of Babylonia developed the same pessimism in regard to justice and the meaning of life as we find in the Book of Ecclesiastes.[2] It is extremely unlikely in view of the contact of Israel with Assyria and Babylonia that the story of Ahikar represents the only debt Israel owes to the apparently much older Assyro-Babylonian wisdom-writings.[3] But the Old Testament itself is not remiss in acknowledging some dependence upon non-Hebrew sources. We are informed that the two small collections of maxims that conclude the Book of Proverbs contain " the sayings of Agur, the son of Jakeh, from Massa " (30 [1f.]) and " the sayings of Lemuel, the king of Massa " (31[1f.]). These are probably of North Arabian authorship. But it is the first Book of Kings

Babylonian letter-writer : " When the dog came to the potter's furnace it barked at the potter," becomes intelligible when we read in the Aramaic Papyrus of Ahikar : " My son, you have been to me like the dog which came to warm itself at the potters' furnace, and after it had warmed itself rose up and barked at them." Cf. Meissner, p. 423.

[1] With Tob. 4[17], cf. Ahik. Syr. 2[10] ; with Sir. 22[14f.], cf. Ahik. Syr. 2[45] ; Ahik. Syr. 2[65], Sir. 4[26], etc. For Prov., cf. Oesterley, op. cit. Gressmann, Z.A.W., 1924, op. cit.

[2] For the pessimism of Bab. Wisdom literature, cf. Ebeling " Berliner Beiträge zur Keilschriftforschung " (B.B.K., i. i. 14, 232 f.). " The heart of God is as the centre /of the heavens, far removed . . . man thinks highly of the word of him who is of high position /who has learned to murder man humbles the weak /who has no sin . . . man gives the fullness of precious metal to him /whose name is " robber," man empties of his gains /him whose sustenance is scant."

[3] As comparatively little of the Babylonian Wisdom literature has been discovered, a just estimate of its influence upon Israel cannot be made. Cf. Oesterley, op. cit. p. xxxvi.

which gives us an indication where, in all probability, the chief
non-Hebrew sources of wisdom from which Israel drew are to
be sought. There (4³⁰) it is said that " the wisdom of Solomon
surpassed the wisdom of all the Orientals (sons of the East—
Moffatt, " *Arabs* ") and all the wisdom of Egypt." The mention
of Egypt here, as distinguished from all the other anonymous
Orientals, is at least striking. Here, in Egypt, the kings were
the actual or reputed authors [1] of didactic works, and such works,
ordinarily composed by the scribes or court functionaries, had
as their purpose the moral and literary training of the youth
who aspired to official positions. In Israel, as we may judge
from Jeremiah's words (8⁹), the " wise " who, in the eighth and
seventh centuries B.C., represent, like the prophet and priest
(Isa. 29¹⁴ ; Jer. 8⁸, 18¹⁸), a definite class, appear to have evolved
from the office of writers or scribes who, since the beginning of
the kingdom, were charged with correspondence, the archives
and, we may assume, the training of pupils in the scribes'
vocation. The intimation of the first Book of Kings in regard to
Solomon as a wisdom-writer, and the close connection of this
monarch's court with Egypt, suggest that it was in Solomon's
reign (972–932), with its establishment of a State properly so-
called, that wisdom-writing in Israel had its beginning, and that
the ancient Egyptian pedagogical literature supplied not only
its incentive but in some degree its models.

The assumption that Egypt influenced Hebrew gnomic
teaching is borne out by the discovery made by Professor
Erman that a considerable section of the Book of Proverbs
(namely 22¹⁷–23¹¹) is a free translation and careful adaptation

---

[1] Amenemhet I. is the reputed author of the " Teachings " for his son
Sesostris I. ; the teaching for Meri-ka-re is also composed by a royal father
for his son and successor. The maxims of the Papyrus Insinger (1 cent. A.D.) are
entitled " Book of the King." With this compare the Hebrew practice. The
collection of maxims in Prov. 1¹ᶠ· and 10¹ᶠ· are attributed to Solomon (cf. 25¹).
Qoheleth (Eccles. 1¹·¹²) adopts the same traditional device. The maxims,
Prov. 31¹ᶠ·, purport to be from Lemuel, a king of Massa. In Sap. Sol. this
literary fiction still holds.

of the Egyptian book, the Wisdom of Amen-em-ope.[1] If we may judge from the verse, " Seest thou a man skilled in his business ? he shall stand before kings " (Prov. 22[29])—a reference to the ideal scribe and his fitness for court appointment—the Hebrew translation would appear to have been made in the time of the monarchy, that is in the pre-exilic period. But besides the Wisdom of Amen-em-ope which presents the only source from which it can be shown that Israel made sustained borrowing, other Egyptian writings dating from the third millennium B.C. onwards have certainly made contribution to the Hebrew Wisdom literature. Notable among these are the teaching of Ptah-hotep,[2] the teaching of Ka-Gemni,[3] the teaching of Meri-ka-re,[4] the teaching of Duauf,[5] and the wisdom of Anii.[6]

Paul Humbert, in his book entitled " *Investigations into the Egyptian Sources of Israel's Sapiental Literature*," [7] points to many parallels in substance and in form between the teachings of the Egyptian " wise " and the Hebrew wisdom-writings, particularly in Proverbs, Job, Ecclesiastes, and Sirach. Though all these resemblances may not prove dependence, and some may be accidental, yet Humbert demonstrates sufficiently that wide use of the Egyptian didactic literature was made in Israel and that not merely of one or two writings. The comparisons which Humbert makes reveal that the chief feature of the Hebrew

[1] Discovered by Sir Wallis Budge. Erman, *Sitzungsberichte der Berliner Akad. der Wissenschaften*, 1924, and Lange, *Das Weisheitsbuch des Amenemope*, think that the work of Amen-em-ope dates *c.* 1000 B.C. Griffith, *Journal of Egypt. Arch.* I. xii. (1926), p. 226, places date much later.

[2] *Circa* middle of third millennium B.C.

[3] *Circa* beginning of third millennium B.C.

[4] *Circa* 1450 B.C.

[5] Before 1300 B.C.

[6] *Circa* 1000 B.C. For comparison of the maxims and teachings of these works with the Book of Proverbs, see Oesterley's *Commentary, op. cit.*; for the wider comparison with the other Hebrew wisdom-books, see Humbert's *Recherches* (below). Cf. also Erman, *The Literature of the Ancient Egyptians* (translated by Blackman), 1927.

[7] *Recherches sur les sources Égyptiennes de la littérature sapientiale d'Israel*, 1929.

wisdom with which we are here concerned, namely its humanism,
has its origin and roots in the international character of the
Oriental wisdom.   To quote Humbert's words: "In both
literatures (Israelite and Egyptian) there is the same ideal of
moderation and prudence, the same utilitarian conceptions and
quest of well-being, the same faith in divine justice and appeal
to human justice.   The pedagogical methods and respect for
tradition are the same.   There are the same literary forms and
type of rhetoric—often indeed the same formulæ.   And all these
elements are animated by the same breath of humanism, and yet
at the same time by a disdain of the ignorant and of those whose
vocation is manual work." [1]   To appreciate Humbert's last
remark, we must compare the favourite Egyptian theme, the satire
on the vocations, [2] which magnifies the office of the scribe by
contrasting it with other callings, with the well-known passage
in Sirach ($38^{24f.}$) on the superiority of the scribe, as student of
the Law, over the labourer and artisan.   The Hebrew writers
were not servile borrowers.   As a study of the Book of Amen-em-
ope shows, they assimilated much, but transformed or rejected
what did not suit their religious beliefs.   We find this same phase
in the later books of 4 Maccabees and the Wisdom of Solomon
in regard to Hellenic thought.   The Hebrew " wise " taught

---

[1] *Op. cit.* p. 178.   Cf. also Humbert, " Weisheitsdichtung " (in *Religion in
Geschichte und Gegenwart*).   " The foreign and especially Egyptian influence is
traceable in the use of certain literary forms—the king as fictive author ;
maxims and a more or less philosophical dialogue with a narrative framework ;
satires on callings ;   praise of the wise (Pap. Anastasi III. 44, iv. 32) ;   descriptions of the feebleness of old age (Eccles. 12, Ptah-hotep, line 8 f.) ;   exhortation
to enjoyments of life in view of the certainty of death."   Cf. the Song of the
Harper (Egyptian) with the *Carpe diem* of Ecclesiastes, and the Gilgamesh
epic (Babylonian), x. col. iii. 6 f.   For the influence of the Egyptian Wisdom
literature on the Book of Ecclesiastes, see Galling, " Koheleth Studien,"
Z.A.W., vol. ix. heft 4, p. 276 f.   Both the pessimism and hedonism of Ecclesiastes are better explicable from contact of the latter with Oriental than with
Greek thought, in spite of Ranston's parallels between Ecclesiastes and
Theognis, etc.   See Ranston, *Ecclesiastes and the Early Greek Wisdom Literature,*
1924.

[2] Cf. " The Teaching of Duauf " in Erman, *op. cit.*

and wrote for the ordinary man rather than for the scribe. To the largely secular character of the Oriental wisdom from which they drew, they added the religious motive as if conscious of the necessity of this orientation of thought. Yet it is beyond doubt that the element of humanism was nurtured by the acquaintance of the " wise " with the wisdom of the neighbouring peoples. It introduced the topic of the worth of life [1] and emphasized the need of man's interest in his own self, of man's regard for man and the belief in God's interest in the individual and in mankind. The god Thoth, the god of wisdom and patron of the Egyptian scribe, had been described [2] as "the Lord of friendliness, the leader of the whole multitude," whose office was " the leadership of mankind " long before the personified wisdom of the Hebrew hymn was thought of as announcing that her " delight was with the sons of men " (Prov. 8[31]). But, above all, it was the humanistic outlook of the Hebrew Wisdom literature which fostered thought upon God as Creator and man as creature, and thus prepared in Judaism the foundation of Christian theology.

1

Through the inherent interest of the wisdom-writings in the individual personality, the idea of God as Creator attained its fuller content. Upon the doctrine that God is the world Creator is founded the teaching of man's duty to man. At the end of the period of the exile the second Isaiah (chaps. 40–55) employed the thought of Jahve as the one Almighty God and all-knowing Creator to support the further conception of Him as the divine providence

[1] See on this subject the excellent treatise of L. Dürr, *op. cit.* p. 7 f. Dürr remarks on the terms " path of life," " way of life," " issues of life," " well of life," " tree of life," " reproof of life," and says, " It is interesting that those terms which almost all occur in the O.T. Book of Proverbs appear in the wisdom-book of Amen-em-ope ; ' The Ways of Life ' is the title of its thirteenth chapter and in the first chapter we find ' a storehouse of life,' " p. 14 ; cf. p. 20.

[2] Cf. Erman, *Literatur der Aegypter*, 1923, p. 186, " Hymn to Thoth " of 18th dynasty.

presiding over Israel's destiny and as giving to this people's history a world significance. The Priestly Code's (Gen. 1) account of Creation, written at some time before the promulgation of this code by Ezra (432, 444 B.C.), transformed elements of the Babylonian mythology of creation, working the whole into a seven-day scheme in order to stress the importance of the Sabbath.[1] But it is the Wisdom literature which developed the ethical significance of the idea of creation, and this, it must be noted, at a date long prior to either second Isaiah or the Priestly Code. With the exception of the few verses in the first Book of Esdras, all the wisdom-books both within and outside the Old Testament enforce their moral instruction by reference to God as the Creator not only of heaven and earth but particularly as the Creator of man.[2] Already in a pre-exilic section of the Book of Proverbs (10–22[16]) we have the teaching (17[5]) that " whoso mocks the poor arraigns his Maker : he that rejoices at calamity (Greek : at him who is perishing) shall not be unpunished." In this same early collection of moral teachings the same thought appears several times (14[31], 19[17], 22[2]). It is quite true, as Oesterley comments (Proverbs, p. 139), that, according to the belief of the times (cf. Sirach 7[11]), the poor existed because it was God's will, so that to deride what was in accordance with the divine purpose was to reproach God Himself. But that Hebrew humanism felt itself to be in no way strictly bound to such ideology is shown by the positive injunction to help the poor and improve their condition. " He who is hard on the forlorn reviles his Maker : he honours his Maker who is kindly to the poor " (14[31], Moffatt). Also it is upon the just and equitable

[1] Cf. Meinhold, *Die Weisheit Israels*, p. 45 f. In second Isaiah we have the Jew " who regards creation as a proof of the power of a God who has set the forces of creation in motion for the benefit of Israel." In Gen. chap. i. the purpose of the author is to present the Sabbath as woven into creation by God who finishes His creative work therefore in six days; cf. p. 50, *op. cit.*

[2] Prov. 14[31], etc. ; Job 4[17], 10[8f.], 12[7f.], 31[15], etc. ; Koh. 3[14f.], 7[13f.], etc. ; Ps. 94[9] ; Tob. 3[11], 8[5f.] ; Arist. 201, 234 ; Bar. 3[32f.] ; 4 Macc. 2[21], 5[25], 11[3], 13[13] ; Sir. 4[6] and often; Sap. 1[14], 6[7], 9[1], 11[17], etc.

treatment of man as man that Job reflects when, in self-examination of his soul for any sin he may have done, he exclaims : " If ever I ignored the rightful claim of any servant, man or woman, what could I do when God rose up ? . . . Did not my Maker make my servant too, and form us both alike within the womb ? " (31[13. 15])[1] This trend of thought continues. Upon the idea of creation, Jesus Sirach, in a passage that bears the spirit style and tradition of the maxim-writers, bases the duty of charity (4[6]) to the afflicted. In the same manner he inculcates the duty of preserving an inner relationship of love to God. " With all thy strength love Him that made thee " (7[30]). And the Wisdom of Solomon exhorts rulers to rule justly—" for the Sovereign Lord of all will not regard any man's person/Neither will He stand in awe of greatness/Because it is He who made both small and great/And alike He taketh thought of all " (6[7f]).

In all these passages which we have considered, there is no trace of man's duty to his fellow-men being limited to race or nation. As we shall see later, in Sirach and the succeeding Wisdom literature, a nationalistic particularism does emerge. But in the pre-exilic section of the Book of Proverbs, which we have cited, and in the poem of Job, the idea of man's duty to man is entirely universal in its range. Meinhold, while re-marking that it cannot by any means be accidental that in the Book of Proverbs the expressions " God of Israel," " Jahve of hosts," which designate Jahve as the national God are absent, yet adds that this universalism has not reached the stage of conscious acceptance.[2] This may be true. Yet that which cannot be regarded as accidental must be appreciated on its own account. It can hardly be supposed that when Job pleads

---

[1] Humbert, *op. cit.* p. 91 f., shows the great similarity between Job's protestations of innocence in chap. 31 as in the Egyptian " negative confessions " (cf. *Book of the Dead*, chap. lxxv.). In Job and the Egyptian writing " there is the same detailed and negative enumeration of sins . . . (*e.g.*) Conf. neg. 1, 11 : ' I have not maligned any servant to his master ' ;   the rights of the poor, Conf. neg. 1,12, etc." (cf. p. 95, *op. cit.*).

[2] *Op. cit.* p. 32.

his innocence, the servants or slaves whom he mentions as not having been wronged by him are all thought of as belonging to his own race. The friends of Job are from different lands. The universalism of these books must rather be explained by the international outlook of these wisdom-writings and by the largely international character of their literary traditions and sources.

That in the development of Judaism the broad humanism of the early wisdom-writers was restricted or modified would seem to be due to the influence upon the " wise " of other competitive religious ideas and to the facts of political history. But the ripest fruit of this humanism, namely, the expression of man's social duty in explicitly positive and universalistic terms, does appear about the second century B.C. in the book entitled the *Testaments of the Twelve Patriarchs*.[1] This work contains, in the main, ethical teaching, and might well have been placed, in spite of an apocalyptic element, in the category of wisdom-writings.[2] It has certainly been influenced by these. The author combines for the first time in history the two commandments of the Law : Thou shalt love the Lord thy God (Deut. 6[5]) and thou shalt love thy neighbour as thyself (Lev. 19[18]),[3] apparently signifying by the " neighbour " all mem-

---

[1] Charles, vol. ii. *Pseudep.*, 109-107 B.C.   E. Meyer, *Ursprung und Anfänge d. Christentums*, pp. 12, 44, on good grounds regards the Testaments (as relieved of its later additions) to date from the last decades of the third century B.C. ; *c.* 200 may seem to be a safe date.

[2] The Apocalyptic element is small. R. T. Herford *Talmud and Apocrypha*, p. 234, rightly regards the " Testaments " as a wisdom-book which adopts the Apocalyptic method as a better way of presenting ethical teaching and increasing the power of persuasion.

[3] Jewish scholars contend that *neighbour*, in Lev. 19[18], was understood in a universal sense. So Herford, *op. cit.* p. 144 f. The only really relevant part of Herford's argument is that Lev. 19[34] (" The stranger that sojourneth with you shall be unto you as the home-born among you, and thou shalt love him as thyself ") points to the duty of loving the non-Israelite. But as Strack and Billerbeck remark, this command concerning the resident stranger proves that the command is not regarded as extending to the universal love of men. See below.   Strack, however, thinks that Jesus was the first to teach the universal love of man.

bers of the human race. This duty of loving the neighbour is inculcated not merely in one passage but in several (T. Iss. 5^2, 7^6, T. Dan 5^3, T. Benj. 3^3). Thus the great commandment which was formulated by Jesus, more emphatically and most perfectly illustrated in the parable of the good Samaritan, occurs more than a century before. Dr. Charles, in his introduction to the Testaments, expresses himself with great care when he says that " possibly in our text (T. Iss. 5^2, 7^6) the sphere of neighbourhood is limited to Israelites, but in our Lord's use there is no limit of race or country." But in view of the fact that the passages concerned are not regarded by Charles as Christians additions and that the injunction is given (T. Zeb. 5^1, 7^2) " to show mercy to your neighbours and to have compassion towards all, not towards men only, but also towards beasts," the contention that in Judaism before the time of Christ the command to love the neighbour appears with full universal significance cannot reasonably be denied. The thought has its roots in the earlier Wisdom literature, in that deduction which the Hebrew moralists of the wisdom-schools drew from, or associated with, the idea of Creation, and which they stated in less positive form. And since the Christian gospels show in other respects a dependence upon the Testaments [1] of the Twelve, it is difficult to avoid the conclusion that in His statement of the great commandment Jesus had in mind the bold enunciation in the Testaments of man's religious and social duty.

Professor Oesterley (*Proverbs*, p. 159) states his opinion that the moral instruction of the wisdom-writers in regard to social life, in particular to championing and sympathizing with the cause of the poor and helpless, bears the marks of prophetic influence. " The wisdom-writers," he says, " take up this burden of the prophets and insist again and again on the duty to the poor which they regard as wisdom in one of its highest forms. . . . He who gives to the poor, who are of God's creation (cf. 22^2), are lending to God " (cf. 19^{17}). Now this opinion seems to be a

[1] See Charles, *op. cit.* Introduction.

case of placing the cart before the horse. Thought, of course, especially in a small nation, can never be confined as in hermetically sealed compartments. Doubtless the wisdom-writers were not uninfluenced by the prophets just as the influence of the wisdom-schools is manifest in certain prophetic writings.[1] But three things appear to belong to the " wise " and to their teaching, as possessions under their own title-deed and right, namely, the individualism which is the inspiration of social justice and equity, the idea of reward and of lending to God as the motive of good or social conduct, and above all the application of the creation-idea to enforce the notion of the obligation man owes to his fellow-creatures. " Laugh not at a blind man and mock not at a dwarf/and harm not him that is a cripple/ . . . Man is clay and straw/and the Deity is his builder." Upon this thought as well as upon the idea of reward and retribution the Egyptian sage Amen-em-ope (25 xxiv. 9, 10, 13, 14) bases his ethical teaching." [2] The Hebrew counterpart is : " Whoso mocks the poor reproaches his Maker :/he that rejoices over him that is perishing (LXX) shall not be unpunished " (Prov. 17[5]). When we view Hebrew humanism as being a native product of the Wisdom literature which has its roots deep in that Oriental wisdom which is much older than the earliest writing prophets of Israel, we may more justly conclude that the prophetic teaching on its social side was inspired and nurtured by Israel's wisdom writers, who as composers of maxims and ethical instructors were active from the time of the establishment of the state under Solomon.

[1] Cf. *e.g.* Jer. 17[5-8] with Ps. 1, and with the words in Amen-em-ope, chap. 4, on the forest tree. See Gressmann, *Israels Spruchweisheit*, p. 31.

[2] Cf. Lange, *op. cit.* Amen-em-ope, *ad loc.* Cf. Fichtner, *op. cit.*, p. 111, " The Egyptian and Babylonian Wisdom literature at several times makes mention of the deities who are especially honoured as Creator-gods, *e.g.* Chnum, Aruru, etc., and on occasion expressly point to the creative function of deity in general." Also (p. 104) " the national character or particular characteristics of the individual deities fade into the general conception of deity, so that we may speak of a tendency to monotheism, or better of a trend towards practical monotheism, in the Wisdom literature of the ancient Orient."

We may not suppose that either the " wise " or the prophets had a monopoly of the moral sense, but a good case might be be made out for the prophetic polemic against the notion that the substance of religion was ceremony, being the fruit of the religious rationalism of the wisdom-schools which both in Egypt and in Israel had expressed, in popular form,[1] the thought that righteousness was better than sacrifice.

2

The doctrine of God as the Creator of all things leads naturally to the question of the moral responsibility of man as a created being and of the responsibility of the Creator Himself for the good and evil which appear in the world of His making. Whenever the absolutely righteous character of God is assumed, some explanation is sought and given for those phenomena of the natural world which seem to conflict with the belief that a just will and protective power presides over the interests of mankind. A theodicy[2] (that is a " justification of God ") is implicit in such explanations. Amos ($4^{9f.}$) in the eighth century B.C., for example, explains the failure and the mildew of crops and the murrain on cattle as the means which Jahve employs to cause His people to return to Him in penitent obedience. Here there is a close correspondence between physical and moral evil.

The religion of the prophets contains no speculation on the origin of evil. God is regarded as the author of all that happens in nature and in history, as the author, therefore, of good and evil (cf. Amos 2^6 ; Zeph. $3^{5f.}$), even accomplishing the hardening of

---

[1] Cf. Prov. 15^8, 21^3, ^{27} and Meri-ka-re, " The virtue of a right-minded man is more acceptable (to God) than the ox (for sacrifice) of an evil-doer," Erman, *Lit. d. Aegypter*, p. 109 f.

[2] Greek, *Theou* (of God), *dike* (justice). Leibniz (see below) appears to have been the first to have used the term in the sense of " the vindication of the divine providence or government in view of the existence of evil." Cf. Theodicy in *Ency. of Religion and Ethics* (Fulton).

the human heart (Isa. 29⁹ᶠ, 8¹²ᶠ). God's action thus manifested
and the assumption of man's free will stand side by side without
becoming the subject of deeper reflection. But that the necessity
of clarifying the relationship of God's will to man's will was in
some degree felt is shown by the Jahvistic account in Genesis
(chap. 3) of the temptation of Adam. Here we may assume,
as is commonly held, that the Genesis account transforms an
ancient myth where the serpent was represented as a divine or
demonic being, and that the original story told of a contest
between two divinities for the obedience of man. In any case,
the Jahvistic myth in making the serpent the symbol of man's
wilful desire displays the interest of the narrator to account for
sin as the result of man's own free choice, while leaving the
ultimate responsibility for the result of that choice with Jahve
who had created man subject to temptation. Possibly it is
with the Jahvistic source in view that the second Isaiah (45⁷),
in the latter portion of the sixth century, in the days when Israel
became acquainted with Persian dualism and its conception of
two opposing personal powers of good and evil, declares, not
without polemical purpose, that God is the creator of good and
of evil, thus reverting to the older prophetic religious ideas.
But in the post-exilic period the problem of evil arises with
greater insistence, for now monotheistic belief outgrows, in
principle, a merely national and monolatrous worship. The
distinction between monotheism and a belief in a god or in
several gods is more than a mathematical difference. Monotheism with its wider outlook upon the world, man, and God,
leads to theories, however veiled these may be, of God's purposes,
of man's relationship to God, of man's responsibility and destiny,
and of the origin of evil. Only when such a belief becomes an
intellectual possession does a theodicy become urgent.

    Karl Gronau, in his work entitled *The Problem of Theodicy*, [1]
remarks that in the application of imagination and reasoning
to the question of theodicy, the antique world penetrated to the

---

[1] *Das Theodizeeproblem in der altchristlichen Auffassung*, 1922, p. 2.

very boundaries of the human understanding, and produced by its own energy the most important of those conceptions from which succeeding ages have drawn—halting before the inevitable contrast of spirit and matter. Gronau, whose task leads him to deal mainly with the abundant material which Greek philosophy and early Christian theology bring to his subject, states that he is convinced that the study of the contribution of the early thinkers would reveal that these had effective influence upon the subsequent course of thought in Christian theology.[1] This conviction is supported when we study the Wisdom literature of Judaism. Here we have seen the idea of God as Creator applied to ethics and developing into the conception of a universal obligation of love of the neighbour. Here also we may see that the idea of God as the One, all-powerful, and omniscient Creator was productive of the main thoughts which human reason has evolved in regard to human and divine responsibility and to the problem of evil.

The doctrine of monotheism placed the post-exilic age under a deep consciousness of the *transcendent* nature of the World-Creator, and gave birth, in the Book of Job, not only to the sense of man's moral limitations before God, whose very angels are convicted of error ($4^{17f.}$), but of the inability of human reason to reconcile the facts of experience with the idea of divine righteousness and responsibility. To understand the will and design of providence is impossible (ch. 38 f.). All that remains is faith in the Creator's will as being wise and good. This line of thought is taken up in Judaism at a much later date in the Fourth Book of Ezra when, after the destruction of Jerusalem by the Romans (A.D. 70), the problem of suffering and of providence lay heavy on the heart of the stricken nation. With St. Paul (Rom. 9), Christian teaching, fortified by the Jewish doctrine of election, works out to the same position. The will of God is inscrutable. God has mercy on whom He pleases to have mercy (*e.g.* Jacob) and makes any one stubborn (*e.g.* Esau, Pharaoh) just as He

[1] *Op. cit.* p. v.

pleases. But we cannot accuse God of injustice. For God may
be compared with the potter who makes one vessel different
from another in accordance with the particular purpose he has
in view for each. The thing moulded may not question him
that moulded it. Man cannot " speak back to God " (v. 20).
Thus the problem of theodicy or justification of God, so far as
it is involved by St. Paul in a deep mystery of election, is simply
laid aside and declared as *ultra vires* or beyond the power of
man to solve. In contrast with the theologians of the Middle
Ages who subjected the question of theodicy to critical reasoning,
the leading reformers, in accordance with the doctrine of the
supreme authority of the Scriptures and their emphasis on faith
and God's purpose of redemption as revealed in Christ, evaded
or discouraged speculation upon God's providence as revealed
in the world. They are conscious of the limitations of human
reason. For Luther, God the all-powerful Creator and world-
governor is a hidden God, a *deus absconditus*, whom we cannot
measure or judge. We can know only God the Redeemer that
is the " God in Christ." There is to be distinguished a world-
ruling and a world-redeeming providence. The first is inaccess-
ible to our knowledge. " It is my custom," he says, " to dissuade
those who wish to know and inquire much about providence,
and I say to them : don't overreach yourself and be in danger
of breaking your neck . . . but go first to Bethlehem and seek
the child Christ." [1] Calvin, too, places the subject of providence
in the light of the belief in redemption, whereby man is persuaded of God's love and enabled to perceive his afflictions as
a divine means of accomplishing his salvation.[2] In the same
manner as St. Paul, and with the same idea of election, he silences
all endeavours to equate the experiences of life with the notion
of a divine justice, except as under one principle : " So much is
God's will the highest norm of righteousness that all that He

---

[1] Luther on Exodus, chap. 9, Erlangen edition, vol. xxxv. 173, " Hebet
nicht zu hoch an, ihr werdet sonst den Hals abspringen. . . ." Cf. W. Staerk,
Vorsehung und Vergeltung, 1931, p. 79 f.

[2] Calvin's Sermon on Job 1[13. 19].

wills, just because He wills it, is to be held as just. When we ask why the Lord has acted in a particular way, the answer is : because He has willed it." [1] The distrust which Luther and Calvin show in regard to attempts to base a theodicy on metaphysical speculation, their resort to the watchword of faith and the doctrine of redemption, bring us, apart from the last-named Christian dogma, no further than to the thought which constitutes the climax of the Book of Job. Man is incapable of assessing the wisdom, justice, and purposes of the Creator and world-governor. Reconciliation of the facts of existence with the idea of a righteous and loving God, as demanded by the ethical postulate, is beyond the power of human reason. Kant, in his work entitled *The Failure of all Philosophical Attempts at a Theodicy*,[2] expresses the same verdict, namely, that " in the question of a theodicy which involves a transcendent subject, a theoretic-objective knowledge is impossible of attainment, and a seeking, groping humanity stands here before an insoluble riddle."

Although the Book of Job stresses the incapacity of man's reason to harmonize the data of experience with the belief in the justice of providence, and thus foreshadows the conclusion to which many thinkers have come as to the futility of attempting a theodicy, this book and the succeeding wisdom-writings work out ideas upon the problem of evil, upon human and divine responsibility, and on providence, which, for the development of a reasonable theistic faith, are of first importance.

That adversity may be sent by God to test man's faith— the probationary view of suffering—or to discipline and train character—the pedagogical explanation—appears to have been an early Hebrew conception. But such reflections were outweighed by the belief that, in general, God revealed the justice of His world-government by meting out well-being for goodness, and

---

[1] *Institutes*, iii. 23. 2.

[2] " Über das Misslingen aller philosophischen Versuche in der Theodizee " (*Berliner Monatshefte*, 1790, Sept., against Leibniz).

adversity for sin. Even the *poem* of the Book of Job (chaps. 3–31)
does not break with this view of a general divine law of reward
and retribution as upheld by Job's friends. But the author of
the poem must certainly have desired the inference to be drawn
from Job's defence of his innocence that, *in certain cases*, suffering
is not suffering for sin. This cannot have been a new thought,
however revolutionary the manner of its setting forth must have
been. Already inherent in the probationary and the pedagogical theories was that physical evil was not always retribution
for guilt. But if we may estimate the influence of the poem of
Job and its argumentative handling of the subject of suffering,[1]
it effected that from now onwards more was put to the account
of the disciplinary purpose of pain and affliction. That this was
the result appears from the fact that the Elihu speeches (chaps.
32–37), which are the work of a later writer (Volz, *c.* 300 B.C.),
and develop the view of suffering as discipline, are inserted in the
book immediately after the poem of Job as a complete answer
to its problem, and that this view becomes more and more
appreciated in the succeeding literature of Judaism.[2] Finally,
when the idea that suffering chastens and refines character is at
length combined with the belief in a future life, it acquired
additional strength and won for itself the permanent place
which it holds in religious apologetic.[3] In the Wisdom of Solomon
(3[1], 4[f.]) we find this consummation : " The souls of the righteous
are in the hand of God . . . their hope is full of immortality ;
and having borne a little chastening, they shall receive great
good ; because God tested them, and found them worthy of
Himself, as gold in the furnace He proved them."

In the New Testament the pedagogic theory, both in the

---

[1] Though, as Volz says (Weisheil, *S.A.T.*, p. 89), the poem is not a didactic
poem (*Lehrgedicht*), its effect was to call forth the didactic poem of Elihu
(cf. 36[3], " I will now justify my creator ").

[2] Cf. Bousset, *Relig. d. Judentums*, 2, p. 442, and *S.A.T.* (vol. ii. 1 Cor. 11[32]),
p. 129.

[3] De Quincey's essay, " Levana," is one of the finest expositions in English
literature of this aspect of suffering.

aspect of suffering as instruction (*paideia*) that is punitive and corrective of sin or defect (Heb. 12[6f.]), as well as altogether unrelated to sin on the part of the sufferer (St. John 9[3]), is advanced in vindication of the existence of physical evil in the divinely governed world.   No doubt, besides the obviously Jewish influence, Stoic ideas upon the uses of adversity in training to virtue and strength of character (cf. 4 Macc. 9[9. 19]; 2 Tim. 2[3]) also operated on early Christian thought.   Even Christ, though He was the Son of God and without sin, learned obedience through the things that He suffered (Heb. 5[8f.]).   For early Christianity and the contemporary Judaism, the doctrine of immortality with its view of the present world of tribulation as being a preparation for the future æon (4 Ezra), and of present sufferings as being nothing in comparison " with the glory that shall be revealed in us " (Rom. 8[18]), dwarfed to small dimensions the *problem* of suffering.[1]   The purpose of the world lay in the future. Then the balance of life would be adjusted.   We have seen that the reformers, Luther and Calvin, concentrated thought upon God's purpose of redemption.   To-day, when to construct a theodicy is generally regarded as a wrestling with an incomprehensible mystery,[2] Brunner, a representative of the Barthian school of theology, returns to that position.   " In the place where philosophy has a theodicy," he says, " the Bible places eschatology—that is, while speculative philosophy regards the contradictions in the world as such as can be mastered by thought,

---

[1] In light of indications in the Gospels the statement of E. Balla (" Das Problem des Leides in der Geschichte der israelitisch-jüdischen Religion," in *Eucharisterion Studien zur Relig. und Lit. des A. und N. Test.*, 1923, p. 260) that a problem of suffering was not known to later Judaism is too strong.   The belief in a future life restored in later Judaism and endowed with greater vitality than ever the fundamental dogma of reward and retribution.

[2] Cf. Staerk, *op. cit.*; Fulton, *op. cit.*; Balla, *op. cit.* p. 260.   Cf. Eucken (*Truth of Religion*, p. 500), " Religion does not so much explain as presuppose evil."   P. T. Forsyth (*Justification of God*, p. 200), a religious theodicy is not " an answer to a riddle but a victory in a battle."   Such statements have religious truth and value, but lead to that pragmatism which is an irrelevant excuse of the practical mind for the lack of theoretical interest.

the Bible regards them as such as can only be removed by the divine act of redemption. Either theodicy or eschatology, but not both." In answer to this it may be replied that while for pantheism and religious pessimism theodicy is impossible or worthless, for theism the effort to construct one, so far as its speculative powers permit, is the more necessary since, besides the practical solution of religious problems by faith, both religious thought and ethics need a theoretic background. Faith must seek to include its *rationale*.

The idea of physical suffering as being, in the purpose of God, disciplinary, can reasonably profess to explain a portion only of the problem of evil. Of great significance, therefore, was the introduction into the prologue of the Book of Job of the figure of (the) Satan. It is true that here he is only a subject of the world-ruler, one of " the sons of God." He is permitted to inflict only physical suffering, yet the possibility of this suffering leading to sin and to moral evil is plainly recognized. That he is described as a servant of the sovereign Lord and not an antagonist of God shows that the dualism of Persian thought[1] was as yet (cf. Isa. 45[7]) subordinated to a strict monotheism. In course of time Satan (cf. 1 Chron. 21[1])—translated in Greek by *diabolos*, Calumniator—designated also Beliar (*Test. XII.*) and Mastema (Book of Jubilees), becomes the fully developed representative of the powers of evil, the tempter of man and the adversary of God. Not without criticism, however, did the belief in Satan as the tempter to evil and the author of sin make headway. " No sin has been sent upon the earth, but man himself has created it," says a writer in the Book of Enoch (98[4]), and a remarkable passage from the hand of Jesus Sirach (21[27f.]) may be interpreted as meaning that every man is his own Satan.[2] But as appearing to relieve God of all responsibility

[1] That primitive Hebrew belief in harmful spirits offered suitable soil for the Persian conception is most probable.

[2] " When the fool curseth his adversary (Satan), he curseth his own soul." But Sirach elsewhere also strongly emphasizes man's own responsibility for sin (see below), without thought of Satanic influence.

for evil and thus enabling man to say that evil was never, and
is never, in the world-Creator's plan, the doctrine of the agency
of the devil became the generally accepted belief.   As such it
enters from Judaism into the Christian gospels and the writings
of St. Paul.   In the thought of Jesus this world is God's creation,
and under the care of His providence are all creatures, even the
sparrow and the anemones of the field—but, nevertheless, this
divine creation is subject to Satan who draws man to sin and
separates him from God.   Satan and evil demons plague the
bodies of men with disease ;   evil thoughts, evil deeds, and un-
belief are their work, and thus the task of Jesus is, by teaching
and healing, to overthrow the kingdom of Satan (Mark 3[23f.]).
In the Fourth Gospel (St. John 12[31]) Satan is " the ruler of this
world " [1] and St. Paul can actually speak of him as " the god of
this world " [2] (2 Cor. 4[4]) " who has blinded the minds of them
that are unbelievers."   Christ's death for our sins was to deliver
us from Satan's power, for so we must understand the phrase
" from this present evil world " (Gal. 1[4]).

The belief in a devil as the originator of evil in God's fair
creation, while it seemed to yield a satisfying theodicy only set
new problems.   It could not be accepted that the spirit of the
Creator and the evil spirit were both eternal and equally
powerful.   The Church fathers, therefore, so far as they did not
simply accept the biblical account, took over from Judaism [3]
the explanation that Satan had been created by God, had been
a holy angel who had rebelled and had fallen from his high
estate.   His fall they attributed to his possession of free-will [4]
and his baneful interest in man to his having had, when an angelic
being, the oversight of this earth.[5]   The problem of evil was
thus only moved a stage farther back, from the human to the
angelic sphere, but was not solved.   Gronau (*op. cit.* p. 95)
states that not seldom we see in the sophistic exegesis of the

---

[1] ὁ ἄρχων τοῦ κόσμου τούτου.   [2] ὁ Θεὸς τοῦ αἰῶνος τούτου.
[3] Bousset, *op. cit.* p. 586.   [4] Origen, *De princ.* 2, 9, 2.
[5] Justin, *Dial.* c. Tr. I. 1 (cf. Philo, *De conf. ling.* p. 346).

Church fathers that the figure of Satan only presented them with new enigmas and that they only retained him in their theodicies through their reverence for the Bible. Doubtless this reverence for the Bible explains in large measure why belief in the devil is not seldom defended to-day, though it yet appears to some, for example to H. Obendiek,[1] that its place is justified in theistic apologetic. Also the historian Eduard Meyer, who observes that it was Christianity which first made the dualistic religious teaching of the Iranian prophet (Zoroaster) a truly effective world-heritage, remarks that "modern religious teaching, in so far as it gives up the old dogma of the existence of the devil, does all that it possibly can to evade the problem of the origin of evil and of the sinfulness of man, and contents itself merely with outlining the conception of God in accordance with individual ethical postulates without asking how these accord with the conditions and circumstances of actual life."[2]

Not only do we have in the Wisdom literature the beginning of that process of thought which applied the idea of a personal power of evil to theodicy and theology and a criticism springing from the healthy intuition of man's own moral responsibility,[3] but in the Fourth Book of Maccabees we perceive the same resort to Greek thought (Platonic, Stoic) which the fourth-century theologians of the Eastern Church also make with the same effect, consciously or unconsciously modifying the belief in the Tempter of men. The author of 4 Maccabees, as those theologians, notably Basil and Gregory of Nyssa,[4] views man's struggle with evil from a psychological standpoint. The Stoics, under Platonic influence, had regarded sin as a blindness of the understanding or reason. In the same way Basil,[5] adopting Plato's illustration of the chariot, teaches that "when a man ceases to hand over the control of the passions to the understanding

---

[1] *Der Teufel bei Martin Luther* (Furche-Studien).
[2] Meyer, *Ursprung*, etc., vol. ii. p. 82 f. ; cf. p. 441.
[3] Cf. Sirach 21²⁷ (above).
[4] Basil the Great, A.D. 330–379; Gregory, A.D. 331–c. 396.
[5] *Const. Monach.*, iv. 1036A.

as to a good charioteer, then the passions bark around the soul like wild dogs." Reason must hold the reins lest it lose its balance and, falling, become entangled in the trapping of the chariot and be dragged whithersoever the steeds of unreason may course. So also the Alexandrian writer of 4 Macc., who is not entirely indifferent to the traditional belief in evil spirits (18[7f.]),[1] presents the conflict with evil entirely as an *inner* struggle. His theme is : " Inspired Reason is supreme ruler over the passions " (1[1]). Modifying the Stoic teaching on which he depends, he regards the passions not as in themselves evil, but as part of human nature implanted by the Creator, and as including all human affections and all our weaknesses and moral defects generally. He speaks of " the bridle of Reason " (1[35]), and likens Reason to a master-gardener who weeds and prunes and waters that he may bring " the thicket of dispositions and passions under domestication."

The idea that man is wholly incapable of grasping the purposes of the Creator, and the idea of a Satan—the first a thought which is taken up by a later writer of a hymn on Wisdom (Job, ch. 28), and which lies behind all subsequent disparagement of theodicy-making ; the second providing an assumption that appeared to be necessary for a theodicy— both receive expression in the Book of Job. The penal and pedagogical views of physical evil also held for " the righteous " [2] a central position in the defence of the Creator's justice as manifested in His dealings with man. But from the time of the composition of the Book of Job (*c.* 450 B.C.) two and a half centuries or more elapse before we have anything like a clear attempt to answer the question : whence sin derives ? and to define human and divine responsibility in relation to moral evil. The work of Jesus Sirach (*c.* 180 B.C.), however,

---

[1] The author of 4 Macc., however, does not bring this belief into his theme. In this respect, also, Basil and Gregory of Nyssa resemble him, for, as Gronau, *op. cit.* p. 92, says, " Bas. und Greg. Nyss. ziehen den Dämonenglauben zur Erklärung des sittlichen Irrtums kaum mehr heran."

[2] Cf. p. 41, 45 below.

reveals that in the interval, probably in the circles or schools where the teachers of " wisdom " exercised their vocation, this question had undergone discussion. In attacking the doctrine of a too pronounced determinism which laid the responsibility for moral evil upon God, Sirach seems to have had opinions of wisdom-teachers in view.[1] His use of the word *yeçer*,[2] meaning *evil propensity*, though appearing for the first time in his book, is obviously not of his own coining, but bears the marks of having been current in the theological vocabulary of those religious rationalists and instructors in ethics to whom Sirach himself belonged.

Sirach knows the importance of the doctrine of free will. He lays down that God is not responsible for the sin of man, and, though he is well aware, as a true humanist, of man's moral obliquity, that man is perfectly able to keep the commandments of God. But along with this tenet he holds another which presents a paradox with which those who have reflected more arduously, if not more deeply, than he upon the subject of free will have seen themselves to be confronted. For, according to Sirach, there has been implanted in man by God an evil propensity or evil tendency. Sirach himself seems to be quite aware of the paradox, for he places the two viewpoints in juxtaposition :

> Say not : " From God is my transgression,"   xv. 11
> For that which He hateth made He not . . .
> For there is no need of evil men . . .   12
> God created man from the beginning   14
> And placed him in the hand of his *yeçer* [i.e. *yeçer hara'* = evil propensity].
> If thou (so) desirest thou canst keep the commandment.

Sirach openly asserts that the evil propensity with which man is born is God's creation. " O evil tendency, why then wast thou created ? " he exclaims (37³). But he thinks that he

---

[1] Cf. Qoh. 7¹³ " Who can make straight what He (God) has made crooked."

[2] Cf. Gen. 6⁵, yeçer=yeçer hara' (evil propensity) occurs *as an expression* earlier than yeçer hattob (good propensity).

safeguards the deity from responsibility for man's sinning, by asserting that man has a perfectly free choice and by a doctrine that over against man's natural propensity to evil God has set the Law—the moral law [1]—as object of obedience. "He that keeps the law controls his (evil) propensity " (21^{11}). Except that the law is more narrowly conceived than it is by Sirach, the same teaching occurs in rabbinic Judaism. In a Talmud tractate (Qiddushim, 30b) the deity is represented as saying : " I created an evil tendency : I created for it the Law as means of healing. If you occupy yourself with the Law you will not fall into the (tendency's) power." The rabbinic psychology taught that in every man there were two opposing principles,—one good and the other evil.[2] This is already supposed in Sirach's contrast of the evil propensity with the Law and is reflected in the moral disquisitions of the Twelve Testaments, the author of which possibly lived at the same time as Sirach. There Judah says in his Testament (ch. 20 ; cf. Rub. 2 f. ; Asser. 1) : " Two spirits are these, which concern themselves with man, the spirit of truth and the spirit of error ; and between both of these stands the insight of understanding. . . . Both the ordinances of truth and those of deceit are written on the human breast ; and the Lord knows them both." Here the illuminated reason is the umpire between truth and error. In Sirach's thought the will is free to obey or overcome the evil propensity innate in human nature. All three, this propensity, free will, and its moral help, are of God. Sin is the rejecting of the last and submission to the first.

Without perceiving any inconsistency with his belief in free will, Sirach combines therewith a doctrine of election whereby God, apparently for reasons known to Himself and apart altogether from man's moral character, blesses some men and curses others (33^{12}). Sirach here puts to use the same

---

[1] In Sirach (cf. Charles, *Apoc.* Intro.) the term Law is frequently used as here in the wider sense.

[2] Cf. *Sayings of the Fathers*, ii. 15, iv. 1.

biblical figure (Jer. 18⁴) of the clay in the hands of the potter,
which St. Paul later (Rom. 9²¹) employs for the same doctrinal
purpose. " Man is in the power of his Creator, to make him
according to His ordinance " (33¹³). This theory of predestination is extended to all creation. God has organized His creation
in a series of opposites, so that over against the good there
will always be the evil. Thus the dualistic thought current
in Sirach's day and which courses as a strong life-stream in the
ethical teaching of the twelve Testaments is applied by Sirach
to all existing phenomena. Evil and good, moral and physical,
are necessary counterparts in God's world :

" Over against the evil (stands) the good, and against death, life ;
Likewise over against the godly, the sinner.
Even thus look upon all the works of God,
Each different, one the opposite of the other " (xxxiii. 14 f.).

Sirach extols the harmony of creation. Every single thing
has been created for a definite purpose (39²¹) so that in the
physical world good things are intended for the morally good,
and good and evil things for the wicked who will turn all things
to evil (39²⁵ᶠ·). " The works of God are all good " (39¹⁶· ³³),
he reiterates, and as each thing has its place and use we cannot
say that one thing is better than another. The goodness of
a thing is relative to its purpose.

The influence of the teaching of Sirach on free will and
predestination may be traced in what came to be orthodox
Judaism as represented by the Pharisees.¹ Also what he had

---

¹ Cf. Josephus, *Bell*. ii. 163 f. : " The Pharisees trace everything to destiny
(*heimarmene*) and God. To do right or not to do right depends in the main
on man himself, but so that always destiny co-operates with him. The
Sadducees reject the belief in destiny completely." *Heimarmene* was for the
Stoics a blind destiny, for the Pharisees it was a divine predestination (cf.
Meyer, *op. cit*. Bd. ii. p. 301). The Pharisees thus taught a synergistic doctrine of limited free will—a *via media* between a doctrine of unlimited free will
(the Sadducees) and the fatalism of the Essenes. R. Aqiba (iii. 14, *Sayings of
the Fathers*) expresses the Pharisaic doctrine thus : " All is foreseen, but the
freedom (of choice) is given." Both Pharisees and Sadducees could appeal
to Sirach.

to say upon human nature bore fruit.[1] He discerned the
conditions out of which sin arises to be entirely within man
and does not summon the adventitious aid of a Satan to explain
sin or exculpate God. He says indeed that " from a woman
did sin originate, and because of her we all must die " (25[24]),
and here we have the spring wells of that thought which,
drawing upon mythology, became a great river carrying a
heavy freight of theological cargo throughout all the ages,
namely, the doctrine that mankind fell in Adam's transgression.
But the teaching that the sin of Adam descended to all mankind
is not found in Judaism, which, though it lays weight on the
consequences of Adam's fall as bringing misfortune and death,
does not admit that it brought any change in human nature.
At most the germs of this idea are contained in the late works
of 4 Ezra and 2 Baruch. Judaism burdened itself with the
notion of an inherited penalty of death. It was left to Christian
theologians to deduce from the Pauline teaching (Rom. 5[12])
the doctrine of original sin.[2]

When we compare the ideas which Sirach contributed to
the subjects of free will and the problem of evil with those of
the greatest teacher of the ancient Church, St. Augustine, we
perceive the influence which Judaism has had upon Christian
theodicy. This would seem to be natural enough since Christianity springs from Judaism and inherited its writings. But to
Augustine's biblicism, as Harnack calls it, his regard for
Scripture, indeed his *submission* to it, must be ascribed a
particular historical significance. " No western theologian
before him had lived so much in Scripture or drew so much
from it." [3] Hence he drew from St. Paul the doctrine of

---

[1] Cf. 4 Macc. (below) and 4 Ezra 3[21], " For the first Adam, clothing himself
with the evil heart, transgressed . . . The law was in the heart of the people
but with the evil germ."

[2] Cf. Bousset, *Rel. d. Jud.* p. 406. " A real doctrine of original sin (*Erb-
sünde*) is unknown to Judaism. We can at most speak of it being there in germ."

[3] Harnack, *Dogmengeschichte*, p. 96. Augustine's principle was, as his
work *de Nat. et Grat.* 26 declares, to submit to Scripture and then ask :
How is it possible ? (*quomodo id fieri potuerit*).

predestination and developed that of inherited guilt. But we may show that, in regard to those topics, free will and the nature of man, in the treatment of which Augustine's chief merit lay, and in virtue of which treatment he has been reckoned justly to be " the psychological genius of the patristic period," [1] Augustine is likewise dependent on Scripture, and that Sirach and his successors of the wisdom-school directed and qualified his thought.

Augustine holds to the tenet of free will even when (De Civ. xiii. 3) this doctrine is in conflict with his Pauline teachings. In the same way as Sirach, he frees God from all responsibility for evil. " If evil has come into the world," he says, " this did not happen in accordance with the divine order ; but after it came it has been woven into that order. . . . That God is the author of evil is a thought more blasphemous than any that can be conceived " (De Ordine, ii. 23, 1005).[2] Sirach also, after stating that God does not need evil, arranges good and bad, saints and sinners in the deity's world-economy.

In his analysis of human nature Augustine associates the will in the closest manner with the natural impulses and desires (cupido, libido, amor, ira, timor), so that these impulses or urges which wish the pleasurable or avoid the painful are regarded by him as being the content of the will but yet distinct from the will itself.[3] The will stands above man's sensual nature and, formally, is free to follow or resist the different urges of that nature, but in concreto is always conditioned by these urges which condition it as motives. The theoretic freedom of choice only becomes real freedom when the love of goodness (amor boni) becomes the dominant motive for the will ; that is, only the good will, the will bound to goodness, is free. The evil will, though unfree, is not without responsibility for it is

---

[1] Harnack, op. cit. p. 104.—remarkably enough in connection with Augustine's dictum " Hominis sapientia pietas est " (Euch. 2, De Civ. xiv. 2), a text under which all the Wisdom literature may be said to have been written.

[2] Translation from Rinn and Jüngst., Kirchengeschichtliches Lesebuch, p. 74.

[3] See Harnack, op. cit. p. 110.

guilty of defect, namely, the omission of response to the love of good (*amor boni*). All this is deeper, more subtle, and elaborate than anything Sirach says about the life of the soul, but, nevertheless, in Augustine's description there is clearly to be discerned the pattern which Sirach presents—the evil urge or propensity, the power of attraction exerted by the moral ideal, and the free will as arbiter. For Sirach, too, the evil propensity and the urge to goodness lie in the will [1] as its content and yet are distinct from the will.

In another respect the psychology of Sirach and the later wisdom-writings had effect upon Christian thought. Christian theological thought applied to the question of the origin of moral evil drew largely from Greek philosophy, especially from the Stoics. Plato had given currency to the view that man's body was the principal source of lust and desire (cf. (*Phœdo*, 66, 83) and of all moral defect. Through the Stoa this view found its way into Neoplatonism and into Christian teaching. But already this Hellenistic thought is found in the contrast which St. Paul makes between the spirit (*pneuma*) and the flesh (*sarx*) which is the source of sin (cf. Gal. 5[13], etc.). This anthropological dualism Judaism did not accept. For Sirach the possibility of sin (what the Germans would call the *Möglichkeitsgrund*) lies within the will of man. The two later wisdom books, the Wisdom of Solomon and 4 Maccabees, both influenced by Stoicism, recognize that temptations to sin arise from man's bodily constitution. " Enlightened Reason is able to master the weakness of the flesh " (4 Macc. 7[18]). "A corruptible body weigheth down the soul" (Sap. Sol. 9[15]). But for these writers the body is not the seat of sin, though it may be the occasion of it.[2] The Church in the East was attracted by the Pauline teaching and by Neoplatonism, but it is to the credit of St. Augustine that influenced though he

---

[1] This is shown by 4 Ezra 3[21] where the *cor malignum* is the equivalent of Sirach's *yeçer*.

[2] Cf. note *ad loc.* to Sap. Sol. in Charles, *Apoc.*, and Bousset, *Rel. d. Jud.*, p. 404 f.

was by Neoplatonism in his view of the nature of sin as " nothingness " or limitation,[1] yet he saw the danger of supposing that
the source of sin was to be found in the inherent qualities of
matter. Sensuality, he argues, is the *effect* of sin. It is not
the flesh which is the cause of sin, for the flesh after its kind is
as good or as bad as spirit after its kind. And if it be said that
not the flesh but the corruption of the flesh, that is, the growth
of sensuality is the root of evil, then for the cause of this corruption of the flesh we must go deeper. " This corruption," says
Augustine, " is not the source of sin but is the punishment of
sin. The sinning soul is the cause of the corruption of the flesh." [2]
For Augustine sin springs from the will of man. A. E. Taylor
in his work, *The Problem of Evil* (p. 13 f.), in speaking of the
paradox of free will formed by the belief that God, who directs
the whole course of heaven and earth and has given man
freedom of will, yet regards sin as having no proper place in
His creation, states that : " It is no more than the historic
fact that Augustine's definite formulation of this doctrine
(that the source of sin lies in the will) is the starting-point for
the whole modern development of the psychology of will, a
subject which had never deeply interested Greek moralists
and philosophers." It was Augustine who made will " of such
capital importance for theology." But this does not represent
the full acknowledgment that should be made or trace the debt
to where it should be placed. Augustine is only pursuing a
line of thought which had been developed by Jewish thought
long since and which we find emerging in Judaism in the teaching
of Sirach.

Both Sirach and Augustine, in placing the cause of sin in
the will of man and in their emphatic exculpation of the deity

---

[1] Cf. Harnack, Bd. iii. p. 209 f., p. 218. The Neoplatonic doctrine of sin
as *Nihil* or limitation, was conceived of by Augustine more deeply. With
him the *nihil* was something " more evil." The nature of sin according to
Augustine is privation of good or of God (*privatio boni, carentia dei*), a freely-
willed diminution of being or goodness, and has a positive aspect, namely,
elatio (pride) or love of self (*amor sui*).   [2] See Grunau, *op. cit.* p. 109.

from all responsibility for moral evil in His creatures, set theodicy at the crossroads where it appears yet to stand. Professor Taylor (*op. cit.* p. 13) says that Plato and Kant are wholly in accord with the traditional teaching of Christianity that sin is something that " ought not to be," is " not in the divine plan " and therefore has no " proper place." The belief that sin is " against God's will," he says, rules out all " naturalistic " doctrines of moral evil which are dangerous in that they enable man to shirk absolute responsibility for sin by casting it upon God or a " step-motherly nature " and thus to evade full shame for his most shameful acts. But it may be questioned if a so-called " naturalistic " doctrine need be irreconcilable with Christianity and if such consequences would necessarily emerge. Troeltsch,[1] a modern theologian of the first rank, says that we must conceive the meaning of the world to be " the raising of the creature out of Nature as eternally ordained by God to participation in God's nature or being," and that this ascent of the creature to freedom in God can only be thought of as a formative, educative, process effected by the Divine Spirit who lets the soul suffer and sin while it learns to sacrifice its finite selfhood, and to make God's will its will. Thus Troeltsch continues : " The suffering in the world and sin are essential elements of the creation, through which alone the rising to personality as outcome of man's own action and of his submission to God can be realized." Now the idea of the world which this theodicy supposes, namely, a world in which suffering and sin emerge as an inner necessity of physical and psychological laws was not within the thought either of Sirach or the Church teachers, but it is no more inconsistent with Christianity than is the modern scientific view of the world.[2]

---

[1] Theodizee, " Systematisch " in *R.G.G.*

[2] Fulton (in *Ency. of Rel. and Ethics*, vol. xii. " Theodicy ") expresses sympathy with a theodicy which recognizes human freedom as real in the sense of implying self-limitation on God's part without implying any finitude on God's part. Fulton adds, " Such a solution still leaves God, as indeed must any theodicy, ultimately responsible for both physical and moral evil."

Finally, as a contribution of the wisdom-writings to theodicy, we must briefly appreciate the idea familiarly associated with the name of Leibniz, who wrote the most elaborate theodicy of modern times, an essay on " The goodness of God, the liberty of man and the origin of evil " (1710).[1] Leibniz held that this world is the best of all possible worlds, and has been chosen by God as being the best of the world-ideas contained in the divine Intellect.   With this doctrine he combined the Neoplatonic conception of moral evil as being a *privation d'être*, a privation of being, that is, as having no real existence and therefore not deriving from God. Moral evil, however, is morally necessary, as it must result where there is free will, and is the counterpart of the good, because where there is no evil there can be no good.   But in the formulation of these ideas Leibniz was only resuscitating the religious philosophy of the scholasticism of the Middle Ages. Abelard [2] combined in the same way platonic thought with the statement that " God could in no way have created a better world than He has made " (*Introductio ad Theologiam*, iii. 5).   And if we read the seventh chapter of Augustine's *Confessions* (vii. 12, 13), we can trace still further back this close association of the Neoplatonic view of moral evil with the teaching of the harmony and goodness of Creation.   For the latter thought Augustine cites Scripture, Genesis (1[31]), Sirach (39[21]), and particularly the 148th Psalm. With this psalm (vv.[13f.]), too, he elsewhere supports the observation that " as no one would criticize a craftsman in his own workshop, so should any dare to blame God in His own world ? " [3] But scriptural support, it may justly be said, is quite a different thing from deduction from scripture. When, however, we find Augustine basing his argument (*De Civ.* iv. 34, v. 23, xi. 18, xiv. 27) in regard to " the ordained beauty of the universe " upon the passage in Sirach (33[15]), where Sirach speaks of the

---

[1] " Essais de Théodicée sur la bonté de Dieu, la liberté de l'homme et l'origine du mal."

[2] A.D. 1079–1142. For Abelard's use of Sirach (19[4]), cf. *Introductio*, ii. 3.

[3] Cf. Staerk, *op. cit.* p. 70, and *De Civ.* xi. 22.

harmony and purpose of opposites, and of physical and moral
good and evil being necessary counterparts in creation, there
can be little doubt whence the notion of the best possible world
entered into Christian teaching and religious philosophy.
Sirach in a considerable portion of his work ($39^{16f.}$) is at pains
to prove the goodness of the cosmos, and that all things, even
pestilence and natural catastrophes, are good for something
($v.^{29f.}$).   After setting forth his thought upon this subject he
says : " Therefore from the beginning I was assured, and when
I had considered it I set it down in writing."   We may interpret this as meaning that he felt that what he wrote had the
mark of some originality.   While the term " evil propensity "
has the appearance of having been a common conception
employed by the wisdom-schools in or before the time of Sirach,
the thought which he develops upon the perfect harmony
and adjustment of creation would seem to be his own contribution to theodicy.

3

With the growth of the conception of Jahve as Creator
there necessarily arose the belief in a supremely good and wise
Providence.   In Israel, after the exile, monotheistic thought
naturally gave fuller expression to the idea of God's creative
power and purpose.   The praise of the Creator in the Book of
the second Isaiah ($40^{12.\ 22.\ 26}$, 41^4, 43^{10}, $44^{6.\ 24}$, 45^7, 48^{12}, etc.) and
the doxologies of the Book of Job ($5^{9f.}$, $9^{4f.}$, $12^{7f.}$, $26^{5f.}$, $36^{22f.}$,
$38^{4f.}$) belong to this period, and in this period may also be
placed the nature psalms 8, 19, 104, 148.   Recent Egyptian
research has shown a remarkable relationship between certain
Hebrew psalms and the Egyptian hymns to the sun which
belong to the Amarna Age (18th and 19th dynasties) and the
following century.[1]   A. M. Blackman concludes from this

[1] Cf. Blackman, " The Psalms in the Light of Egyptian Research " (in
D. C. Simpson, *The Psalmists*, Oxford, 1926) ; A. B. Mace, " The Influence of
Egypt on Hebrew Literature " (*Annals of Archæology and Anthropology*, vol. ix.
Liverpool, 1922) ; Humbert, *op. cit.* p. 100 f. ; Erman, *Lit. d. Aegypter*, p. 185 f.

relationship that Egyptian literature has had a manifest influence upon Hebrew lyric poetry. But in regard to Psalm 104 it has now for long been generally admitted that the author, who lived in the post-exilic period, was dependent upon the ancient hymn of Pharaoh Amenhotep IV. (c. 1370 B.C.) in praise of the sun-god as creator and preserver of the world and of all life.[1] In both poems, with the application of identical pictures, the deity is described as the paternal providence who provides for all beings, fish, reptiles, birds, quadrupeds, and man. The psalm in its expression of the care of God for all creatures, and His wisdom and goodness in giving them food and sustenance in due season (cf. Ps. 136[25], 145[15], 147[9]) is typical of a more abundant Egyptian hymnology upon divine providence. Characteristic of this praise of the deity as Creator and Provider in the Egyptian nature hymns is a passage from the great hymn to Amon-Râ : " Thou art He who made the grass for the herds and fruit-trees for men ; who brings forth that from which live the fish in the river and the birds in the heaven . . . who makes that which the mice need in their holes and feeds the birds upon all the trees ; who watches at night when all men sleep and who seeks that which is best for his cattle ; who has made men all of them and has created all that is." [2]

But it is in the Wisdom literature both of Israel and Egypt with its inherent interest in humanity that the idea of a divine providence presiding over each individual person reaches its fullest development, and appears in every respect to be on a level with the New Testament assurance that the very hairs of man's head are numbered and with Jesus' saying that no man by taking thought can add a cubit to his stature. We have already seen that in the earliest collection of the Book of Proverbs moral conduct is based upon the thought that God is man's Maker, and upon a doctrine of personal retribution

[1] Staerk, " Psalms," S.A.T., p. xxi. ; Hempel, Altheb. Lit., p. 13. Gunkel, Ausgewählte Psalmen on Ps. 104 for dependence on Gen. 1.
[2] Erman, p. 352.

and reward. The Book of Job, in a passage (12[7f.]) in the style of the nature psalms, speaks of the beasts, the wild birds, the crawling creatures, and the fish of the sea as all having a sense of God's government and care, " in whose control lies every living soul and the whole life of man." [1]   In the contemporary Elephantiné fragment of the story of Ahikar we read that " nothing lies in a man's power, to lift up his foot or to set it down [namely, without the will of the gods], " and the Book of Proverbs records that God has perfect knowledge of the thoughts of man for He weighs the hearts of men (24[12], etc.).   A phrase that occurs in an Egyptian hymn, namely, *sealed by his seal*, and which indicates that " all living beings are under his (the divinity's) hand " [2] may, as Humbert suggests, underlie the thought of Job 37[7] : " He (God) seals the hand of every man that all men may know His working."

A remarkable utterance of the Egyptian sage Amen-em-ope, describes the divine providence as all embracing in its scope and minutely comprehensive in its omniscience and power. " Whoso does evil, the harbour casts him out, and its slime returns him (back). The north wind descends that it may bring his (life's) hour to an end " (iv. 12, 13).   Fichtner (p. 112) says that only in this Egyptian saying and in the biblical wisdom-writings (cf. Job 37[11f.], Sir. 39[21f.], Sap. Sol. 16[17. 24], 19[6] ; 4 Macc. 4[10]) can he find the idea that the Creator exercises absolute power over the world's resources and forces, employing them in the interest of reward and punishment.   This is hardly true, for in the prophecy of Amos (4[7f.]) Jahve brings drought, locusts, corn-blight, plague, and earthquake to chasten Israel, and in the Book of Jonah (*c.* 420 B.C.) where the forces of Nature, the sea, and the great fish combine to bring Jonah back to his task at Nineveh and to obedience to the divine will, we have the very substance and meaning of the Egyptian moral.   But

---

[1] Moffatt, *ad. loc.*

[2] *Hymn to the God of Thebes*, Erman, p. 365. Cf. Humbert, *op. cit.* p. 104, and Hebrew text of Job 37[7].

it is the case that in Israel's Wisdom literature a strongly individualistic view of providence led to the expression of a belief that the natural forces and the moral purposes of the Creator are complementary powers. A particularly clear statement of this is made by the author of the Wisdom of Solomon. "The cosmos," it is here said (16¹), "fights for the righteous," and "creation, ministering to . . . its Maker, strains its force against the unrighteous . . . and slakens it in behalf of them that trust in Thee, for beneficence" (16²⁴). Sirach, as we have observed, is imbued with the thought (39²¹ᶠ·) that the world is a cosmos, an ordered system in which the powers of Nature and the ethical laws are in perfect union.

That the biblical faith in providence owes much to the non-Hebrew Wisdom literature, and was fostered by it to become one of the most powerful articles of religious belief, may be concluded not only from the traces of contact which we have noted between the Hebrew and the Oriental wisdom, but also from another characteristic which is common to this class of writing. We refer to the discernible modification of the particularism which attaches to all national deities and which in consequence hampers thought in its ascent to the conception of an all-powerful and all-knowing providence. In the Egyptian and Babylonian wisdom-writings there appears what may be called a monotheistic tendency which shows a marked preference for the general description of the deity as " God " or as " the God." The individual names of the gods do not completely disappear. In the Babylonian Wisdom literature, Shamash the sun-god receives mention ; in Ahikar reference is made to " the gods " ; and in the Egyptian writings, even to the latest times, gods, especially the god Thoth, are named. The tendency, however, is unmistakable. The same feature is to be observed in the Hebrew wisdom-books. The name Jahve occurs exclusively in the oldest collections of the Book of Proverbs, but the preference for the general term expressive of deity and Godhood (Elohim, Eloah, El) gradually

becomes apparent.[1] Later, in the second century B.C., there is
a partial return to the name Jahve, a fact upon which we shall
have afterwards to remark. That the removal of the name
should become so marked a characteristic is the more noteworthy since " Jahve," as the deity of a monolatrous, and then
of a monotheistic, worship was already predisposed to absorb
all the highest attributes of deity. But the use of the general
term for divinity was more suited to convey the thought of a
universal providence. We have thus not only testimony to the
influence of the wisdom-schools as being the main source of the
deepening and developing of the doctrine of providence, but
also to that international relationship which helped this
development.

The question, important from the point of view of the
history of religion, may now be set : what addition, if any, did
Christianity make, apart from its particular doctrine of the
Incarnation, to the doctrine of providence which came down
to it from Judaism ? The teaching of the Gospels could hardly
be expected to contribute anything to the subject deeper than
the ideas which Judaism had developed concerning the oversight of the Creator over His creation and over each person,
his thoughts and actions. The wisdom-writings had taught
that God has perfect knowledge of each person and his ways.
When we are asked in the Sayings of the Fathers to remember
(ii. 1) that " there is an Eye that sees, an Ear that hears, and
that all actions are inscribed in the (celestial) book," this does
not go beyond previous thought, and but repeats the question
of the wisdom-psalm (94[9]) : " He that planted the ear shall

[1] In the older collections of Prov. " Jahve " is used exclusively without
reflection upon any particular or national characteristics (cf. Fichtner, p. 104).
In the poem of Job " Jahve " (except 12[9]—perhaps *lapsus calami*) and in
The Divine Speeches (except introductory formulæ) is dropped. So also in
Qoheleth. In Sirach and Sap. Sol. in half of the cases the general term is used
(Hempel, *op. cit.* p. 53). From the time of Sirach in the Wisdom literature
the consciousness that the world-creator gave Israel the Law and is Israel's
God and " our God," the " God of the Fathers," brings the particularistic
element in " Jahve " back into the realm of religious thought (Fichtner, p. 113).

He not hear ?   He that formed the eye, shall He not see ? "
(cf. Sap. Sol. 1⁶).   Moreover, Judaism expressed the thought
that the deity has sympathy with human nature.   " We know,"
says the author of the Fourth Book of Maccabees " that the
Creator of the world as Giver of the Law feels for us according
to our nature " (5²⁵, cf. Ps. 103¹⁴).   That God loves all His
creatures is the teaching of a beautiful passage in the Wisdom
of Solomon (11²³ᶠ·) :

> " Thou hast mercy on all men, because Thou hast power to do all things,
> And Thou overlookest the sins of men, to the end that they may repent.
> For Thou lovest all things that are,
> And abhorrest none of the things that Thou hast made.
> For never wouldst Thou have formed anything if Thou didst hate it.
>
> ·   ·   ·   ·   ·   ·   ·   ·
>
> O Sovereign Lord, Thou lover of souls,
> For Thine incorruptible Spirit is in all things."

Besides this, in the wisdom-psalm (127), there is the thought
which is parallel to Jesus' call to men to trust the providence
of God and not to be overcome with the mundane cares and
anxieties of life, for " God's gifts come to His loved ones as they
sleep " (v. 2).

Now in the gospels three elements stand out as the substance
of Jesus' teaching—the coming kingdom of God with its judgment, the fatherly providence of God, and the religious ethic
of repentance, holiness, and loving service.¹   All these have
considerably more than their roots in Judaism, and this is
particularly evident in regard to the doctrine of an individual
providence.   But it is exactly here that Karl Holl, one of the
most thorough of the researchers in the history of religion,
regards the contribution of the teaching of Jesus to have been
altogether new, and on account of its newness and appeal to
have effected the rising of Christianity to first rank among the
religions of the world.²

---

¹ Cf. Harnack, *Ausbreitung*, 3rd ed. p. 35 f.
² " Urchristentum und Religionsgeschichte," *Die Antike*, Bd. i. Heft 2,
1925, p. 161 f.

Holl observes that when we dissolve the Christian teaching and sacraments into their elements, comparing them with Jewish and Hellenistic teaching and religious practice, the question becomes acute : how did Christianity gain its ascendency over the competitive faiths ? He regards it as one of the chief defects of the study of the history of religion that this simple question has been almost entirely overlooked. Serious thought, he says, will quickly abandon the idea that the victory of Christianity was due to the helping power of the state, or due to its power of assimilating ideas from the religious world of the time. This ability to assemble loans would only mean that in itself it was one of the poorest of religions. Nor was it its high ideals and strict morality that attracted the masses, for the masses are not attracted by these alone. The special feature in Jesus' teaching, Holl sees to be preserved in that which seemed to His day so strange as to raise astonishment and attack, and therefore as fact is the best historically accredited. Jesus was called by His opponents " the associate of publicans and sinners." He Himself acknowledges that He came to seek " the lost," that He had not come to call " the righteous," and states that the publican and the prostitute would enter into the kingdom of heaven sooner than the patterns of righteousness, the Pharisees. This —although the standard of entrance to that kingdom was the highest imaginable, namely, the perfection of God Himself and a purity of inner disposition. The idea of God as offering Himself to the sinner, familiar as it has become to Christendom, presented the greatest contrast to Judaism. In the Old Testament, God is described as Father, the nation is called His son ; in the course of time the king is called son of God, and at length in the Psalms of Solomon the individual righteous person is given that title (cf. also Sap. Sol. 2^{18}). This brings us near to the time of Jesus. But Jesus, in addressing His gospel primarily to sinners and not to " the righteous," placed the idea of the personal relationship to God on a broader foundation. The parables of the prodigal son, of the Pharisee and publican in the Temple, His words concerning the woman who was a great sinner, and on the forgiveness of God in the story of the unforgiving servant, describe what was His special teaching in this respect. He placed the relationship of God and man not on the distinction between pure and impure, righteous and unrighteous, but upon forgiveness, and the thankfulness that proceeded from the gift of forgiveness. Right conduct had here its motivation. He thus placed the idea of relation to God on another plane than that constituted by the view that the more morally perfect the nearer man is to God. For Judaism, if the Law was to have any meaning at all, it announced that God acknowledges only those who do righteously. The doctrine of the divine providence which Jesus held, in its emphasis upon the love of God for the unrighteous, seemed to put an end to all moral striving. That was the blasphemy against God for which, according to Holl, the Jews crucified Christ. To what is reckoned to be the common-sense view, Jesus' extended conception of the relation of God to man may still seem to transgress against reason. The Church itself in its later practice tended to modify the teaching of Jesus.

Holl's contention in regard to the new element which Christianity introduced and which was the cause of its expansion, loses nothing in the way of confirmation when it is qualified as we think it should be. It is always difficult to prove that an *idea* is new. Some Jules Verne always precedes even the pioneers of discovery. In the passage which we have quoted from the Wisdom of Solomon, where God is named the Lover of souls, who has compassion on all men and loves all things that are, and overlooks the sins of men that they may repent, the thought that the goodness and mercy of God are calls to sinners to repentance appears apparently for the first time [1] in Judaism in the pre-Christian era. It is true that the author

---

[1] Cf. Holmes, *ad loc.* note in Charles, *Apoc.* vol. i.

in later parts of his work resiles from this high ethic,[1] and
otherwise clothes himself in Jewish particularism, but he does
express the idea which seems to be the root of Jesus' teaching.
That this teaching ran counter to the tradition of Judaism
may be observed in the fact that the application of it to history
by the author of the Wisdom of Solomon in his succeeding
chapters overturns the Old Testament historical accounts.
That the application of it by Jesus to the conditions of life in
Palestine in His time offended the spirit of Judaism is shown
by the New Testament narrative. But Jesus' message of the
love of God for sinners in its development and in its very
doctrinal nature was certainly new and felt to be so. We
can gather this from the satire which the upright and astute
Jewish scholar Celsus launches against Christianity. He
complains that Christians depict God as if He were a robber
captain who would regard it as a slur and reproach were any
of his followers to confess to having done no crime. Further,
we observe in the statement of St. Paul, that God " commends
His love toward us, in that, while we were yet sinners, Christ
died for us " (Rom. 5[8]), that this special element in Jesus' teaching was maintained in Christological doctrine. Repentance as
constituting the right relationship to God, Jesus demanded,
but this was the response to the love of God who sought the
souls of men. The newness of the idea lay in the thought of
the approach of God to man and not of " the righteous " to
God. The initiative lay with God. Holl remarks that not
only the Jewish converts but those from the Hellenistic religions
must have appreciated that in the Christian gospel was something
other than that expressed in the familiar formulæ of the mystery-
cults : " He who has lived well and justly," " He who is free
from all iniquity " let him approach and partake. A *mysterium*
for the forgiveness of sins, states Holl, " as we have it not only
in Baptism but in the earliest conception of the Lord's Supper,
was something which was entirely foreign to the Greek

---

[1] Cf. Holmes, *op. cit.* and Siegfried in Kautzsch *Apok.*, Sap. Sol. 11[23f.].

mysteries." The Church indeed later felt uncomfortable under
the Gospel teaching, and returned to the beaten track of religious
forms—hence penance, asceticism, etc.—moulding its thought
anew after the pattern of " He that is pure, only he can approach
to God," [1] but the Church dogma of the Incarnation (" *became
man for us men and for our salvation* ") preserves the authentic
teaching of Jesus on the providence of God as exercised toward
sinners. From the religious-historical viewpoint this teaching
of Jesus represents the development [2] and fruition of the
humanism of the wisdom-writers, the centre of whose religious
thought was the interest of God in the individual.

We have already shown that even in pre-exilic times (*e.g.*
Prov. 17[5]) and in the Book of Job, and, above all, quite explicitly
in the *Testaments of the Twelve*, man's duty to man is conceived of in a universal sense. But the broad humanism,
which is common to the Hebrew and the Oriental wisdom, and
which in Israel and the Book of Amen-em-ope finds general
expression in the view that every man and all his ways are
under the oversight of an all-knowing Creator, underwent in
the process of Hebrew thought change and modification. This

---

[1] In the Eucharistic office, according to the forms of the primitive Church
(see the excellent compilation *The Divine Service*, by Dr. H. J. Wotherspoon),
it has to be noticed that after the *sancta sanctis*, " Holy things to the holy,"
there come the words " There is one Holy, one Lord, one Jesus Christ, etc."
The so-called " Fencing of Tables," as practised two generations or so ago in the
Church of Scotland, with some such general formula as : " He that is guilty of
etc. etc., I do hereby debar him from coming to the Lord's Table " was in
principle a return to the idea of the mystery religions.

[2] Interesting and illuminating in this regard is the comparison which
Edward Norden (*Agnostos Theos*, p. 277 f.) makes between Matt. 11[25f.] (Q)—
a literary product and not an extempore saying—and Sir. 51 (cf. 51[26] with
its Gospel parallel Matt. 11[29]," Take my yoke upon you," etc., and its invitation
to " all that labour and are heavy laden "). See also E. Meyer (*Ursprung*, etc.,
Bd. i. p. 280 f.) on " The rejoicing over the success of Christianity (Matt. 11[25f.]=
Luke 10[21f.]) and Jesus Sirach." Norden and Meyer agree that there is literary
contact between the two passages, with a wider religious appeal on the part
of Q to the mass of men and the lower strata of society. This appeal reaped
its fruits in the first Christian centuries, and gave the Christian faith ascendancy
over its competitors (Meyer, *op. cit.*).

modification was effected in three ways—the heightening of
the national consciousness of Israel that it was an elect people,
a result which the wide outlook of second Isaiah upon the world
to which Israel was to be missionary only intensified ; the
growing regard for the authority of the Law and the value
of the cultus ; and the growth within the nation itself, since
the days of Nehemiah, of the class of " the righteous." Much
of the debate between Jewish and Christian scholars
concerning the presence or absence of universalistic thought
in Israel appears to be due to ignoring these intransigent elements
on the one hand and the unique nature of the wisdom literature
on the other.

The Book of Proverbs in its several collections, forming
originally separate works, extending from pre-exilic times to
the date *circa* 300 B.C., is itself a mirror of the increasing esteem
for the cult in the wisdom-schools, and probably reflects a
process taking place in the nation at large. There are collections which take no notice at all of the cult, others which mildly
criticize it by affirming that goodness of conduct is above
perfect ritual observance. It is only in the latest collection
that we find the one and only direct exhortation to honour
Jahve with offerings ($3^{9f.}$). This paucity of appreciation of
the cult is noticeable in all the canonical wisdom-writings.
But in the second century B.C. a change takes place. Sirach,
though striking the traditional note by teaching that offerings
without morality are worthless, nevertheless rises to poetic
heights in describing the temple-service on the day of Atonement. Later, in the Wisdom of Solomon, the cultus, sacrifices,
and Levitical purity (18^9, ^{21}, 9^8, $3^{13f.}$) receive full recognition,
and the *Sayings of the Fathers* opens with a saying that purports
to be from Simeon the Just (*c.* 219 B.C.) : " On three things
the world stands—on the Law, and on the Service, and on the
doing of kindnesses."

But, along with this trend of thought as revealed by the
Wisdom literature, other changes occur which emphasize Jewish

religious nationalism. From the time of Sirach onwards the
deity is called " our God," a term, common elsewhere, but not
used hitherto in this class of writing, and He who created
heaven and earth and all things is the " God of the fathers "
(Sap. Sol. 9^1; Bar. 3^{32}; Job 8^1). For the author of 4 Macc.
He who is the World-Creator and has sympathy with our human
nature is the " Law-giver," the God of Israel *par excellence*.
Wisdom who had been in Prov. (8, 9) a personification of God's
creative purpose or Helper in creation is now identified by
Sirach with the Law.   Thus, along with a widening view of
God's providential government and care for man, there is an
opposite tendency, an increase in nationalistic and particularistic
thought.   Sirach can rise to a doctrine of universalism :

> An honourable race is what ?   The race of men !
> An honourable race is that which feareth God (10^{19}).

But his view is that while God has poured out Wisdom upon
all nations in measure, He grants her "without measure to
those that love Him " ($1^{9f.}$), that is to Israel, for the heavenly
Wisdom-Law whom the Creator created had been caused by
Him to descend to earth and to take up her inheritance in
Israel (24^8).   Whatever, therefore, is given or seems to be given
in the larger spirit of universalism is later taken away or reduced.
So in the Wisdom of Solomon, while God is the sovereign Lord
who is the lover of souls and hates nothing that He has made,
we learn further that He has hated the Canaanites as an accursed
race from the beginning (11^{24}, 12^{11}).

That which we see in the Jewish Wisdom literature in its
latest products, namely, a universalism curbed and restrained
by nationalistic elements, we may observe to be reflected in
Jewish religious history.   The Judaism of the time immediately
before Christ was enthusiastic in making converts among the
nations.   " The period in which the Christian preachers began
their work," says Schürer (*Z.N.T.W.*, 1905, p. 40 f.), " is exactly
the time when the Jewish propaganda had reached the high
point of its success."   Hillel (20 B.C.) and his school spurred

on the Jewish mission to the heathen. One of his sayings (*Sayings of the Fathers*, i. 12) is : " Love the creatures (mankind) and lead them to the Law." But as Harnack remarks in his *Mission and Expansion of Christianity* : [1] " In the time of Christ and the apostles the forces that strove to advance were intermingled with those of a nationalistic character which contrived to retard." The figure which Axenfeld [2] employs in his description of Jewish propaganda as a precursor of the Christian world mission is that of a conquering army keen for the offensive, but continually hampered by having to keep in touch with its base. The front line of the attacking forces may be represented by the great ideas : the one spiritual God, the Maker of heaven and earth, His holy moral law, and His judgment to come. The base of operations in the rearward were represented by the notions : the God of our fathers, our God, the holiness of the Sabbath, and circumcision. While the devout or " God-fearers," as those converts were called who accepted a partial measure of Jewish ritual, were numerous, much fewer in comparison were those who took the rank of proselytes by accepting the whole law and the mark of circumcision. Outside Palestine, conditions were favourable to freedom and laxity,[3] but if among the Jews of the diasporate there was any weakening of the nationalistic and particularistic ideas and practices, this was efficiently counteracted by the growing influence and authority of the Judaism of Palestine where the Pharisees were the champions of the national religion and where historical memories of the Maccabean wars, in behalf of the Law and against Antiochus Epiphanes' policy of the uniformity of religions, were very much alive.[4] The Sadducee movement,

[1] Third German ed. p. 19.

[2] " Jüdische Propaganda als Vorläuferin der urchristlichen Mission " (*Missionswiss. Studien*, 1904), p. 8 f.

[3] *e.g.* The Wisdom of Solomon, 6[1f.], in the address to rulers has the lax Jewish magnates of Alexandria in view.

[4] 4 Macc. is an example of an excellent sermon on the example of the martyrs in the time of Epiphanes (*c.* 167 B.C.); cf. 2 Macc.

as Hölscher shows, was not popularly hated because of its
negative religious tenets, but because these tenets were largely
inspired by a freer outlook upon, and friendliness with, the non-
Jewish (Roman) world.[1] The resurrection of the dead, which
they denied, belonged to the Messianic programme with its
vindication of Israel as against the heathen. The Sadducees
rejected this programme.

It is against the Palestinian background of religious thought
that we must view the Christian teaching. The teaching of
Jesus on the doctrine of Providence was twofold. On the one
hand it deepened the conception of God's care for His creatures
by extending the divine care and interest to sinners. " Many
that be first shall be last and the last first." This cut at the
roots of the distinction fixed by the age-old division of " the
righteous " and " the unrighteous." On the other hand the
nationalism of orthodox piety was attacked and dissolved.
The blessings of the End-Time will not be for the sons of Abraham
alone ; Many shall come from the East and the West and shall
sit down with Abraham and Isaac and Jacob in the kingdom
of heaven (St. Matt. 8$^{5\text{-}13}$ Q). The parables of the vineyard
(St. Matt. 21$^{33f.}$) and of the Great Supper (St. Luke 14$^{16f.}$; cf.
St. Matt. 22$^{2f.}$) teach the same universalism. God's guests
come from the highways and byways. His invitation goes
out to mankind and not to Jews only.

Harnack shows conclusively that the universalism of Jesus
did not include a *mission* to the heathen. The oldest source
of the Gospels (namely, Q) relates to a mission to the Jews in
Palestine only, a mission which Jesus believed would be the
last. The early Church in promoting a mission to the heathen
saw that " the missionizing of the world had of necessity to
result from the religion of Jesus." " That it so resulted, in
contradiction to many of His words," says Harnack (p. 36 f.),
" is a strong witness to the manner, power, and greatness of
His teaching." But if in the days of Jesus an obstacle to the

---

[1] *Der Sadduzäismus*, 1906, pp. 12 f., 106 f.

practical application of the doctrine of the universal providence of God, through a mission to the heathen, lay in the belief that the End-Time was at hand, Jesus had removed the obstacle of nationalism and had liberated those spiritual forces which flowed particularly strongly in the wisdom-writings. That this liberation was something " new " can be seen from the fact that the Christian world mission conquered the territory which Jewish propaganda had prepared, entering by the breach which Judaism left unclosed, the gap between its universalistic teaching and its particularistic religious doctrine and practice.

In the period after the rise of Christianity Jewish thought in regard to non-Israelites followed the more rigid conceptions of the school of Shammai rather than the liberal tendencies of the Hillel school. The term " stranger " (gēr) is more narrowly conceived than in the Old Testament and indicates the full proselyte who has accepted baptism and circumcision. In the period of the Mishna it is clear from the prescribed practice (Halakha), which is normative for Judaism, that the word "neighbour" as found in the Law (Lev. 19[18])—"Thou shalt love thy neighbour as thyself"—does not mean every man, but only the Israelite and the full proselyte. Modern Jewish scholars seek to show that in the New Testament period the command to love the neighbour was understood in a universal sense and that it bears that sense in the passage in Leviticus. The relevant passages of Jewish literature which Billerbeck and Strack have collected prove that this thesis cannot be held in its entirety, and particularly not for the New Testament period.[1]

[1] Cf. p. 12 above, note [3]. Cf. Strack-Billerbeck, op. cit. p. 354 f. (as against Elbogen, Bacher, etc.) on the dispute whether Judaism (Hillel, etc.) interpreted Lev. 19[18] in a universal sense in the N.T. period. Hillel (Sab. 31a) said, " What is hateful to thee do not to thy fellow (haber)." Strack-Billerbeck hold that apart from this negative form of statement saying nothing about love for the neighbour, Hillel says nothing that leads us to think that he goes beyond the general view that " the neighbour " includes the Israelite and the proselyte, but excludes all others, even the resident stranger (gēr toshab) who as not accepting Judaism was a " goi " or pagan. " Only from the second century A.D. onwards do we hear a voice here and there which perhaps can be taken as

Universalistic thought does appear in the Old Testament, in second Isaiah, in the Psalms, in the Book of Jonah. The Wisdom literature was its foster-mother. The author of the Twelve Testaments, we have observed, evidently did interpret, if he did not understand also, the command of Leviticus in a universal sense. But thought has always a relationship to history, and the period of the Maccabean wars, in defence of the Jewish religion, had a most profound and lasting effect. The effort of Antiochus IV. to abolish the Law, and in particular the practice of circumcision, had the effect that a Judaism living on its hard-gained victory laid an immense importance and weight on all the marks of adherence to the religion of the fathers. Judaism from the Greek period presents in its development a narrowing down and a continuous qualification of the idea of universalism, a qualification by no means restricted to moral requirements. The experiences of this period, and the political experiences of a later date, only sharpened for the orthodox the ancient contrast between Israel and the nations.

The development of thought in Judaism of the New Testament period is of a piece with that which we discover later. That the particularistic trend was, in spite of individual expressions of an opposite character, maintained for centuries, may be observed in " the premier text-book of medieval Jewish mysticism " called the *Zohar*.[1] Here the argument that the

preaching the universal love of man," *e.g.* Ben 'Azzai (*c.* A.D. 110)—Siphra Lev. 19[18]—who taught that God's making man in His own image represented a higher general principle than the love of the neighbour in Lev. 19[18]. This itself shows that Lev. 19[18] was not generally conceived of as having universal significance. Dr. Herford (*op. cit.* p. 150) admits that in rabbinical literature there are " bitter and angry words," and violent hatred against Gentiles, and is right in attributing much of this to persecution of Jews at the hands of the Romans and later of the Christian Church. But while this could account for such a saying as Ben Jochai's (*c.* 150), " the best of the Goyim (non-Jews) deserve death " (Mek. Exod. 14[7]), it hardly can account for Siphra Lev. 20[10], " If any one . . . commits adultery with his neighbour's wife, that excludes the wife of others " (*i.e.* of non-Israelites).

[1] The following translation is that of Harry Sperling and Maurice Simon, vol. i. (Soncino Press, 1931), with Introduction by Dr. J. Abelson.

Zohar is not representative of Judaism as a whole cannot be urged, for it far surpasses the Mishna and the Talmud in its liberal independent thought, and may be regarded as the flower of Jewish religious thinking. In setting forth the cardinal precepts of Judaism, this exhortation occurs : " The eighth precept is to love the proselyte who comes to be circumcised and to be brought under the wings of the ' Divine Presence ' (*Shekinah*),[1] which takes under its wings those who separate themselves from the impure ' unholy region ' and come near unto her, as it is written : *Let the earth bring forth a living soul according to its kind*.[2] Think not that the same ' living soul ' which is found in Israel is assigned to all mankind. The expression ' after its kind ' denotes that there are many compartments and enclosures, one within the other, in that region which is called ' living ' beneath its wings. . . . There are besides, under each wing, other concealed enclosures and divisions from whence there emanate souls, which are assigned to all the proselytes who enter the fold—these are indeed termed ' living soul,' but ' according to its kind ' ; they all enter under the wings of the Shekinah, and no farther. The soul of Israel, on the other hand, emanates from the very body of that tree [the celestial Tree of Life].[3] . . . It is for this reason that Israel is called a ' darling son ' for whom the bowels, as it were, of the Shekinah yearn,[4] and that the children of Israel are called ' those who are born from the womb ' and not merely from the outer wings. Furthermore, the proselytes have no portion in the celestial tree, much less in the body of

[1] " To bring under the wings of the Shekinah " is a particularly frequent formula meaning to make a heathen a proselyte. " When a proselyte desires to come over to Judaism, we stretch out our hands to bring him under the wings of the Shekinah " (Lev. R. 2, 12 Ben Gamaliel, c. 140 A.D.). Cf. 2 Bar. 42³.

[2] Cf. Gen. 1²⁴.

[3] In 1 Enoch 24³ this tree is on a high mountain. " Its fruit shall be for food for the elect " (25⁵). In 2 Enoch 8⁴ it covers all paradise and bears the fruit of all trees.

[4] Cf. Jer. 31²⁰, cf. Isa. 46³.

it ; their portion is only in the wings and no more. The righteous proselytes,[1] therefore, rest under the wings of the Shekinah and are united to it there, but penetrate no farther, as has already been explained. Therefore, we read : *Let the earth bring forth a living soul according to its kind,* namely, *cattle and creeping things and beast of the earth after its kind,* that is to say, all derive their soul from that source called ' living,' but each according to its kind, from the grade appropriate to itself." (*Zohar,* Prologue, Part I. 13a.)

" The *Zohar,*" says Dr. Abelson, " was a people's book." He compares it with the great medieval philosophical treatise of Moses Maimonides, the *Guide to the Perplexed,* which was not known to the Jews in the mass. The passage we have cited speaks for itself. The difference between the sons of Abraham and even the perfect proselyte is fundamental, and rests on the fact of Israel's election. There does not appear to be anything in this thought that distinguishes the *Zohar* from the rabbinic tradition.[2]

---

[1] " Proselyte of righteousness," term. tech. = full proselyte (*gēr*) who submits to circumcision, the bath of purification or baptism, and the laws regarding offerings.

[2] In the Midrash, Num. R. 8, the proselyte is given the full promise of, Blessed is every one that feareth the Lord " (Ps. 128[1]) in this and the next world, but whereas the Israelites inherit the merits of Abraham, the proselytes' present and future benefits are circumscribed by, " For thou shalt eat the labour of thine hands " (Ps. 128[2]).

CHAPTER II

THE IDEAS OF INDIVIDUAL RESPONSIBILITY AND OF REWARD AND RETRIBUTION IN THE OLD TESTAMENT

A QUESTION of importance to the examination of the ideas of reward and retribution in Hebrew religion is : When in Israel's history does the individual become conscious of being the subject of the deity's favour and anger ? Writers upon the religion of the Semitic peoples have emphasized the power of the conception of the blood-bond that bound the individual to the family, tribe, and race.[1] In the Old Testament one feature appears to stand out more prominently than any other, particularly in the historical books and the prophetic writings, and that is the solidarity of the nation and its members. Hence it has become a generally current opinion that only late in the day, in exilic and late pre-exilic times, did the individual gain a personal religious value. Thus the prophet Jeremiah has been hailed as " the father of religious individualism." In regard to the proverb which in the days of Jeremiah and Ezekiel served as a popular skit upon the belief in solidarity or as a support of piety in face of calamity : " The fathers have eaten sour grapes, and the children's teeth are set on edge," Professor Peake says : " The doctrine [of solidarity] had affirmed the mutual responsibility of the members of the group which formed its social unit. The individual had but little independent significance." [2] Also Eissfeldt in a recent essay on the *Growth of the Biblical Conception of God* (1931, p. 13 f.), after remarking that Jeremiah and Ezekiel gave the decisive impulse to the

[1] Cf. W. R. Smith, *Rel. of the Semites.*
[2] Jeremiah, *Cent. Bible*, vol. ii. p. 100.

growth of individualistic and universalistic thought, writes :
" Previous to these prophets the individual brought his private
concerns before Jahve, but the religious individualism which
we first recognize in Jeremiah is something new."

We certainly observe in the Book of Jeremiah what may be
taken as an indication of the growth of thought upon man's
relation to God. The prophet in his intimate descriptions of
his communings with God presents a picture of the dependence
of the individual soul upon the divine guidance and help. The
prospect also of the future which Jeremiah holds to be in store
for Israel, a new covenant of Jahve with His people, which
has its guarantee of being kept by the nation by the fact that
it will be written in each individual's heart, is a high point of
Old Testament aspiration and reflection.[1] But when Eissfeldt
says that previous to Jeremiah the individual brought his
private concerns before Jahve we must ask how much or how
little is meant by this bringing of private concerns. Eissfeldt
evidently wishes to signify that before Jeremiah the consciousness of an individual relationship to Jahve was barely existent.
All the writing prophets of the eighth century, though they are
representatives of Jahve to the people, have a close personal
relationship to Jahve, whose word they receive and proclaim.
Isaiah's account of his call to be a prophet, his response to God,
" Here am I ; send me," the forgiveness of his sins, the cleansing
of his lips that he might be Jahve's spokesman, all exhibit the
marks of a religious individualism. But inasmuch as prophets
and others chosen to be instruments of the divine purpose are
not ordinary persons, it may be held that no deductions of a
general nature may be based upon their exceptional experiences.
We must therefore seek to establish from other data that
religious individualistic thought is present even in ancient

---

[1] The New Covenant passage (Jer. 31[31-34]) is regarded by Smend and Duhm
as not genuine but as a post-exilic addition, presupposing the destruction of
the Old Covenant with the fall of Jerusalem. But with Peake (*Problem of
Suffering*, p. 15 f.) and others we may regard the verses as a genuine forecasting
of the future.

Israel and is quite apparent from the beginning of the monarchy onwards. Naturally, the idea of a personal relationship and responsibility to Jahve was subject to increasing development and purification. The belief in deity was in Israel increasingly enriched with new thought and higher conceptions of the nature of Godhood, but no one on that account would deny a true belief in deity to a primitive stage of culture. Similarly with the consciousness of religious individualism, unless we are prepared to point to a time in Israel's history when a person did not bring his private concerns before Jahve nor regard himself on account of his actions or omissions as subject to divine reward and retribution, we cannot say on the ground of the enrichment of the notion of man's personal relationship to God, that once the idea of a personal relationship did not exist. It is impossible, unless we draw up some very refined definition of religious individualism, to indicate any point in Hebrew history as known to us by its records where we can say, " Here emerged religious individualism "—that is, the consciousness of the deity's interest in and claims upon the individual person who seeks the deity's favour and fears the deity's wrath.

The question with which we are dealing is one of major importance from the point of view of our estimate of the influence of the Wisdom literature in its earliest products upon Hebrew religion. For although Löhr [1] and, in lesser measure, Gunkel [2] have both shown that even in ancient Israel the idea of corporate responsibility did not destroy that of individual responsibility, however much on occasion it limited it, the dogma that religious individualism only emerged with Jeremiah and Ezekiel is still employed as a literary criterion, with the result that the earliest collections of maxims in the Book of Proverbs, with their highly individualistic outlook, are placed

---

[1] *Sozialismus und Individualismus im A.T.*, 1906.

[2] Cf. Genesis in *S.A.T.*—" Ausgewählte Psalmen "—and in article on "Vergeltung " in *Die Religion in Geschichte und Gegenwart* (abbr. *R.G.G.*).

in the late pre-exilic or in the post-exilic period. Hempel,[1]
for example, states that the fact that in these earliest collections
the notion of collective responsibility, against which Ezekiel
in the sixth century wages warfare, plays no rôle, is a warning
against giving these too early a date. He therefore would
place that section of the Book of Proverbs which reflects dependence upon the wisdom of Amen-em-ope and Ahikar
(Prov. 22^{17}–24^{34}) at the end of the fifth century, and the two
earliest collections (10–22^{16}, 25–29) somewhat earlier. Hempel's
criticism fails to appreciate that proverbs usually and normally
have reference to individual and not to corporate life. A
collection of proverbs, all of which referred to the family or
nation, would be a literary rarity, to say the least. The very
character of the Hebrew and Oriental wisdom is its regard for
the person and his well-being—an inalienable feature. It is
true that the collective view of responsibility has no prominent
place, but it is present. Though typical of these maxims is
that " he who tends a fig tree gets the figs " (27^{18}), yet it is taught
that a man's house and children reap security or destruction
through his virtue or vice ($14^{11.\ 26}$). His descendants benefit
from his uprightness (20^{7}). Had the earliest collections of
maxims (10 f., 25 f.) borne any traces of Ezekiel's polemic
in favour of a purely individual responsibility, then it would
be necessary to place them in the sixth century or later. But
there are no such traces, either of this polemic being about
to emerge or having emerged. The individualism, religious
and secular, which characterizes the Hebrew maxim literature,
a product which Hempel himself recognizes to be originally
foreign to Israel, must be explained as largely due to its antecedents, the Oriental, primarily the Egyptian, wisdom-writings.
Sellin, who regards Proverbs, chapters 10–22^{16}, as belonging to
the Solomonic period (c. 950), and the nucleus of chapters 25–29
as dating from the period of Hezekiah (c. 722–699), implicitly
puts out of action the literary canon supplied by the tenet that

[1] *Althebräische Literatur*, Potsdam, 1930, p. 55.

Jeremiah is the father of religious individualism and Ezekiel its first exponent. The Wisdom literature shows us, Sellin observes, " that the intellectual life of Israel was much richer and more many-sided than we are apt to imagine from attending too exclusively to the evidence of the prophetic and historical writings." [1] The task of giving ethical instruction, particularly to youth (Prov. 23, 24), naturally prescribed for the maxim writings an individualistic outlook, just as for the prophetic and historical works their interest in the *people* Israel made the collective aspect of responsibility, reward, and retribution necessarily predominant. For the bulk of the Old Testament indeed, the Law, the prophets, and the historical accounts, the centre of thought is provided by the one great contrast, Jahve and His people, the divine providence and the race; but this constitutional characteristic of these writings must not blind us to the evidence that religious individualism is traceable quite early.

The solidarity of the individual with his family and tribe is in ancient Israel so great a reality that upon critical occasions the single personality seems to be of little account. The story of Achan (Josh. 7[24]) is a typical example. For the appropriation of spoils which in the warfare of Joshua against the Canaanites had been placed under a religious ban, not only Achan, the author of the deed, but his sons and daughters, his oxen, asses, and sheep are put to death. As retribution for sin against Jahve the sinner's punishment would in no wise have been complete if Achan's posterity had been allowed to survive and perpetuate his " name," or, as primitively conceived, his " life." But that the fate of Achan's sons and daughters, who are presumably innocent, is shared by his cattle shows that not merely the idea of the bond that links a man with his family is involved, but the primitive belief in taint and *tabu* which embraces all Achan's possessions. The antique mind magnifies the effect of the individual's acts. In this age,

[1] *Introduction to O.T.*, p. 207.

though the innocent may suffer with the guilty and considerations of morality are not separate from those that concern the observance and breach of the cultus, the bond of communion which holds the single member to the family and clan has by no means the effect of entirely suppressing the individual's significance. As in ancient Hebrew psychology the soul of a man is thought of as being in each part of his body, so, says Pedersen, the family is thought of as being "embodied in every man, with all its substance and all its responsibility." [1] Thus the fact and consequently the sense of individual responsibility is heightened. Jonathan's action in breaking the religious fast by partaking of honey disturbs the whole life of the community. The reward of Rahab's individual act of treason in betraying Jericho to the Hebrews (Josh. 2) is reaped by all her father's house. In both these incidents the individual is given excessive importance. The idea of solidarity was thus capable of developing what may be called a super-individualism. [2]

While in critical circumstances such as warfare a whole people (1 Sam. 15) or city might be subject to the ban (*herem*) and thus condemned to death, the innocent suffering with the guilty, and while the sin or error of one person (Josh. 7; 2 Sam. 21; 2 Sam. 24; cf. 1 Chron. 21[17]) could cause the wrath of Jahve to fall upon the whole community of Israel, there is ample proof that in pre-prophetic times the individual regarded himself as dependent upon the deity's providence and protection and as personally subject to reward and punishment for his actions. When Stade, [3] speaking of the earlier period of Israel's history, says that "the piety of the single individual is inseparable from the sense of unity with the nation," he omits to reflect that at

---

[1] *Israel*, p. 277.

[2] A phase of this super-individualism, indeed a derivative of it, is the rôle of the king in Israel. Cf. *The Labyrinth* (S.P.C.K., 1935), article by A. B. Johnson on "The Rôle of the King," p. 73: "The well-being of the nation as a social unit is bound up with the life of the king" (cf. 2 Sam. 21[17]).

[3] *Alttest. Theol.*, p. 193.

all times religion comprehends a vast area of private interests and concerns. It is true that a person cannot be completely separated from the group of persons to which he belongs, and that in ancient Israel, as with other peoples, the connection of the person with the clan or race was a bond of the most real and potent kind, but it is psychologically improbable that the Hebrew conception of religion, namely, "the fear of Jahve," had at any time within the range of history an absolutely communal significance. What, then, is the nature of the evidence that can be brought to prove the existence of religious individualism in the pre-prophetic period of Hebrew religion ?

Religion at a primitive stage provides man with the necessary ritual to free him from sickness and from evil spirits. The maladies that afflict his body are a personal affair. Nicolsky in his work, *Traces of Magical Formulæ in the Psalms*,[1] regards a number of psalms as containing numerous traces of magical formulæ which once belonged to the nomadic or semi-nomadic period of Israelite history. That the Psalms which are hymns, complaints, and prayers of a much later date should preserve such traces is consistent with the fact that religions outgrow and transform, but seldom entirely abandon, former modes of expression and belief. One of the magic formulæ to which Nicolsky points is "Jahve my Refuge" in Psalm 91 (v.[2]). In this he sees an expression of hoary antiquity which once indicated that within a magic circle constituted by the appropriate ritual and thus placed under the protection of the deity invoked, no demon or evil spirit had power. It is not incumbent upon us to accept as proven all that Nicolsky takes to be traces of magical formulæ in the Psalms, but it is certain that Hebrew religion in passing through its earliest phases, especially that associated with magic, which is essentially individualistic in what it seeks to acquire or to avert, did not abandon the purely personal outlook implied. In the present form of the story (Ex. 4[25] J) which narrates how the demonic

[1] *Spuren magischer Formeln in den Psalmen,* 1927.

Jahve attacks Moses in the inn, and that Zipporah, Moses' wife, placates the offended deity by circumcising her son and casting the bloody foreskin at Moses' feet, we have an instance of apotropaic magic restoring a personal relationship.[1]

The promotion of private interests constitutes a large part of ancient religious practice. A function of the priesthood which attached to that office even more securely than the duty of offering sacrifice, which could be offered in early times by a layman (Jud. 6[19], 13[19]), was to give instructions (torōth) in respect of the will of the deity in the varied circumstances of life. Childless women, for example, like Hannah, pilgrimaged to the shrine (1 Sam. 1[9f.]), made petition, and sought to move Jahve's compassion with vows. Probably Hannah's vow was a usual and general formula : " O Jahve of Hosts, if Thou wilt indeed look on the affliction of Thine handmaid and remember me . . . then I will give . . ." The title of the deity here unites the petitioner with her people, but the petition itself and its form is in personal terms. So also is the formula with which the priest dismisses the petitioner of a like nature : " Go now in peace ! The God of Israel vouchsafes unto thee the request which thou hast made of Him " (1[17]). The first chapter of the Book of Samuel here appears to have preserved the type of petition and answer made and given at the sanctuaries in the remote past in the land of Canaan. The fact of the person's solidarity with the race did not exclude the manifestations of personal religion. Nothing is more revealing in this respect than the form and significance of personal names. Such names as Jonathan (Jahve has given), Ishbaal (man of Baal), and Samuel (heard of God—El) bear their own witness to a personal piety that cannot have been a novelty of the early monarchic or late pre-monarchic period.

The literature which reflects the religion of Israel in the period before the writing prophets, shows the presence of a deep belief in the divine providence as presiding over individuals

[1] Cf. Hölscher, *Geschichte d. isr. und jüdisch. Religion*, p. 25, note 5.

and in a God who rewards and punishes personal conduct. Gunkel remarks of the old sagas of the book of Genesis contained in the Jahvistic and Elohistic sources that though they reflect the early traditions of tribal life, they equally testify to the lively sense of God's providential care for the single person. Jahve is interested in the small domestic affairs of Abraham, Isaac, and Jacob. Jahve guides Abraham's servant in his errand of finding a wife for Isaac (Gen. 24 J). "Er, Judah's first-born, was a wicked man before Jahve, and Jahve cut him off." What Onan did "was wicked before Jahve, who cut him off also" (Gen. 38 J). The whole of the Joseph narrative has the idea of reward and retribution and of divine providence woven into it. God hears the cry of the child Ishmael, the son of the outcast Hagar, when the child and his mother are perishing with thirst in the desert, and sends them aid (Gen. 21 E). If we date the beginning of the writing of the Jahvistic source about 1000 B.C. and its completion from Genesis, chapter 2, to 1 Kings, chapter 2, a century or so later,[1] we must suppose an explicit religious individualism with its corollary doctrine of retribution to have been current for a considerable time before the Solomonic period.

Similarly in the oldest historical records. These have been subject to redaction by the so-called Deuteronomist school, which interpreted the history of the race by the theory that the people's obedience to Jahve brought national prosperity and their faithlessness disaster. But the records, in places where we have no reason to suspect any redaction, appear to reveal that the idea of divine reward and retribution as applied to the individual person's behaviour had been a religious tenet of time immemorial. David (2 Sam. 3[39]) says of Joab, Abner's murderer : " May Jahve requite the wrong-doer for the wrong he did." The seven thousand who in the days of Elijah had not bowed the knee to Baal are promised salvation because of their loyalty to Jahve (1 Kings 19[18]). Already as early as 797 B.C. King

[1] Cf. Sellin, *Introd. to O.T.*

Amaziah of Judah, in putting to death the murderers of his
father, spared the children of the assassins, evidently ad-
judging the law of community to be too harsh and unjust
(2 Kings 14⁶). Thus at this early stage, in a case where extraordinary, retaliatory, measures might have been deemed
advisable or excusable, and a considerable time before we find
upon the statute book (Deut. 24¹⁶, cf. 7¹⁰) a law expressly
forbidding the punishment of children on account of the crimes
of parents, the ethical sense, which normally must be developed
long before its effect appears in legal codes, has modified the
old notion of family solidarity in one aspect. The idea of
communal responsibility is found to be impracticable from the
point of view of civil law as actually administered within the
race. Nor need we necessarily assume that the action of
Amaziah signifies a change for the first time in the general
practice of the law of his day. That which was novel and
remarkable in the king's action consisted in his clemency in
omitting to institute the customary blood-bath or " purge,"
associated then and long afterwards with eastern dynastic
conspiracies and political *putsches*. Doubtless there was danger
that in such and in other cases the old " law " of community,
affecting not only an offender but his family, could be invoked,
and thus the Deuteronomic law forbidding its operation was by
no means unnecessary, but Dr. S. R. Driver doubts whether,
even in the much earlier period of Hebrew history represented
by the accounts of Achan and of the slaying of the seven sons
of Saul (Josh. 7²⁴ᶠ·, 2 Sam. 21¹⁻⁹), we have here anything more
than a record of instances of an exceptional nature. These
cases, he says, " hardly authorize an inference as to the ordinary
judicial procedure." [1] On the other hand, the Book of Deuteronomy in its present form, where along with the law against
punishing a man's family for the man's crime (24¹⁶) there
appears, in the context of the ten commandments (5⁹, cf. Ex. 20⁵),
also the conception that Jahve visits the iniquity of the fathers

---

[1] *Deuteronomy*, in I.C.C., p. 277.

upon the children, probably reflects both the ordinary judicial procedure and Hebrew thought upon communal responsibility, at least since the days of Amaziah. We may conclude that at this time, if not, as Driver's observation suggests, much earlier, so far as the administration of justice by the State was concerned, the principle of solidarity had fallen into desuetude, but that so far as the action of *Jahve* was concerned it was recognized that the law of consequence, the working of Providence, was wide and far-reaching in its scope and divine reward, and retribution were manifested not only upon the person who did good or ill but upon his posterity. This religious belief remained in Judaism a tenet against which the protest of Ezekiel beat in vain. We find it in the latest period of Old Testament writing, for example in Malachi (2^3)—the sins of the priesthood will be visited upon their seed. All through the Apocryphal and Pseudepigraphical writings the idea of collective responsibility presents itself.[1] As the doctrine does not prevent a religious individualism appearing in late writings, neither did it do so in the centuries before Ezekiel.

What we have observed in the sagas of Genesis and in the old historical sources, namely, that the single person in the pre-prophetic period had moral value, was responsible to Jahve for his conduct, was object of Jahve's interest, His favour, and punitive action and sought His help in time of distress, is supported by an examination of the older Hebrew legislation contained in the so-called Book of the Covenant (Ex. 20^{23}–23^{19}). Here we have laws in respect of the male and female slave, the slave's wife, the kidnapped person and the injured person (ch. 21). These laws deal with what would in modern thought be regarded as secular matters, but it is to be noted that they are not conceived of as being, in character, secular. They are given as divine statutes. They represent the deity's will and are expressive of a true religious individualism comprehending

---

[1] Cf. Couard, *Die religiösen und sittlichen Anschauungen der alttestamentlichen Apokryphen und Pseudepigraphen*, p. 121.

the least powerful members of society. Sellin, on the ground that the administration of justice in this code of law is still in the hands of the priests and not of secular officials, and that not a king but rather tribal leaders (22²⁸) are in authority, says that we cannot place the Book of the Covenant in the monarchic period. Sellin, therefore, dates the code from the time of the Judges, when " Mosaic principles were combined with early Canaanitish ' common law ' into a legal *corpus.*" [1] Most critics, however, regard the Book of the Covenant as belonging to the period of the kings.[2] It is a code of an agricultural and commercial people. But, so far as our purpose is concerned, namely, to demonstrate the early appearance of religious individualistic belief in the pre-prophetic age, this variance of opinion makes little appreciable difference for it is widely recognized that this Hebrew legal code exhibits points of contact with the Babylonian code of Hammurabi (c. 2000 B.C.) and the Hittite laws (*c.* 1300–1270 B.C.), that is, with laws which had been current in western Asia since the second millennium. Even Hölscher, who thinks that the Book of the Covenant in its present form dates as late as early exilic times, regards its kernel (chaps. 21¹–22¹⁶)—the part which exhibits a strong sense of individual responsibility and respect for justice as done to the individual—as being an older collection of statutes of civil and penal law closely related to the old Babylonian Code and representing in part the customary law of the Canaanites.[3] An example of the statutory law of the three codes mentioned may be given to show their similarity and difference. The Book of the Covenant ordains that " If a man strikes and destroys the eye of a slave of his, male or female, he must let the slave go free for the sake of that eye ; and if he knocks out the tooth of a slave of his, male or female, he must let the slave

---

[1] *Op. cit.* on Book of the Covenant, p. 42 f.

[2] See *Hebrew Religion,* Oesterley and Robinson, p. 141. " It is now widely held that this Code was formulated in a later age, long after Israel had made its home in the promised land."

[3] *Op. cit.,* § 57, p. 129 f.

go free for the sake of that tooth "(21²⁶). The Codex Hammurabi lays down that " in the case of a man injuring the eye of the slave of another, or breaks a bone of the slave of another, he must pay the half of the slave's value " (199). And the Hittite laws enact that " if any one injures a male or a female slave or knocks out his or her teeth, he must pay ten shekels silver " (1⁸). A comparison of the statutes of the Book of the Covenant, in chapters twenty-one and twenty-two, with those of the Babylonian code and the Hittite laws will show a like similarity in content and form, with such divergencies as correspond to differences in national genius and sociological conditions. All three recognize the single person's rights, responsibilities, and obligations, and apply the principle of restoration or reparation by making good the material damage done. The Israelite code distinguishes itself from the Hittite laws by its preference for retaliation, the visitation upon the offender of the same personal injury incurred. When now we ask : At what time did the Israelites make resort to the Canaanite common law and form it to their purposes—in other words, what is the date of that early kernel of which Hölscher speaks ? We must answer that an early date is more probable than a late. Whatever be the period in which the Book of the Covenant attained its present form, and doubtless like every legal code that continues to be a living document it has been brought up-to-date and reflects the latest stage of its use, we may reasonably conclude that the Canaanite common law was adopted by Israel after the end of its nomadic period but not long after its settlement in the land of Canaan in its villages and towns. Such common law as was at hand would be the only possible legal instrument regulative of the perfectly new conditions of life.

Professor Hempel, who considers the present text and arrangement of the Book of the Covenant to belong to the period of the kings, thinks that the ordinance in Ex. 21² relative to the purchase of Hebrew slaves reflects the time before the absorption

of the Habiru (Hebrew) people by the Israelites, who, as
1 Sam. 14[21] shows, were, in the eleventh century in the days of
Saul, still distinct and separate from the Hebrews with whom
they were racially related.[1] Hempel, therefore, seems prepared
to regard the beginning of the formation of the Book of the
Covenant as at a very early stage in the monarchy or before it.
But another consideration leads us further. That the Israelites,
say, in the reign of Solomon, when the state was in a highly
organized condition and no doubt developed new legislation,
suddenly scrapped their old nomadic laws and adopted the
customary law of Western Asia is not possible. Laws do not
drop from the blue but have some relationship to the conditions
of life that have been before. They grow gradually and naturally, and the traces of antique origin in the code to which Sellin
points, support the view that the nucleus of the code (ch. 21[1]–
22[16]) which reflects contact with the Canaanite common law
must be regarded as dating a considerable time before Solomon's
reign.

We have remarked upon the individualism of the Book of
the Covenant including what Hölscher takes to be the older
kernel and stated that this individualism is *religious* in character.
Hölscher explains this religious element by supposing that the
older kernel has been placed by a priestly editor, in a priestly
interest, within a literary frame of sacral and ethical nature (viz.
20[22-26], 22[17]–23[19]), and provided with an exhortatory conclusion
(23[20-33]). The ancient nucleus (21[1]–22[16]) Hölscher thinks was
entirely secular, representing laws administered formerly by
the elders, but now, in the present form of the code, has lost
its original worldly nature, having been brought under the
principle enunciated in Deut. (1[17]), namely, that " the judgment
(*mishpat*) is God's." A glance, however, at the kernel reveals

[1] Cf. Hempel, *op. cit.* p. 80. The *Habiru* Hempel (p. 8) regards as having
invaded Canaan earlier than the Israelites, as capturing Jericho and Ai, and
as inhabiting the mountains. While remarking that the relationship of
Habiru and 'Ibrim (Hebrews) is yet subject of debate, Hempel takes Ex. 21[2]
and 1 Sam. 14[21] as referring to the Habiru.

that what is certainly a primitive and original characteristic of it is the connection of the priesthood with the administration of the law. The slave, for example, who is entitled to freedom but prefers to continue in his master's service, comes to the local sanctuary (to the gods ; the God ?) to have his decision ratified by the priest (21⁶). The priesthood represents not merely a court of last instance (22⁷ᶠ·) but, " whatever the offence be—whether an ox or an ass or a sheep or clothes or any lost property is claimed—the case must go to the local sanctuary " (22⁹).¹ In the code of Hammurabi,² in its introduction and its conclusion—very suitable places in which to state the idea of the ultimate source of law—the laws are affirmed to be of divine institution. The Book of the Covenant distinguishes itself even from the Babylonian code in its emphasis throughout of the religious nature of the ordinances governing private rights and obligations. This feature cannot be regarded as secondary or late. Even if the present introduction and conclusion have been worked over by a priestly editor and made more religious, it is probable that in its earliest setting, after the manner of the codex Hammurabi, the Book of the Covenant had some prefatory remarks referring to the divine revelation of the Israelite statutes and introductory of what we assume to be the primitive nucleus of the book. Hempel confirms this. " In the history of Israelite legislation, " he says, " the priesthood not only were the authors of the sacral law (laws of the cultus) but also the secular statutes are, in the older period, in its hands."³ Though the authority of the tribal elder, the king in the city, his officials and overseers, could on occasion by their " natural " right modify the priests' power " a separation of secular from divine law cannot be made " : " All law is holy since all law is regarded as a command of God." The statutes are derived from the priestly oracles given at the independent shrines

---

¹ Moffatt's translation.
² Cf. Gressmann, *Altorientalische Texte zum Alten Testament*, p. 380 f.
³ *Op. cit.* p. 73 f.

throughout the land rather than from any royal decrees, and this feature differentiates the Israelite laws from those of the Oriental codes. The priesthood is from the first the custodian of the faith in Jahve. Their position as custodian of His law Hempel traces back to the time of the taking over of the Canaanite shrines, and the gradual substitution of " Levitical " priests for the former Canaanite priesthood.

The conclusion to which we are led by the Jahvistic and Elohistic sagas of Genesis, the old historical writings, and the early legislation of Israel, namely, that at a time very much earlier than the first of the writing prophets (Amos, 750 B.C.) there had developed a religious individualism which consisted in the belief that the individual person was subject of the deity's care and oversight, was liable to the divine reward or retribution, blessing or curse, was governed in his civic relationships by laws that were of divine provenance, is of much importance for our judgment of the nature and influence of the earliest wisdom-writing and teaching in Israel. Sellin, we saw, places the earliest collection of the maxims of the wise (Prov. 10–22^{16}), with its strong individualistic outlook, in the period of Solomon ; and Gressmann regards it as belonging to the pre-prophetic period. The question, therefore, now requires to be asked : Was the individualism of the wisdom-writings, in their first beginnings, of a religious character ? With the exception of the teachings of Meri-ka-re and of Amen-em-ope the wisdom of Egypt was prevailingly secular, and Gunkel[1] is of opinion that " the Hebrew proverb-literature . . . was in its beginning altogether secular, and it was not the reward of the righteous man but the recompense of wisdom, that is, of worldly wisdom, which was preached. The religious motive was introduced later, and the belief in the worth of wisdom was united with the belief in God as Judge. Thus at length the idea of divine reward and retribution became fundamental to the teaching of wisdom, and hence the dual aspect of this wisdom,

[1] *R.G.G.* (Vergeltung).

its earnest piety, and its secular utilitarianism." Here, in
Gunkel's statement, we have a view presented corresponding
to that of Hölscher in respect of the legislation in the Book of
the Covenant. It would mean that the earliest collection of
proverbs (Prov. 10-22) is not representative of Israel's first
wisdom-writing, or that its plentiful references to Jahve as one
who demands and rewards goodness and punishes evil are later
additions, or that the collection itself must be given a comparatively late date when, it might be inferred, the religious
element was due to prophetic influence. Substance is given to
Gunkel's supposition by the prudential and worldly nature of
the maxim-writings in general. But since Gunkel himself has
demonstrated the early appearance of religious individualism
in Israel as shown by the sagas of Genesis, and concludes that
" the belief in divine reward and retribution in regard to the
single person did not arise at any definite time in the history
of Israel but attached to Israel's religion from the beginning,"
we have no reason to assume, in the absence of actual evidence,
that at any time there was in Israel a purely secular proverb-
literature. That the bulk of the maxims in the earliest collection
is of secular character is no doubt due to contact with the oriental
wisdom-writings, but the religious element in Prov. 10-22[16]
does not appear to have been woven in, or tacked on later, as an
afterthought. On the contrary it would seem that as in the
analogous case of early Hebrew legislature this was primitively
distinguished by its religious nature from the eastern customary
law, so also from the very outset in Israel's wisdom-writings the
religious sanction of right conduct, the motive supplied by the
idea of God's blessing and curse, was present. We cannot say,
that this was peculiar to Israel's early Wisdom literature since
the Egyptian *Teaching for Meri-ka-re* (15th cent. B.C.) is
remarkable for its religious tone, and even if we were to give
the Wisdom of Amen-em-ope a later date than 1000 B.C. (say,
600 B.C.—Griffith: *Journal of Egyptian Archæology*, xii. 3–4,
1926), we are not justified in supposing that Amen-em-ope was

an innovation in Egyptian religious wisdom-writing or had no previous models.

Since both outside the Wisdom literature of Israel and within it the idea of God as Guarantor of reward and of the individual as personally responsible to the deity for his conduct is current in pre-prophetic times, the view, which has done service as a principle of literary criticism,[1] that Jeremiah and Ezekiel are the first exponents of personal religion and personal responsibility, must be abandoned. This means that the relation of the prophetic writings to those of the wisdom-school must be viewed in a different light. The position is as Gressmann [2] states it : " The prophets were not the originators of the teaching of divine reward and retribution but rather made it their starting-point." They found it already at hand. But when Gressmann proceeds to say that the prophets took over the individualistic teaching of the wisdom- (maxim) writers with which they were familiar,

---

[1] The application of this canon of criticism to the Psalms is seen in the contention (Reuss, etc.) that the " I " of the Psalms never refers to an individual poet but to the whole Jewish community assembled for prayer in the Temple. But the tendency of criticism in the twentieth century is to see in the Psalms not only a nucleus of pre-exilic psalms but to admit psalms of the Davidic period (cf. Briggs, "Psalms," *I.C.C.*; Sellin, *O.T. Intro.*) and psalms which before their enrolment in collections or adaptation for general use were " on the lips of men." Both Briggs and Sellin regard Ps. 7, 18, 23, 24[7-10] as having claims to be of the Davidic period. If this be accepted it is clear that already we have a noteworthy expression of religious individualism long before the prophetic period. But how tenaciously the dogma against pre-exilic individualism continues is seen from the following statement of Oesterley and Robinson, *op. cit.* p. 302 : " The view is rapidly gaining ground that where such ' individualistic ' psalms are to be assigned to the pre-exilic age, that either they present the community under the guise of an individual or that they form part of the regular ritual carried out in certain forms of legal process whereby Jahve was invoked." The last part of this statement exhibits a consciousness of the weakness of the communal theory, and leads inevitably back to the early appearance of religious individualism—in the form of legal process. Cf. Hempel, *op. cit.* p. 72, who regards Ps. 7[3-4f.] (one of the oldest of the psalms) as presenting the formula of an oath taken in the presence of the priest by an individual who invokes Jahve to send punishment and disaster upon him if he be guilty of some alleged offence.

[2] *Israel's Spruchweisheit*, p. 56 f.

that they applied it in " grandiose independence " to the life of the nations, and that through the influence of the prophets the notion of divine recompense was deepened so as to become in the wisdom-writings so predominant as almost to be called a " dogma," this seems to be in part psychologically unsound and in part historically doubtful. In the era before the prophets religious individualism was not confined to the earliest maxim writing. We may assume that the strong individualistic interest of the wisdom-schools did have effect upon the prophetic preaching of social justice, and also that the value which the wise placed upon right conduct and possibly their mild criticism of the cult[1] are reflected in the prophetic polemic against the religion of ceremony. But the Wisdom literature, particularly in its earlier products, is radically different from the preaching of the prophets in orientation of thought. To propose that the prophets applied the teaching of individual recompense, as taught by the wise, to the life and destiny of the nations is to disregard this difference and to mistake where the root of the prophetic preaching lies. The prophetic message had always been the " Word of Jahve " to Israel, the nation. The idea of national solidarity and responsibility is a natural extension of the notion of clan and family solidarity, and has all the antiquity which those who see nothing except it until post-exilic times claim for it. Alongside of an exact and often grotesque individualism, the code of Hammurabi recognizes the principle

[1] Prov. 15[8] (" The sacrifice of the wicked is an abomination," etc.), 21[3], " Justice and fairness please Jahve more than sacrifices " ; 21[27]. See p. 13 f. above. On the question of the relation of the Law (Decalogue, Book of the Covenant, Deuteronomy) and the Prophets to the ethical teaching of the Wisdom literature, see the important pages (25–35) in Fichtner, *op. cit.* Fichtner (p. 25) says : " The ethics of the wise are, as is conditioned by the nature of the case, in great part the same as those of the Law and the Prophets . . . but if we glance at the Oriental wisdom, the correspondence between this and the ethical instruction of Hebrew wisdom is striking, not only in regard to content but in formulation." Fichtner (p. 35) for this reason regards the international wisdom as supplying the essential background and inspiration of the ethical teaching of the Hebrew Wisdom literature.

of family solidarity (cf. § 116, 210, 230) and lets children suffer death for the crimes of parents. In the development of the religion of Israel the idea of family solidarity was, so far as the administration of justice by man was concerned, abandoned but not outgrown, for its execution was left to Providence, to Jahve, in whose hands the application of the wider principle of national solidarity could alone be conceived as resting. This wider principle is the religious " dogma " of the prophets. Its origin is not to be thought of as the application of individualistic thought to the life of the nation and nations. In the religious political message of the writing prophets, because of the political nature of their message, the principle of national solidarity occupies the foreground. Their general scheme of thought is : that unless the nation repent of its disobedience it will, in whole or in part, become a subject people, be punished and led into captivity and consequently future generations will reap the result of the guilt of the fathers. The wickedness of King Manasseh and his generation was accounted by both prophet (Jer. 15[4]) and writer of religious history (2 Kings 21[11f.], 23[26f.], 24[3f.]) as the pledge of national disaster. When in the days of Jeremiah and Ezekiel the disaster did come, the facts of the situation provided the means of testing the principle of communal responsibility and the doctrine of reward and retribution attached to it. It was asked : Were Jahve's ways just ? The recent God-fearing generation of Josiah had effected no good for posterity. Were the best of the nation who in 597 B.C. had been led captive with King Jehoiachin to Babylon to be regarded as morally and spiritually inferior and those who had been left in Jerusalem to be regarded as the meritorious remnant ? The transported exiles were no worse, indeed in the eyes of Jeremiah (ch. 24) were better than those who had been spared to remain in Jerusalem. In the extremity of the times and in an atmosphere born of war and defeat, when thought becomes unbalanced, Ezekiel produced an unacceptable variety of religious individualism aimed against the whole conception of vicarious suffering and the idea of solidarity. Jahve makes each individual suffer for his own sins ; neither his past goodness nor past badness counts, but only his present state. Ezekiel does not further clarify his thought or make it consistent. He relates the sin of the people, Israel, throughout all its history and makes Jahve address the " house of Israel " as if it possessed corporate responsibility (cf. chs. 16, 23, 36^{32}). Except valuable criticism and an unacceptable theory of Jahve's relation to the individual, Ezekiel brought nothing substantially new to the idea of reward or to that of corporate and individual responsibility. Judaism continued to think collectively and as regards the individual conceived of a balance of merit that took into account past and present, a preponderance of good over evil, or *vice versa*, as influencing divine reward and retribution.

It is to be observed that it is within the prophetic school that the criticism of the doctrine of national solidarity is dealt with, for this doctrine was the warp and woof of the prophetic message. On the other hand, it is within the Wisdom literature, in the Book of Job, that discussion of the idea of reward and retribution with reference to the individual finds its most notable expression (cf. Ps. 37, 73). It is to be assumed that contact between prophecy and wisdom-teaching took place and fructified the thought of each, but each must be held responsible for the development, along its own line of thought, of what was its own particular subject of interest. It would seem to be more probable that the resort to religious individualism that was forced upon prophecy in a period sceptical of divine justice, as represented by the belief in national solidarity, was dependent upon inspiration from the Wisdom teachers, than that, as Gressmann supposes, the idea of reward and retribution as this appears in the Wisdom literature was deepened, made more religious and dogmatic through prophetic influence.

We must distinguish between what had been for centuries the content of religious piety and belief, namely, a religious individualism, seeking Jahve's blessing and fearing His punishment, and that theological speculation which emerges later under the threat of national catastrophe and criticizes the notions of reward and responsibility in both aspects, collective and personal. In the antique mind there is little or no tension between these two aspects, and there they rest peacefully together as they do in the code of Hammurabi. Speculation, criticism, and theories ordinarily appear long after the content of religious belief has been an undisturbed possession. From the time of the Exile onwards the inconsistencies between belief and the facts of national history, between belief and personal experience, are felt acutely and find utterance. The problem of suffering, presented by the belief in reward and retribution, becomes the one great problem.

Without doubt, the work of the prophets in purifying the conception of Jahve, and investing that conception with a high spiritual ethic had forged the means and even to a certain extent the necessity of dealing with the religious difficulties that arose from the fundamental belief in reward and responsibility. But in the earliest wisdom-writing the conception of Jahve is a high one, and in the older legislation the moral element in Jahve is notably strong. In primitive times, the moral element in Jahve is only one characteristic of the divine nature among others, but the view which, on this account, would deny an antiquity to the idea that the individual is the subject of divine reward and retribution, must, in view of the evidence, be reckoned as a strange and dogmatic aberration. If religious individualism had developed so late in Israel as to appear only in the exilic and post-exilic period, then Hebrew religious thought would occupy an anomalous position in the history of religion. L. Schmidt, in his work on the Ethics of the Greeks, remarks, that in the belief of the ancient Greeks, as the Homeric poetry shows, the firmest of presuppositions obtains, that a strict justice rules the destinies of men, rewarding goodness and punishing evil. Even though the gods are, as individuals, full of whims and human affections, the world of the gods (*die Götterwelt*) pursues and punishes the impious man, and protects and loves the good man.[1] Further, when we turn to the general history of ethics, we discover that the notion of divine reward and retribution, as applied to the single person, does not limp so far behind the first awakening of the moral sense, as the theory we have been combating suggests. Paulsen, in his *System of Ethics*, states that " the belief that *it fares well with the good and ill with the evil* is the first great fundamental truth to which reflection upon morality leads all peoples. In numberless maxims and proverbs, this truth receives expression as being the sum of life's experience." [2] It is needless to add to Paulsen's statement, that maxims and proverbs are of their nature the vehicle of individualistic thought. Again, in his description (*op. cit.* p. 371 f.) of the development of thought in that aspect which he calls the " Individualizing of the Conscience," Paulsen defines three stages. First, there is the stage at which the individual conscience is a reflex of customs and laws, of the objective morality of the people. Next, the ideals of the race as contained in its religious and poetical products are appropriated by the individual as his own ideal. Thirdly, when the content of life becomes richer, the individual begins to express his own thoughts, in short, begins to philosophize. These three phases of development, as depicted by Paulsen, cannot of course be taken to be sharply chronologically distinct, but the second stage very accurately represents in the history of Hebrew religion, a phase reached so far back as the time when the legends of Genesis were current in popular oral tradition—say, a considerable time before the beginning of the first millennium B.C. The final stage in Paulsen's analysis is, so far as Hebrew thought is concerned, representative of an extended period. It is to be discerned already in the individualistic requirements and safeguards of the older law-making, in the older products of history-writing, and particularly in the earliest example of wisdom-writing,

---

[1] Cf. Paulsen, *System der Ethik.*, p. 403, vol. i.
[2] *Op. cit.* p. 403.

which presents us, in the form of maxims already of a literary character, in its very beginning, with a rudimentary philosophizing on the welfare of the individual life, how it is to be attained and how it is lost. This individualism is, as far back as we can trace it, of a religious quality. In the process of time, when thought becomes more critical, this religious individualism is forced to face the difficulties presented to a this-worldly ethic, by the concept of divine reward and retribution. Under the title, "Theories of reward and retribution in the Old Testament and in later Judaism," we shall describe in the following chapter those varieties of thought which the growth of reflection upon the notion of divine justice and recompense occasioned.

CHAPTER III

THEORIES OF REWARD AND RETRIBUTION IN THE OLD TESTAMENT AND IN LATER JUDAISM

THE ancient belief that it fares well with the good and ill with the wicked has, when the Old Testament writings are concluded, come to expression in various forms. There is first of all the simple and thorough-going theory that righteousness brings to individuals and to people material reward, and that evil brings material loss and penalty. Hosea's admonitions, " They sow the wind and reap the storm " (8[7]), " You have been ploughing evil and you reaped disaster " (10[13]), probably echo the belief of the age-old proverbial wisdom. In its considered application it may be termed for the sake of convenience the Deuteronomist theory, since it is applied to Israel's history, as consistently as seemed possible by the Deuteronomist redactors of Israel's historical records, as a religious interpretative principle, and is elaborately worked out in the twenty-eighth chapter of the Book of Deuteronomy itself (cf. Lev. 26). As the prophets interpreted the way of Jahve with His people from the book of the world-happenings of their day, the Deuteronomist school surveyed the past from the viewpoint of the same religious philosophy. The cause of national disaster was disobedience to Jahve's commandments and the breaking of the people's covenanted promise to obey. In Deut. 28, which as peroration of the Deuteronomic legislation[1] is the summing up of its religious teaching, it is important to note the detailed elaboration of the theory. The blessings of obedience are prosperity in every department of

[1] Cf. Driver, *Deuteronomy* (in Int. Crit. Comm.) on Deut. 28.

the national life; the offspring of men and of cattle and the produce of the soil will be healthy and abundant; Israel will gain victory over its foes, the respect of the world, and be vouchsafed prosperous seasons. The penalty of disobedience will be defeat in battle, pestilential fevers, barrenness of the soil, failure of crops, incurable diseases. Disobedience and disloyalty to Jahve will be visited with physical suffering, with the " boil of Egypt," with "tumours, scurvy, and itch " "from head to foot," with " fever, ague, and erysipelas " (vv. 22, 27, 35).

The oldest collections of maxims (10–22^{16}, 25–29) and the maxim-literature in general, although they do not give so systematic a presentation of the consequences of good and evil conduct, agree in the main with the religious outlook of Deut. 28. For the maxim-writers the content of reward is " life " to which is attached that which invests life with worth, namely wealth, honour, the good name and the continuance of a man's " name," or life, in his posterity. Long life, length of days is the chief good; early death and destruction is the destiny of the fool and the impious. " Righteousness saves from death " (Prov. 11^4). With this simple and less particularized picture drawn by the proverb-writers, the Book of Deuteronomy has a close connection. Recurring formulæ of this Book, in its motivation of good conduct, are : " That thou mayest live," " that it may be well with thee," " that Jahve may bless thee," " that thou mayest prolong thy days." [1]

Though the twenty-eighth chapter of Deuteronomy in its bolder appreciation of the working of the law of recompense represents in this respect an advance upon the early maxim-writings, neither in this chapter nor in the Books of the Kings as edited by the Deuteronomist school has the belief that benefits reward righteousness and punishment falls on evil-doers crystallized into the very different theory that material

---

[1] The contrast " life " and " death " in Ezekiel (see below) has the same value as in Proverbs.

well-being is of itself an indication of righteousness [1] and suffering an indication of sin. But under a this-worldly ethic, where the only available means of testing the doctrine of recompense are the outward circumstances and events of a person's life, the idea that divine reward and retribution are manifested in an outward manner passes rapidly and naturally into the idea that the outward circumstances of life are an index of character. The affliction of disease with which Deut. 28 threatens the nation if it should disobey Jahve provides the topic of discussion in the Book of Job, which reflects the prevalence of a popular belief that at least extraordinary calamity must be the result of sin. Job's malady is described, we may note, in language reminiscent of the Deuteronomic passage. Jahve smote him with " painful ulcers from the sole of his foot to the crown of his head " (2[7]). That the Deuteronomist theory of reward was developed into a belief in the rigid correspondence of sin and suffering is most strikingly illustrated by the work of the Chronicler. The Deuteronomist redactors of the Book of the Kings pass a good judgment upon Uzziah, king of Judah, as having done right in the eyes of Jahve and are quite content to report without comment the fact that Jahve struck the king with leprosy. For the Chronicler, however, this leprosy was the punishment of sacrilege. Uzziah by offering incense in the temple had usurped the functions of the priesthood. The Book of the Kings narrates that king Manasseh did evil in the sight of Jahve, and that this brought disaster on Judah and Jerusalem, but has nothing to say of any penalty having fallen upon Manasseh himself. The fifty-five years of Manasseh's long and prosperous reign are an awkward fact for the Chronicler, but he helps himself out as well as possible. He reports that Manasseh was brought in fetters to Babylon and in the day of trouble humbled himself before

---

[1] Also in the maxim literature, while in Prov. 13[18] poverty is a mark of shame or punishment, wisdom (28[11]) is better than riches. In the maxim-literature there is what Bertholet (*Bib. Theol.* p. 91) describes as a pronounced *ebionitic* strain. This appreciation of pious poverty appears to be due to contact with the Oriental wisdom (cf. Prov. 23[4f.], 15[15f.] with Amen. 6, 7). Cf. Boström,*Prov. Studien*, p. 53 f.

Jahve, realizing at last that Jahve was God. Jahve listened to his prayer of repentance, restored him to his kingdom, and Manasseh, reformed, did some good works. So with king Josiah. The Book of the Kings records his goodness and his defeat and death at Megiddo. The Chronicler's review of this part of Israel's history reaches in the interest of his theory what may well seem the height of absurdity. Josiah's death, he tells us, was on account of paying no heed to the words of Pharaoh Necho, who, in warning Josiah against intervention in the Egyptian campaign against Assyria, had intimated to Josiah that this campaign was by order of God. And, finally, as an example how exactly suffering corresponds to sin and how careful Jahve is to mete out exact justice in this world, the Chronicler brings what he must have regarded with some satisfaction as a wholly invincible proof. The years of the exile were seventy in number. This was the number of Sabbatical years which, according to pious tradition (cf. Lev. 26[34]), Israel in the past had disobediently omitted to observe.[1]

Apart from the artificial constructions of the Chronicler's narrative which presses the history of the past, from which time held the writer aloof, into a theological system, and apart from that form of popular piety which was prepared to hold that at least every grave case of misfortune could only have sin as its explanatory cause, the plain Deuteronomist theory that goodness was rewarded with good and evil with evil laid a sufficiently heavy tax upon belief. But there is no sign of any religious problem being presented until the time of Jer. (12[1-6]), and thereafter in certain psalms (37, 49, 73), where the prosperity of the wicked and the condition of the righteous are felt to be in need of some religious apologetic. Fichtner[2] points to three

[1] 2 Chron. 36[21] (cf. Bertholet, *Bib. Theol. d. A.T.*, p. 82) should be translated " Till the land has received (paid) back her sabbatical years," etc. So Kautzsch, *Textbibel*, and Max Haller, *S.A.T.*

[2] *Op. cit.* p. 73. In the collection Prov. 22[17]–24[34] the advice is given not to envy the wicked (23[17], 24[1, 19]), but this does not occur in the part adapted from Amen-em-ope.

places in the early maxim-writings (Prov. 10–22^{16}, 25–29) where suspicion of the truth of the doctrine of reward on account of the prosperity of the wicked (11^{18}, 20^{24}, 29^{1}) appears to be implied; but the reminder that the success of the wicked is not real or lasting (11^{18}), that man cannot understand but must trust the divine providence (20^{24}), that punishment may be delayed but comes at length suddenly and surely (29^{1}), must from the beginning have accompanied the doctrine, reconciling it with the facts of life. In the early maxim literature, and in this form of writing as a whole, an optimistic atmosphere prevails and there is little trace of any deep religious questionings far less of the idea of the exact correspondence between suffering and sin which we meet with in Job and the Chronicler. The proverb (26^{27}), " the stone a man sets rolling will recoil upon him," has not the literal interpretation which it received in later Judaism and which might have served as the Chronicler's motto.

The Deuteronomist theory that the nation and the persons within it were in material fashion rewarded or punished, according as their conduct was good or evil, was not so ill fitted, as this bare description might lead us to suppose, to become a principle of belief. The theory had appendices, and it was these appendices that made it elastic and durable and, until the centre of gravity of the belief in divine recompense was changed by the idea of a future life, constituted it the most efficient and popular article of faith. It was recognized that since the events of life were subject to the control of the divine intelligence, it was not always possible for a man to understand the ways of Providence (Prov. 20^{24}). A man's good and evil deeds might not be observed to bear appropriate fruit in his lifetime, but Jahve would bring them to light in his descendants with whom his personal life was bound up. As yet the idea of divine recompense was not, as it was sometimes conceived in later Judaism, that of a mechanical force immanent in the nature of things.[1] The Guarantor of reward and retribution was Jahve, a living and watchful Personality. He could delay action, bringing sudden destruction on the wicked or revealing His judgment " at the latter end." He could change His mind on man's repentance and be merciful and forgive. God gave ample room for repentance and was patient and long-suffering. The theory connected well with the eschatological ideas of a coming judgment (Ps. 1) when the sovereignty of Jahve would be made manifest, a judgment that would establish the prosperity of the righteous and destroy the wicked.[2] The drama of the judgment which through the oracles of the prophets became more and more the symbol and seal of the doctrine of recompense and which in periods of crises could be infused with an expectancy of a more or less immediate rectification of the balance of justice, vindicating Israel as against the nations, the righteous over against the wicked, had only reference to those who would be alive at the End-Time. But the idea of a coming judgment, restricted as it was and concerned as it was more with the nation than the persons who composed the nation, represented an orientation of thought to the future in which every strong belief in God as Judge and consequently as Vindicator of the righteous is compelled to take refuge (cf. Mal. 3). The two religious conceptions however, which, in what we have called the Deuteronomist theory, must be held as having been most effective in reconciling the facts of national and personal history with belief in Jahve as Rewarder, were that Jahve *tests* fidelity and faith by suffering, and *disciplines* through misfortune. The early wisdom-writers thought of adversity as serving the divine purpose of reproof and admonition (Pr. 15, 29[1]). Amos appears to be familiar with the thought. Jahve has sent calamities upon

---

[1] Cf. *Der Vergeltungsgedanke bei Paulus,* 1912, by G. P. Wetter, p. 9 f. Due to the influence of Hellenism which even affected Pharisaic thought and spirit " God's punitive justice in the world was acknowledged but was apparently conceived of as working mechanically through immanent laws " (p. 10). Cf. p. 46, *op. cit.*

[2] Cf. Ps. 25[13], 37[9f.], 69[35f.].

His people in the vain hope that they would return to Him ($4^{6f.}$).
The Deuteronomist editor of the Book of Judges (2^{22}–3^6) accounts
for the Canaanites not having been driven out of the land by the
Israelites by saying that it was Jahve's plan to prove Israel.
The story of the projected sacrifice of his son Isaac by Abraham
(Gen. 22) is furnished by the Elohist narrator with the religious
motive : God sought to test Abraham. Represented respectively
by the so - called Folk-tale of the Book of Job (1–2^{10}, $42^{10f.}$)
and the Elihu speeches (38–42^6) in that book, the probationary
and the disciplinary views of the purpose of suffering turn to
account the many references in Hebrew literature to testing,
warning, cleansing, refining, and teaching. Both affirm that
misfortune *may not* be retribution but may befall the pious to
reveal the reality of faith or to train and improve.

With all its adjuncts[1] the Deuteronomist theory was,
within the limits of a this-world outlook, an extremely serviceable
and adaptable instrument. It realized the difficulties that arose
from life's actualities. It could be held with sincerity and conviction. The expression of it could be offensive, as when the
author of the thirty-seventh Psalm, who throws into light what
is its weakest element, declares (v. 25) :

> I have been young and now have become old,
> Yet have I never seen the pious man forsaken,
> Nor his children begging bread.

But such extreme optimism must be set against the theory as a
whole. As we shall see, neither does the Old Testament, in spite
of new attainments of thought in regard to suffering and responsibility, outgrow the Deuteronomist theory of recompense ; nor
does later Judaism, with the now wider vision of a belief in a
future life, dispense with the main features of its teaching.

Criticism of the current belief in reward and retribution is

---

[1] Others are : misfortune may be punishment for sins of youth, or those
man is unconscious of having committed (Ps. 25^7, 44^{22}, 90^8) ; no man is pure
before God (Prov. 20^9 ; Job 14^4 ; Ps. 51^7), and thus none can claim exemption
from punishment.

met with in the Book of Ezekiel (chaps. 14, 18, 33). The task of this prophet in exile, before as well as after the destruction of Jerusalem, was set by the conditions of the times. The breaking up of the community, and then the final dissolution of the State, and the cessation of the temple cultus, weakened the whole idea of solidarity, and cast into deeper prominence the individual Israelite and his relationship to Jahve. This was all indeed that appeared to be left. Ezekiel's rôle is not solely that of a prophet but also that of a teacher who encourages and warns his fellow exiles in the midst of a heathen surrounding. He has to appeal to the individual conscience and repel the notion, laming and conducive of despair and apathy, that those in exile, as children of their fathers, are merely bearing the punishment of the deeds of their ancestors. He has to meet the criticism of the divine justice as urged or implied by some, and the spirit of complacency of others who were glad of any convenient religious tenet which would relieve them of blame for their present condition. Psychologically, Ezekiel's teaching was in such circumstances the best possible. It was born of the situation, and this accounts for its onesidedness and its not having permanent effect, however effective it may have been at the time. Each person, he asks the exiles to believe, suffers for his own sins only. No one is penalized for the guilt of the fathers. In a community against which Jahve sends pestilence or famine or war as retribution for evil-doing, the merits of the righteous will not atone for a single sinner, not even shelter and protect a member of their own families. The righteous alone will escape from such calamities. Penitence, followed by obedience, will at once restore a sinner to God's favour and he will " live," but a good past will not save a man from dying for his iniquity. It is the present moral condition of a man that counts.

We may observe from Ezekiel's teaching that while it strengthened individual responsibility by permitting it neither to be crushed by the idea that punishment for the actions of others in the past descended upon their progeny, nor to be sapped by a willing acceptance of that idea, this teaching could not prove so adequate as the Deuteronomist reading of national and personal history. It defended the divine justice, but gave no interpretation of history as under the divine government and under divine laws. The Deuteronomist tenet that Jahve visited the iniquity of the fathers upon the children was true to the conception and fact of corporate responsibility, and nothing that has happened before or since Ezekiel's day has diminished the truth of this belief. In its moral and physical aspects it suffers little, even in the form of the parody : " The fathers have eaten sour grapes and the children's teeth are set on edge." Ezekiel, as we have previously shown, himself cannot avoid the thought of corporate responsibility. What Eissfeldt (*op. cit.*) calls the " atomistic mechanical " feature of Ezekiel's doctrine of reward, its separating the national past from the present, its supposition that the past does not count in the judgment of God but only the present state of the individual's soul,[1] is evident also in his isolating the individual from the community. His picture, which nevertheless accords faithfully with his teaching, of all the righteous citizens, and only the righteous citizens, escaping with their lives when Jahve sends pestilence or war against a community, is a crude conception that can never have been substantiated in the world's history. His rigid individualism, though it had the merit of performing a needful service in the exigency of his time, compares unfavourably with the very sane individualism of the wisdom-writers, and sank below rather than rose above the elastic and adaptable Deuteronomist theory which took account both of the nation and of the individual as subject to Jahve's judgment. In other respects Ezekiel's teaching remained within the scheme of Deuteronomist thought. His contrast (18[21f.]), life for the righteous and death for the wicked —" Have I any desire for the death of the wicked ? " says

---

[1] Cf. the extra-canonical (Agrapha) saying of Jesus : " In what I find you, therein I judge you " (Hennecke, *Neutest. Apokryphen*, p. 9).

Jahve. If he gives up his evil life, shall he not live ?—is the same as was employed by the wisdom-teachers (cf. above), and indicates strictly material well-being and misfortune as the means of Jahve's rewarding and punishing. If Ezekiel's isolation of the individual personality quickened the sense of responsibility, it was not without baneful result also, as may be perceived in the inventive spirit of the Chronicler who conceives it to be incumbent upon him to provide sins, transgressions, and good actions to explain the separate histories of the personalities of the past.

Anders Nygren, the Swedish theologian, in an essay on the independence of the ethical viewpoint,[1] asks : " Why is it that in Israel the problem of the suffering of the righteous, the problem of the Book of Job, became so acute ? " " The reason is," he says, " that the union of the ethical and the eudæmonistic viewpoints was regarded as an axiom." " If the false axiom be removed, the problem is immediately solved, or, rather, cause to set the problem vanishes." Though we may not be able to accept Nygren's view that, under the circumstances which he mentions, there would be no problem or cause to set the problem of theodicy, his statement is abundantly true that the union of the ethical and the eudæmonistic in the Old Testament is axiomatic. This characteristic is traceable very much farther afield than in the Old Testament. Progress, however, is made within the Old Testament itself towards appreciating the ethical or religious and eudæmonistic motives of conduct independently and thus of modifying the Deuteronomist standpoint. This movement of thought, nevertheless, only throws into clearer light the hold which the Deuteronomist theory continued to exert upon the mind and the value which it was estimated to have and in fact had. The portions of Hebrew literature which reveal this new departure, or at least make progress towards effecting it, are the Book of Second Isaiah (40–55), the seventy-third Psalm, and sections of the Book of Job.

[1] *Zeitschrift für systematische Theologie*, 1926–27, p. 211 f.

At the close of the period of the exile the anonymous author of second Isaiah, viewing the history of his race, alights upon the idea that suffering can be vicarious and atoning. He has evidently reflected deeply upon this tragic history, and concluded that it cannot be explained merely by the categories of reward and retribution. The Servant of Jahve, Israel, had suffered more than his deserved punishment. So far as this punishment was undeserved, Israel suffered for the sins of others, and this suffering served the plan of God's redeeming love which was to make His people, as bearers of the revelation of the living God, the missionary of true religion to the heathen world. Israel's afflictions atone for the guilt of God's adversaries. But the author of second Isaiah, who makes room for the idea of vicarious suffering, does not reject the Deuteronomist view of the place and purpose of reward and retribution. Torrey (*Second Isaiah*, p. 146), who refers to the thought that Israel bears the penalty of the sin of the world and through his woes makes atonement to God for the heathen nations as " a profound solution of the hardest problem in Jewish Theology," leaves unquestioned the authenticity of verses which are challenged on dogmatic grounds by Duhm because of their Deuteronomistic character. These verses (48[18. 19]) declare :

> Hadst thou but hearkened to my bidding,
> Thy peace would have been like a river,
> Thy righteousness like waves of the sea.
> Thine offspring had numbered as the sand,
> And the fruit of thy loins as its grains.
> They would never be cut off nor destroyed from before me.

If this passage, which may be translated either as referring to the past (so Torrey) or to the future (cf. Moffatt), be woven into the text by an editor, this editorial addition is none the less significant as exhibiting a constant watchfulness in the interest of that doctrine of providence which in the Old Testament is the most representative and rational. Yet there is every reason to regard the verses as genuine. Israel's vicarious suffering is not regarded by second Isaiah as a continuing and general principle of existence. This suffering is now over. It was for a specific purpose now to be realized, but it itself is now an accomplished thing. The Deuteronomist teaching of reward and retribution denotes still the general principle of God's government.

A complete departure from the Deuteronomist teaching is made in respect of that aspect of it which is the most important by the writer of the seventy-third Psalm. The author of Ps. 73 concludes that virtue, the life in obedience to God, is its own reward, or, expressed in religious terms, the reward is a consciousness of the possession of God and of nearness to Him:

> But I remain ever by Thee . . .
> Whom have I but Thee in heaven,
> Besides Thee I desire nought else on earth (vv. 23, 25).

The idea of reward is spiritualized, the conception at least of its invariably utilitarian character is abandoned. But here, again, we may observe that otherwise the writer has no other notion of Jahve's world-régime than the way marked out by the Deuteronomist scheme. He is unable to account for the despite done to the idea of divine providence by the prosperity of the wicked than by assuming that at their latter end (v. 17) they will be brought low in ruin and destruction. On the side of retribution there is no departure from the traditional dogma. For himself, though he may hope that God will yet bring him to honour,[1] the author answers the question as to whether good conduct can be disinterested—the question put into the mouth of the Satan in the prologue of the Book of Job (1⁹)—in the way in which religion can best answer it.

Old Testament thought upon the subject of reward and retribution as the means of God's reaction to human conduct and

---

[1] Possibly we should read v. 24b (see note in Kittel's *Heb. Bible*; cf. Moffatt's translation) as, "Thou wilt bring (lead) me after Thyself by the hand," but *honour* (*Kabod*, cf. Job 19⁹) appears to be the preferable reading, according with the value wisdom-writings place on the personal reputation. Cf. Pederson, *op. cit.* p. 363 f.

as the method of His providence, operative, so far as the individual is concerned, within the limits of his earthly experience, receives the fullest treatment in the Book of Job. The purpose of the book is very generally stated as being to lodge protest against the current dogma of retribution. But this view cannot be upheld by any strictly impartial reading of the dialogue (chaps. 3–31), which is the original work of the author of Job, or of the so-called folk-tale [1] (represented by the prologue and epilogue 1–$2^{10.\ 13}$, $42^{10f.}$) which the author of the dialogue employed to provide an introduction and conclusion to his work. As Baumgärtel in his book on the Job-dialogue (*Der Hiobdialog*, 1933) conclusively demonstrates, the Job of the dialogue never deserts the dogma of reward and retribution which is for himself, as it is for his friends, the common ground of belief and discussion. Here Baumgärtel is supported by Köberle,[2] Budde,[3] Volz,[4] and Pedersen.[5] The presupposition upon which Job and his friends alike proceed is that in accordance with their belief in the retributive justice of God " the blameless, righteous man could never fall into misfortune." Therefore it is that Job, who knows himself to be free from guilt, feels the injustice of his suffering. His complaint against God is sustained to the last. His demand that he be re-established in his " rights " is only conceivable on the ground of the belief shared by all participants in the argument. He has no rights apart from such belief, and in the dialogue he maintains his rights to the end (31^{37}).

---

[1] *Folk-tale* is a convenient expression to denote the popular tale known to Ezekiel ($14^{14.20}$), the substance of which is presumably contained in the prologue and epilogue of the Book of Job. That the prologue and epilogue in their present form constituted the folk-tale it would be rash to conclude, for they exhibit great literary art (cf. Hempel, *op. cit.* p. 176). König (p. 465 f., *Das Buch Hiob.*) suggests that the Satan passage is an interpolation. It is more likely that this passage is by the author of the dialogue who wrote in the Persian period.

[2] *Sünde und Gnade im religiösen Leben des Volkes Israel*, 1905, p. 377.

[3] *Das Buch Hiob*, 2nd ed. 1913, pp. xxxii. xxxv.

[4] *S.A.T.*, 2nd ed. 1921, p. 19.

[5] *Op. cit.* p. 370.

When in the epilogue, following apparently the old folk-tale, restitution of Job's prosperity is made, the retention of this feature appears to be no inartistic blunder on the part of the author of the dialogue, as it otherwise would be had he denied the current belief in the relationship of prosperity and righteousness. It is true that in his criticism of the divine justice Job brings forward instances where flagrant wickedness remains unpunished (21), but this brings us no farther than do the complaints or reflections upon the prosperity of the wicked made by upholders of the orthodox creed (cf. Jer. 12^{1-6} ; Ps. 37, 49, etc.). When Job invokes just retribution and God's wrath upon his defamers with the warning, " Fear ye the sword ! " (19^{29}) we perceive that he does not discard the familiar doctrine. The dialogue is assuredly a protest. It is, on the face of it, the most vehement protest of a sufferer that in his case suffering has not been merited. Also for the author of the dialogue, even though primarily this be no didactic writing, we can only reasonably conclude that his work would have been without point unless it was to contend that suffering was not a token of sin in every individual case. An explanation of such suffering by the righteous he does not give ; but, unless we separate the so-called folk-tale from the dialogue altogether, the author of the dialogue must have desired to show, as Hempel [1] puts it, that " it is the honour of the sufferer that by his endurance in trial he justifies God against the wager of Satan " that the righteous man, broken under the severest trial, " has something he can give to God, namely, his witness to God, as God Himself at length will appear as ' witness ' of the sufferer's innocence." The *general validity*, however, of what the author of the dialogue conceives to be a divine law as expressed by the belief of his day is not questioned. The questioning of this would have destroyed the background against which the writer sought to present his picture. Baumgärtel [2] appropriately remarks on Duhm's view (*Commentary on the Book of Job*,

[1] *Op. cit.* p. 179.   [2] *Op. cit.* p. 187, note 151.

p. x.) of the dialogue as a highly remarkable attack on the prevalent teaching in regard to sin, and that thus it occupies an isolated position within the history of religion, that this supposition of isolation should be sufficient of itself to cause us to pause before coming to such a conclusion. The traditional doctrine of reward and retribution does receive dismissal within the Old Testament, but this is in a writing (Ecclesiastes, Qoheleth) which is characteristically unrepresentative of Old Testament piety.

Another observation must here be made. The argument of the dialogue is constituted by the acceptance of the *developed form* of the theory of reward and retribution, which later in the work of the Chronicler we see applied to history and which regarded righteousness and prosperity, or wickedness and misfortune, as representing, as it were, two sides of a mathematical equation. " The blameless, righteous man could not fall into misfortune." The Deuteronomist theory proper had no such uncompromising teaching. It recognized the two religious palliatives, the probationary and disciplinary aspects of misfortune. Both are appreciated by the author of the dialogue, but are overshadowed, and their effect reduced and lost. Volz notes the contrast between the patient Job, whose suffering was in the old folk-tale the test of faith, and the impatient, rebellious Job of the dialogue.[1] Also in a passage of the poem, which Budde describes as " the most beautiful and comforting in all the friends' speeches ". (5^{17-26}),[2] Eliphaz speaks of the disciplinary purpose of suffering after the manner of the Proverb (3^{12}) : " Whom God loves, He chastens." Ball says[3] that this " section 5^{17-27}, which reads almost like a psalm (cf. Ps. 1, 91, 92, 112, 128), might conceivably be a quotation of a then well-known piece." Baumgärtel goes farther, and on the

---

[1] *S.A.T.*, 1911, iii. 2, p. 1. " The one Job could not possibly change into the other."

[2] *Op. cit.* p. 24.

[3] *The Book of Job*, Oxford, 1922, p. 154 f.

ground that this section has no organic connection with what Eliphaz has said before, he regards it as a later interpolation.[1] But there is no need to seek to decide the issue. The Job of the dialogue, though he knows himself to be innocent, regards suffering only from the punitive aspect. Possibly the late author of the Elihu-speeches (32–37) found in the dialogue as it lay before him no references to the pedagogical aim of suffering. It is, however, perfectly certain that, in promising to make good the defects of the friends' arguments by making his theme that God in love sends suffering to discipline man, he saw the need of bringing the whole subject on to the broad basis of the Deuteronomist theory. His speeches attempt to mitigate the hardened or rigid form of the doctrine of reward and retribution which in the dialogue we see has already developed, and which in later Judaism develops further into a tit for tat, measure for measure, conception of divine justice.

In his notable essay of more than forty years ago on " Hebrew and Greek ideas of Providence and divine retribution," [2] Mr. C. G. Montefiore states that " we may note that no theistic religion has ever wholly dispensed with the necessity of retribution, however much the idea itself may have been spiritualized and refined." In Psalm 73, upon which, though it probably belongs to the Greek period and is therefore later than the dialogue of Job, we have already remarked for the purpose of better contrast with the dialogue, we meet for the first time with the refinement of the idea of reward. The author of the psalm appears to have profited not only as he himself reveals (v.[17]) [3] from contemporary thought, but also from such earlier discussions as the dialogue of Job presents upon the great topic of the revelation of divine justice in personal life. But in the Book of Job, in its present form and with all its parts, there is as yet no endeavour to refine the idea of reward. There,

---

[1] Baumgärtel, op. cit. p. 15 f.
[2] Jewish Quarterly Review, 1893 (July). p. 553.
[3] Cf. Commentaries, and below.

it is still held that reward and retribution must have effect in the outward condition of man. The spiritual tension caused by Job's belief that he suffers unjustly, and nevertheless that God must be just is kept up in the dialogue to the last. In spite of his inability to let go his hold upon God, in spite of a sense of communion with God, he does not attain to the thought of Psalm 73 that the supreme and ample reward is the possession of God though body and spirit should perish. The tension of the dialogue is indeed relieved by the later additions to the poem, the Hymn on Wisdom (chap. 28) and the Divine Speeches (38–42[6]), but this is due to the writers of these pieces leaving the subject of recompense and concentrating not on God's justice but on His almighty power and wisdom. Human wisdom, finite and inadequate, is contrasted with the infinite wisdom witnessed in the physical realm. The highest human wisdom is attained in the fear of the Lord and in the avoidance of evil (28[28]). In the works of creation God's operations are seen to be fraught with surpassing wisdom, with peculiar care and deep design. Man may therefore conclude, it is implied, even from the small portion of the divine plan so marvellously purposeful, that he can comprehend that all that befalls him is likewise in accordance with divine wisdom and justice (40[8]). This, the Book of Job in its present or final form regards as the answer to the general problem of suffering. " Now," Job can say, " mine eye has seen " (42[5]). We are thus directed to the need of faith in God, founded upon what can be perceived of the divine intelligence in the works of creation. The effect of the Divine Speeches in their dropping the categories of reward and retribution is to separate the problem of theodicy from these categories. But in consequence we are left with faith and not with a refinement of the idea of reward, and it would be reading too much into the Divine Speeches if we were to conclude that the author desired to deny the current Deuteronomist theory of God's retributive justice (cf. 38[12f.]).

It is significant that it is in the Book of Ecclesiastes, where the ethical teaching is reduced and tenuous, and where pessimism dwarfs piety, the Deuteronomist theory finds rejection. The inclusion of Ecclesiastes within the canon has, however, placed there what might have been expected to emerge from the normal course of thought, namely a development of previous reflections upon providence on their negative side. Though in the work of Qoheleth the living streams of Old Testament piety do not flow, there are lively rivulets of rationalistic thought engendered by those contrasts of life and belief, fact and doctrine, which we meet with in the wisdom-writings. The scepticism of Qoheleth has its precursor in the pessimism that pervades many an utterance in the Book of Job. The theme of the Hymn on Wisdom had been that man can discover many things but not wisdom ; wisdom is only with God. This, indeed, is as Sellin describes it, " a declaration of bankruptcy on the part of a teacher of wisdom." [1] Ezekiel had thought of God as bending the whole course of history for His own glory and to magnify His holy name.[2] In the Divine Speeches of the Book of Job, though God is yet an active personality who talks with Job, He is also the inscrutable power and intelligence behind nature. It was natural that this conception should, as in Ecclesiastes, advance a stage farther and that God should become the being who determines all things, a being bereft of personal quality, a sort of *Fatum*, or impersonal power. Pedersen [3] accounts for the origin of religious pessimism as being a growth from the conception of the omnipotence of God, before whom man is nothing and feels his nothingness. This was, no doubt, one of its roots in Judaism. But the strange phenomenon of pessimism in Jewish thought, appearing as it does in the Wisdom literature, directs us to seek here, and in the writings (*e.g.* Jeremiah, Habakkuk) influenced by this

---

[1] *Einleitung in das A.T.*, 1929, p. 140.

[2] In Ezekiel " the original idea of the Holy One as subject to passion and emotion . . . is reduced " (Ritschl).

[3] *Revue de l'Histoire et de Philosophie Religieuses*, 1930, p. 361.

source, for the immediate cause. We find it in that struggle for faith which is seen in the Book of Job and in those psalms for the writers of which the prosperity of the wicked and the sufferings of the righteous was a shock to faith that had to be overcome, that is, the principal cause of pessimism in Judaism lay in the practical difficulties which beset the Deuteronomist theory of reward. Pessimism is bound to arise where a rational reconciliation is sought between the idea of divine justice and the facts of national and personal life. Though Qoheleth, doubtless, owes much to the spirit of the Hellenistic age [1] and the surrounding Orient, his thought can only be understood in its connection with the Old Testament ideas upon the omnipotence of God, of man as of the dust and returning to the dust [2]; upon the value of wisdom and upon divine providence in relation to the individual.

Due to Qoheleth's own inner contradictions of thought, and possibly to later additions within the body of his book, his conception of the working of providence tends to be elusive. Within the framework of a belief in a God of judgment but in loose attachment to this belief the following positions are however represented. Moral and religious qualities have no necessary relationship to man's outward condition of well-being or ill-being (9^2).[3] God may call to account (5^5) and even reward (8^{12b} addition ?), but there is no evidence of a scheme of retributive justice. What happens has been determined long ago and has to be accepted. Man " cannot argue with one mightier than himself " (6^{10}) is possibly a reflection upon the dialogue of the Book of Job. Wisdom, Qoheleth admits, is profitable to man in many ways, but it is often of no profit to him through no fault of his own, and in any case it is

---

[1] See Commentary 1932 by Hertzberg on *Der Prediger* (*Qoheleth*), p. 47, on " The Relation (of Qoheleth) to non-Hebrew Literature " for criticism of Ranston (influence through Theognis) and others.

[2] Cf. Hertzberg, *op. cit.* p. 37 f. for Qoheleth's appreciation of the Creation story in Genesis.

[3] Cf. Hertzberg, pp. 37, 151.

absolutely useless, one of the vanity of vanities, as a means of understanding the ways of providence (8[17]). All that appears as special evidence of God's providence—and here Qoheleth deals his severest blow to the notion of reward—is God's giving to some, apart altogether from their merit, the ability to enjoy what in life can be enjoyed. Also death is a divine provision, for it is God's process of judgment whereby He sifts out,[1] that is, brings to an end the periods or lives wherein justice or injustice rules—for both these phases of life are in accordance with His predetermining purpose. Finally, but not least as a contribution to the thought of the Old Testament, is Qoheleth's observation that there is always an incalculable element in life—*mikreh*. He does not define this. Hertzberg (p. 78) describes it as "a mixture of chance (*Zufall*) and destiny (*Schicksal*)." But it is evident that if in relation to God who causes all things it is destiny, as having no relationship to man's conduct it is pure contingency or chance.

While there is ample admonition to "fear God" in Ecclesiastes, and without doubt the author regards man as accountable to God, these fragments of religious thought count for little when taken as governed by the idea of God as a determining fate. They amount to little more than the recognition of the law of consequence. There is no place left for the rigid form of the Deuteronomist theory. This is denied and cast forth. The later writer, who attached to the end of the epilogue (12[13]): "Fear God and keep His commandments, for this is the duty of every man. For every work will God bring to judgment, with respect to every hidden thing whether it be good or evil," does his best to retrieve from the fragments of piety that which in Ecclesiastes at least appeared to him to be consistent with the elastic general form of the theory of reward—a striking testimony in itself to the watchfulness and care with which Judaism guarded what it judged to be the essential basis of religion and ethics.

[1] Cf. Hertzberg on 3[18] p. 91 f.

The higher spiritual values which emerge from Old Testament thought upon the subject of reward and retribution might be held to be the notion of vicarious suffering, the contrast of the finite wisdom of man with the infinite intelligence whose wisdom is manifest in the universe of which man is only a part, and the idea that virtue is its own reward. But when we weigh these values in respect of their effect upon conduct and upon the subsequent course of thought, they are found to play a secondary rôle in comparison with that complex of ideas which had as its centre the belief in reward and retribution as the mode of God's reaction to man's thoughts and actions, and as the principle of His government in relation to man. While the teacher of religion rightly sets emphasis on the higher attainments of religious thought, drawing the mind upwards to the hills, and while, when observed in retrospect, advance in religious and moral ideas seems to have been made over the summits, from the point of view of the history of religion humanity in the mass moves onward on the beaten track. We may observe this in later Judaism, even when the idea of immortality has widened the horizon of thought and placed a new factor at the disposal of theology. That which remains vital is the Deuteronomist theory which adapts itself to the new conditions, or rather to which the new conditions adapt themselves.

CHAPTER IV

THE DEVELOPMENT OF THE DEUTERONOMIST THEORY IN LATER JUDAISM

OF the religious ideas which the Old Testament bequeathed to later Judaism one of the purest was that of Ps. 73, that the consciousness of the presence and approval of God was its own reward, a thought which, since the contrast drawn by the Psalm is between the wicked and the righteous, we may fairly interpret by the moral principle, " virtue is its own reward." This conception, separating the moral and religious from the eudæmonistic motive of conduct, offered a solution of the problem of theodicy, so far as the Old Testament felt the problem in respect of individual lives, from within the personal experience. Weiser, in his essay on " The problem of the moral order of the world as presented in the Book of Job," [1] thinks that this is the end result of this work as it now stands. The appearance of God is vouchsafed (ch. 38) to Job and leads him from his claim upon the goods of life to the supreme Good and with this Job is satisfied. But later Judaism, so far as can be judged from extant literature, did not avail itself to any great extent of this outlet. If the Deuteronomist doctrine, reinforced by the rigid individualism of Ezekiel and in its less compromising form, was faced with the insuperable difficulty of the supposition that a man's moral character could be estimated by his fortune or misfortune, it at least wrestled with the problem of the justice of God as reflected in this actual world and in the observable events of human life. The idea of reward and retribution supplied the only means of judging whether there

[1] *Theologische Blätter. Jahrgang* 2, 1923, p. 157 f.

was a moral world-order at all. To be persuaded of God's
providence through the assurance of being near to God or
possessing Him, and that this is the reward of righteousness
is to take refuge in an inner personal experience, that is, in
an area which is well known to be the residence of all delusions.
This, we may believe, was one reason, though not the only
reason, why upon this highway where the soul is left alone
with its own inner experience, we find in Judaism so few way-
farers. There are, however, traces of teaching along this line
of thought or on lines parallel with it.

If we limit ourselves to the consideration of the period before
the Christian era and to the first two centuries after it, we find
three examples of teaching to the effect that man should do
good and serve God without looking to a reward. All three
examples are given in the Sayings of the Fathers. Antigonos
of Soko (3rd cent. B.C.) taught : " Be not as servants who serve
their master on condition of receiving a gift, but as servants
who serve their master not on condition of receiving a gift,
and let the fear of God (Heaven) be upon you " (i. 3). Rabbi
Jose (A.D. 100) said : " Let all thy actions be for the sake of
God " (to the name of Heaven, ii. 16), and Simon ben Azai (c.
A.D. 125) is responsible for the saying : " The reward of a commandment is a commandment and the reward of a sin is a sin "
(iv. 2), by which we may understand that God rewards obedience
and service by giving a man fuller opportunity to obey and
serve.[1] In accordance with such teaching later teachers made
much of the technical terms *lishmah*,[2] meaning " for the sake of,"
that is, the performance of a religious or moral duty for its own
sake, and *Simchah shel Torah*, meaning " the joy of the law,"

---

[1] Eleazar ben Pedath (*c.* 250 B.C.) explains Ps. 112[1], " that delighteth greatly
in His commandments," as intending the man who delighteth in God's commandments and not in the reward of God's commandments. If this saying
be ascribed to Eliezer ben Hyrkanos (*c.* A.D. 115), it comes within our period.
Cf. *Abod. Zar.* 19a. Also Baeck (in *R.G.G.* on " Vergeltung ").

[2] *e.g.* Rab (A.D. 247). See Strack and Billerbeck, *Kommentar zum N.T.
aus Talmud und Midrasch*, vol. i. p. 591.

the inward joy felt through compliance with the will of God.

In valuing these recommendations to disinterested goodness we are confronted with two extremes of opinion. Bousset, in his *Religion of Judaism in the Hellenistic Age* (p. 415), regards the passages cited as merely " occasional and accidental," while Jewish scholars at times tend to convey the impression that the sentences of Antigonos, Jose, and Azai represented the accepted and normal principle of rabbinic teaching.[1] Occasional the admonition to serve God without an eye to reward certainly was, but we cannot view with Bousset the sentences in question as being accidental. In the Testaments of the Twelve, where the commandment to love God is joined with that of love of the neighbour, we have already evidence of the growth of a very high ethic. Also in the work of Sirach, where the utilitarian and eudæmonistic motive of right action is always either expressed or in the background, there is, nevertheless, the appeal to the categorical imperative, the commandment of God. The priests are to be given their portion and the sacrifices are to be maintained because " it is commanded " (7^{31}). " Remember the commandments and be not wrath with thy neighbour " (28^7). In the Wisdom literature after Sirach, where the Law and Wisdom are one, the Law appears as the norm of conduct, not indeed separate from the idea of reward, but there is the tendency to appreciate it independently as norm. This is perceptible both in the Book of Tobit and in the Wisdom of Solomon. The festivals are kept as has " been ordained in all Israel by an everlasting decree " (Tob. 1^6; cf. 4^5, 6^{13}, 7^{11}), and Wisdom is that which understands " what is right according to Thy (God's) commandments " (Sap. 9^9). But it is in the Fourth Book of Maccabees, written at latest before the fall of Jerusalem in A.D. 70, where we see the fruit and result of this trend of thought. Here, it is true, the reward of obedience to God, " the prize of virtue " (9^9, $19^{29f.}$) is immor-

---

[1] See Schechter, *op. cit.* below and T. Herford, *op. cit.*

tality. But the Law of God has absolute authority. For this men must be prepared to die as died the martyrs in the Maccabean Age. They must be prepared to sacrifice all worldly gain, the joys of life, and the ties of family affection. That virtue is its own reward comes here to explicit announcement. One of the martyrs is described as saying to the tyrant Antiochus : " For I am supported under pain by the joys that come through virtue, whereas thou art in torment whilst glorying in thy impiety " (9³¹).[1] When, therefore, we place the three sentences in the Sayings of the Fathers in the light of that development of thought which appears in Judaism since the writing of the 73rd Psalm, and especially in the light of the Maccabean struggle (c. 164 B.C.) [2] in behalf of the Law, when loyal Jews had everything to lose by their loyalty, the view that these sentences are an accidental element in Jewish teaching represents a very grave error. They are natural products of preceding thought and history. On the other hand, to present them as setting forth the principle upon which later Judaism based its ethical and religious teaching is to ignore this teaching in the mass as well as the history of thought from which it sprung. The doctrine that man should serve God without hope of reward remained a rare doctrine, and when Schechter,[3] in tracing it throughout Judaism, makes a sudden leap from earlier Rabbinic sayings to the Middle Ages, when it becomes general in devotional literature, we become aware how occasional it was. Representative of the bulk of the sayings in the Sayings of the Fathers and of Judaism before and after New Testament times is the injunction of Rabbi Judah (c. A.D. 150) : " Keep in view three things and thou wilt not come into the clutches of sin ; know what is above thee, an eye that sees, and an ear that hears, and all thy deeds

---

[1] Cf. 7²² " It is a blessed thing to endure all hardness for the sake of virtue."

[2] i.e. in the case of Jose and Azai.

[3] *Some Aspects of Rabbinic Theology,* chapter on " The Joy of the Law," p. 163.

written in a book " (2¹).   God keeps reckoning of all the actions
of man.   Nothing escapes His retributive justice.   Hillel
(c. 30 B.C.), seeing a skull floating in the water, makes the
pronouncement :   " At the last they that drowned thee shall be
drowned " (2⁷).   God is a faithful rewardèr of all service done
for Him.   " The day is short and the work is great, and the
labourers are slow and the hire is much " (2¹⁹ ; Rabbi Tarphon,
c. A.D. 100).   The diligent student of God's word, the Law,
" has gained for himself the life of the world to come " (Hillel,
2⁸).   Even the words of Antigonos, the teacher of disinterested
service, conclude upon the note :   " Let the fear of God be upon
you," and reference to " the sake of God " does not rule out
the promise of reward (cf. 2²), or of " the glory (that) will come
in the end " (Sifre 84a).   For Judaism, in the centuries with
which we are here concerned, moral action was action in the
fear of God.   Its first principle of ethical teaching was as
expressed in the Wisdom literature :   " The fear of the Lord
is the beginning of wisdom."   So long as reward and retribution
retained their established place and worth as explanatory of
God's providence there was no chance of their being displaced
as man's motives of conduct.

Dr. Travers Herford, in his comparative study of the Jewish
ethical teaching in the early centuries (*Talmud and Apocrypha*,
p. 275 f.), says that for the Rabbis " reward denoted the better
condition in which a man found himself who did the will of
God as compared with a man who failed or neglected to do
it."   This formula, wide enough to include the finer and less
refined notions of reward, describes what everywhere by most
people is signified by reward—an improvement in a man's
condition, whether this be compared with what befalls others
or not.   Now we have observed that the ethical teaching of
Judaism worked with the conception of reward, and that
instruction with this motive in the foreground or in the background is immeasurably more abundant than admonitions to
do good without expectation of reward.   It was, as Herford

says, a question of a man's better condition, of the " That
it may be well with you " of the Deuteronomist teaching. But
when Herford adds that " the expectation of reward was never
regarded [by the Rabbis] as the motive for doing the action,"
this neither accords with the relevant literature nor with
psychology. A teacher may intimate to his pupils that there
will be a prize for good conduct, or, that good conduct is its
own reward, but if he intimates both, as Herford admits that
even the Rabbinic teaching in its most exalted form does, the
mental gymnastic of separating the two forms of good may be
for the pupils intellectually possible, but in practice will not be
attempted. The intimation of a reward is altogether purpose-
less unless it be to inspire excellence. Judaism was perfectly
able, as we see from the Fourth Book of Maccabees, to teach
that the better condition of the doer of the Law was a present
inner condition of soul, but this was not the normal doctrine.
In 4 Maccabees itself this teaching does not stand alone. The
author encourages his readers to emulate those who, in the time
of persecution, died for righteousness' sake, " knowing well
that men dying for God live unto God, as live Abraham and
Isaac and Jacob " (16^{25}).[1] This thought of a hereafter and
the plentiful references to reward [2] contained in the book
are not intended to be without motivating power any
more than is the author's mention of God's retributive
justice when he relates that " vengeance pursued the
tyrant Antiochus upon earth and in death he suffers punishment " (18^5).[3]

The writer of the Fourth Book of Maccabees, steeped though
his thought is in Stoic philosophy which had risen to the conception that only virtue is a good and only vice is an evil,[4]
exhibits that Jewish independence of his teachers which is a

---

[1] On 16^{25} and 7^{19}, see Kautzsch, vol. ii. p. 162, and Charles on 4 Macc.
[2] 10^{15}, 13^{17}, 17^4, 17^{18}, 18^{23}.
[3] (Punishment), $9^{8. \ 32}$, $10^{11. \ 15}$, 12^{19}, 13^{15}, 18^{22}.
[4] See Gronau, *op. cit.* p. 9, on The Teaching of the Stoic Chrysippus.

characteristic of his work,[1] when, alongside of the notion that
virtue is its own reward, he sets the Jewish traditional teaching
on reward and retribution as the motive of conduct and as
the mode of the deity's reaction to man's well-doing and wrong-
doing. We see here the distinction between that which was
acquired as a philosophical idea and that which was held and
applied as a living religious belief. It is a distinction which
Herford, towards the end of his book to which we have referred,
at least comes near to making. In contrasting the Rabbinic
teachers, for whom *doing* the commandments of God was the
main purpose of life, with Philo, whose ethic was founded on
Stoic thought, he states that " for Philo, virtue was a condition
of soul which God helped man to acquire, or even developed
in him, in proportion to his ascent in the scale of wisdom and
goodness towards more perfect knowledge of God " (p. 314).
Certainly in Philo the difference between Jewish and Greek
thought is made most apparent through his attempt to blend
them. But how difficult it was for the Hebrew mind to rest
completely even in the simpler position of " virtue is its own
reward " becomes obvious not only from 4 Maccabees, the work
of an able scholar and orthodox Jew who stated the doctrine
in its purest form, but from a passage in a work written near
the end of the first century by a Jew who expressly wrote for
the Greek reader and the Roman world. Josephus (Ant. iv. 8)
makes direct contact with the subject of virtue and reward.
He describes Moses before his departure from mankind as
addressing the Israelites with these words : " Virtue indeed
is the principal and the first reward, and after that it bestows
abundance of others ; so that your exercise of virtue towards
other men will make your own lives happy and render you
more glorious than foreigners can be, and procure you an
undisputed reputation with posterity." In this passage, that
virtue *of itself* is a reward is affirmed, but thereafter, in the

---

[1] See Charles, *Pseudep.* vol. ii. " Intro. to 4 Macc." on the author's
independent treatment of the Stoic doctrine of Reason and the Passions.

rest of the speech, it is not considered apart from the other conditions it can procure.   Josephus starts out by making obeisance to the philosophic idea and then immediately follows in the familiar path of wisdom-teacher and the Deuteronomist.

Although, as we have shown, the idea of serving God without hope of reward cannot be described as arising accidentally in Judaism, and can be accounted for by the trend of thought since the writing of the Book of Job, it has to be noted that when this idea comes to clear expression, namely in Psalm 73 and the saying of Antigonos, we are in the Hellenistic Age. The writer of the Fourth Book of Maccabees, who probably lived in Alexandria, was well acquainted with the Stoic philosophy.   It may, however, be conjectured that also in Palestine the idea of *lishmah* or goodness for its own sake was not entirely uninfluenced by Greek thought.   The Pharisees who owed their origin to the need of protecting the faith of the fathers from attempts at Hellenization appeared too late to stem the tide entirely, and while safeguarding that which was traditional and old, they themselves were unable to remain wholly unaffected by the subtle strength of the Greek spirit.[1]   But the traditional did remain and nowhere is this so evident as in the teaching in regard to reward.

We may here remark briefly, that what has been said of Judaism in regard to its attitude to the ideas of " virtue for its own sake " and " for the sake of God " is borne out by the Gospels.   The New Testament presents in this respect the same picture as does the Judaism of its time.   Jesus' approach to publicans and sinners and to some of those who are addressed in the Beatitudes (Matt. 5[3f.]), responds to conceptions that were not accepted by Judaism.[2]   The nature of His teaching was such that it has two opposite effects.   It made access to the " kingdom of God " easy (My yoke is easy) but in another aspect more difficult (Except your righteousness shall exceed that of the Scribes and Pharisees ye shall in no case enter into

[1] Cf. Wetter, *op. cit.* p. 9 on the Pharisees.   [2] Cf. chap. i. above.

the kingdom of heaven). This comprehensiveness and this narrowing affected the number of those to whom reward would apply, but it did not affect the idea of reward and retribution as a motive of conduct. The popular Jewish notion that misfortune must be retribution for sin, Jesus rejected (Luke 13[1f.]; John 9[3]); the notion of reward He often refined (*e.g.* that ye may be the sons of your Father in heaven) [1] but the hope of divine reward as a motive of right action persists. As in Judaism we meet with the admonition to do well without hoping for a reward followed at once by the words "and let the fear of God be upon you" (P. Ab. 1[3]), in the Gospel we have the injunction to lend to our enemies without expecting any return followed at once by "then you will have a rich reward" (Luke 6[35]). Suffering and self-denial endured for Christ's sake (for my sake and for the sake of the gospel, Mark 10[39]) is rewarded a hundredfold in the present world and in the world to come. Those who seek the kingdom of God will have the earthly necessities of food and raiment over and above (Matt. 7[33]). On a line of thought which comes very near to the conception of virtue as its own reward is the notable saying of the fourth Gospel : "This is life eternal that they know Thee the only true God and Him whom Thou hast sent, even Jesus Christ" [2]—a saying which gives a present reference to the notion of eternal life, and which in its formulation is held to show Hellenic influence.[3] Of the beatitudes in the synoptic Gospels, Johannes Weiss points to "Blessed are the pure in heart for they shall see God" as almost wholly overcoming current reward conceptions and concentrating upon the condition of the soul itself.[4] Weiss thinks that Jesus'

---

[1] Matt. 5[45], cf. 5[9]; Luke 6[35], etc.   [2] John 17[3], cf. Moffatt.

[3] Cf. Sap. Sol. 15[3] : "For to know Thee is perfect righteousness, yea to know Thy dominion is the root of immortality." Cf. Charles, vol. 1. p. 572, on dependence of John and Sap. Sol. On Hellenistic influence see Heitmüller (*Schr. d. N.T.'s* vol. ii. p. 758 f., 760), Johannis-Evangelium.

[4] Matt. 5[8], cf. *Schr. d. N.T.* 1907, p. 262 ; cf. Paul (1 Cor. 13[12]); 1 John 3[2] Rev. 22[4].

teaching must have reflected this quality more often than the Gospel reveals. This is possible. But what is clear is that for the Gospels and contemporary Judaism the idea expressed by " for the sake of God " (of Christ, the Gospel—Heaven, the Commandment) had no intention of excluding the hope of divine reward as a motive of conduct, and that while the content of reward could be refined, the conception of virtue as its own reward remains occasional, qualified, and rare. The reason for this is twofold. Neither Judaism nor early Christianity, particularly Jewish Christianity, was capable of separating morality from religion. Duties towards man and God, as in the Ten Commandments, were both alike imposed by *God*. They were His commandments. He would safeguard them. The Deuteronomist teaching of reward and retribution represented the normal teaching as to the manner in which He would do so, and in which He would act according to His knowledge of the hearts or inner dispositions of men. When even, as in 4 Maccabees, the suffering of martyrdom for " the prize of virtue " is commended, there is the reward of a future life in view as the motivating consideration. The New Testament and 4 Maccabees stand here upon the same plane. Suffering for the sake of truth is never regarded apart from God's reward.[1] The idea of virtue being its own reward can be taught without any reference to God at all. Where morality and theistic religion are one and inseparable, this position cannot be taken without creating the consciousness of an awkward breach. Therefore in Judaism and in the New Testament, when the idea of righteousness having its own value in itself does appear, it does so in a synthesis in which it is related either less closely or more closely (*e.g.* Ps. 73 ; John 17[3] ; Matt. 5) with the notion of man's personal relationship with God. The other reason for the rarity of the thought that virtue has its own value apart from any other consideration, was that both Judaism and Christianity had inherited from Israel's past a conception

[1] Matt. 10[39] ; Phil. 1[20f.]

which was for them, as it was for the religion of Zoroaster, of
inestimable power, inasmuch as it connected God in a very
special way with world-history and personal destiny. God
would manifest His righteousness and consummate His plan
in a final Judgment which would have regard to Israel and the
nations, peoples and persons, the righteous and the wicked.
In both Judaism and in the teaching of Jesus, the Divine Judgment was put forward as something to be feared. We perceive
from the Gospels that it was easier to refine the content of
reward than it was to refine the idea of retribution.[1] But
wherever the notion of Judgment, whatever form it may take,
is retained and valued, it is psychologically impossible to
abandon the idea of reward and retribution as a motive of
conduct. Moreover, both Judaism and New Testament writers
justly felt that the conceptions of reward and retribution, from
the point of view of a religious philosophy of history, had
necessarily more living connection with the scheme of life, with
providence, and with God's plan of world government than
could possibly be disclosed by a purely inner personal experience,
or perceived from the remote vantage ground of the fragmentary
truth *præmium virtutis ipsa virtus.* In Greek thought this
truth had its natural and congenial soil. The Stoic ideal of
" the wise man " had been taken over by the Stoics from the
Cynics and through the Stoics it received its full development.
The wise man was unconditionally free and capable of all good
actions, and his God-like attributes were the subject of the
most exalted praise. To this Stoic ideal attached the teaching
that "Happiness is based upon the perfection of virtue, and
this is only possible for the wise. Virtue is the only good, and
as such is unconditionally sufficient for happiness." [2] In this
description we may further detect that which accounts for
this product of Greek thought striking no deep root in the

---

[1] Cf. Mark 9[43f.] ; Matt. 13[41f.]
[2] See *Geschichte des hellenistischen Zeitalters*, 1901, p. 125, Bd. i., by Julius
Kaerst.

Hebrew mind. The Stoic ideal and appreciation of virtue did not commend itself either to Judaism or Christianity because of its quality of self-sufficiency which is ultimately repellent to religion,[1] and because its idea of happiness or blessedness ran counter to those new-age conceptions which were common to both religions in their emphasis on the expectation of a coming " kingdom of God."

.   .   .   .

We must now retrace our steps to the channel in which the main stream of thought upon reward and retribution flows, in order that we may trace the development of the Deuteronomist theory which, in spite of the occasional tendency to separate the ethical from the eudæmonistic motive of conduct, and in spite of the ever-present problem of the sufferings of the righteous and the prosperity of the wicked, remained the tenet of orthodox theology.

The Maccabean period sees emerge in the Judaism of the second century B.C., the belief that at least some particularly righteous persons, who had experienced death, would, after a judgment that was to precede a new æon or age (Dan. 12 cf. Isa. 26), rise from the dead to participate in the bliss of an everlasting kingdom of God. The Old Testament writings bring us so far. In the first pre-Christian century, the belief in a future life has become a mark of the new orthodox (Pharisaic) Judaism and to this belief the Deuteronomist theory, which hitherto envisaged the divine justice as manifesting itself in the events of this life only, had to adapt itself. In the Second Book of Maccabees, in the Psalms of Solomon, and above all in one of the finest works of the Wisdom-school, the Book of the Wisdom of Solomon (Sap. Sol.), we perceive what adaptations were made. These writings show that the belief in a hereafter

[1] Cf. A. E. Taylor, Gifford Lectures, *Faith of a Moralist*, 1926–28, 1st series, p. 229 f. " A man cannot receive power to rise above his present moral level from his own inherent strength."   " Except in the New Testament and in Plato the indispensability of τροφή (nourishment) from without for the moral life seems never to have found adequate recognition," p. 231.

did not have the effect, as it tends to have in later ages, of
removing to a future stage of existence all that has to do with
divine reward and punishment, leaving to God the task of
adjusting the balance of justice in another world. The Book
of Énoch and the later apocalpyses indeed seldom, or never,
refer to the punishment of sinners in this life, committing them
to judgment in the beyond. But these apocalypses do not
represent the normal line of thought. God's justice, it is
demanded, must be manifest in the moral order of this world
over which His providence completely presides.

The first psalm of the Psalms of Solomon, written probably
soon after the invasion of Palestine by Pompey (63 B.C.), still
reveals the close connection, in thought, of righteousness and
prosperity, and accounts for the tribulation suffered by the
taking of Jerusalem as due to the secret sins of its inhabitants
and their insolence in prosperity. The author describes the
city as saying :

> I thought in my heart I was full of righteousness,
> Because I was well off and had become rich in children.
> Their wealth spread to the whole earth,
> And their glory unto the end of the earth.

The author's religious philosophy is that, " According to their
sins, He (God) hath done unto them " (2⁷), and the violation
of the women of Jerusalem by the Gentiles he regards as a just
judgment of God upon the city's immorality and harlotry
(2¹³ᶠ·), an apt example of *quid pro quo* ! Written a decade
or more earlier than the earliest of the Psalms of Solomon, the
Second Book of Maccabees (100–64 B.C.) sets forth the view
that God does not delay long with His retributive justice. For
the author, the present world exhibits the plain writ of the
law of recompense. One of his heroes, the ninety-year-old
Eleazar says : " Were I for the moment to evade the punishment of men, I should not escape the hands of the Almighty
in life or in death " (6²⁶). The doctrine of a hereafter does not
prejudice the law of recompense operative in this world. In

the very passage where the hope of resurrection is expressed, and the story of the seven brother martyrs is told, the author makes two of the brothers affirm : " We are suffering this on our own account, for sins against our own God " (7^{18}); " we are suffering for our own sins " (7^{32}). Since this " we " includes not only the martyrs but the nation, the Deuteronomist teaching of corporate responsibility becomes more evidently plain.

But it is in the Book of the Wisdom of Solomon [1] that the best opportunity is offered of viewing the interaction of the belief in immortality and the traditional Deuteronomist conceptions. In the first part of the book (chaps. 1–10) the author departs from the traditional view that childlessness and a short life are tokens of God's displeasure. In general, long life had been the *summum bonum* of the old theory, but now the idea of " life " is spiritualized, and is not to be reckoned in number of years, but as a perfection of soul ($4^{13f.}$). In the case of the righteous, early death is not a punishment (3^4), but proceeds from the love of God (4^{10}), in whose hand their souls are and where they remain in peace ($3^{1f.}$). But these thoughts modify only slightly the age-old teaching of the doctrine of recompense. The reason which the author gives for the early death of the righteous man is, lest living longer " wickedness should change his understanding or guile deceive his soul " (4^{11}), that is, in other words, lest he sin and so become subject to retribution. There is also no notice taken of Ezekiel's strict individualism. " The children of adulterers shall not come to maturity," do not take root, and are witnesses of wickedness against their parents (4^6). Immortality is " the wages of holiness " (2^{22}). The misfortunes of the righteous are the " mysteries of God," the " little chastening," after which " they shall receive great good, because God tested them and found them worthy of Himself " (3^5). The second portion of the book (chaps. 11–19), which appears to be by a different but later contemporary writer,[2] presents a distinct tightening of the conception of

[1] 50–30 B.C.   [2] 30 B.C.–A.D. 10. See Intro. in Charles, *Apoc.*

retribution, the artificiality of which demonstrates how firm a hold the traditional method of defending God's providence possessed. The punishments which God exacts, it is taught, are extraordinarily appropriate, and the misfortunes which befall men are in no wise arbitrary. For " by measure and number and weight Thou (O God) didst order all things " (11[20]). The river Nile turned by God to clotted blood was His vengeance upon the Egyptians for their slaughter of the Israelite babes (11[5f.]), for " by what things a man sins by these he is punished " (11[16]). This thought is carefully worked out by the Book of Wisdom,[1] and Philo also (Vita Mos. 1[17]) is attracted by it. The teaching that the righteous attain immortality (15[3]) and that the misfortunes which at present they experience are admonitory (11[10]) or disciplinary (12[21]) does not modify the belief of the writer of the second part of Sap. Sol. that Providence manifests itself here on earth in reward and retribution. Nature (the world) itself, the writer affirms, fights for the righteous (16[17]), and "creation, ministering to its Maker, strains its force against the unrighteous for punishment " (16[24]). Hardships and troubles may be chastening, but suffering does not appear to be thought of as ever being undeserved. Thus the author of these chapters offers the completest defence of the traditional Deuteronomist doctrine which later Judaism possesses. It is significant that he draws so largely upon biblical history in setting forth his ideas upon the world-order. The more Judaism became a " religion of the book," the deeper must have been the impression made by the grand interpretation of Providence which the Old Testament presented.

If on the surface the Deuteronomist theory appears at the end of the first pre-Christian century to be unshaken, yet nevertheless we see from the literature examined that the idea of an after-life had worked a deep alteration in the old Israelite view of the scheme of divine justice. The difficulty presented

---

[1] Cf. also *Test. of Gad*, chap. 5, and Jub. 4[31]: " With a stone Cain had killed Abel and by a stone was he killed."

to faith by the misfortunes of the righteous was in great part overcome. The thought that God had the " wages of holiness " in reserve, and that present afflictions as a means of chastening prepare the soul for the life to come, deepened immeasurably the older disciplinary view of earthly sufferings. The writer of the first chapters (1–10) of the Wisdom of Solomon does not relate the sufferings of the righteous to sin at all. Their calamities are a testing, but are not considered as remedial and the reward of righteousness—though heavenly wisdom bestows temporal advantages (7^{11}) and the righteous escape the temporal penalties of wickedness—is " life," that is immortality in the world beyond. The righteous indeed only *seem* to die (3^2). As in the Fourth Gospel, eternal life is regarded as a quality or state to be enjoyed already in the present world.

It is at this stage of Jewish religious thought as reflected in the Wisdom of Solomon that we are able to appreciate the cause which led to a further development of the Deuteronomist theory through Rabbinic Judaism in the first century of the Christian era. The author of the first ten chapters by his doctrine that spiritual life and spiritual death are states of soul which exist already here and now and continue in the hereafter [1] had united the present and the future into one whole. But, inasmuch as he recognizes that, from the point of view of the rewarding of the righteous, this world presents no proof of God's justice, the writer disconnected the present world from the world to come, and left these two aspects of existence separate and unbridged. If, as the literary criticism leads us to conclude, the different spirit and thought of the second part of this book is due to that part being by a different writer, we may infer that its being appended to the first ten chapters had the same editorial purpose as the last part of the Epilogue of Ecclesiastes, namely, to bring the book more into the lines of the traditional theory. Hence the measure-for-measure doctrine of the concluding chapters ; hence, espec-

[1] See Intro. in Charles on the *Theology of Ch.*, 1–10.

ially, the teaching that all creation, all Nature, that is the present world as constituted, is so ordered that goodness is defended and supported and evil punished. The author of these chapters appears to have sensed that the probable effect of the first chapters would be to foster the thought that this world provided no clue to God's providential justice, and that, for the vindication of this, men must look solely to the life to come. The idea of justice demanded that there should be no such deep cleft between the present world-order and the next, if both were under the government of God. The Deuteronomist teaching of providence had been the bulwark of optimism. It was therefore felt, we may assume, that if it were believed that reward and retribution only became realities in the distant future and beyond the confines of this present life, the result would be an intolerable pessimism. That the danger of this was real may be perceived from the Fourth Book of Ezra, in a portion that dates from the end of the century (A.D. 100). The writer, pondering the question of the suffering, evil, and sin in the world, concludes that the ways of God are inscrutable, the future world must be patiently awaited for the solution of all difficulties, the present world order is so hopeless that it cannot be renovated or purified. This world is doomed to be dissolved that the incorruptible age of true life and immortality may dawn.[1] It is in the light of this tendency of thought that we must regard the endeavour of rabbinic Judaism to relate the present and the future life as two connected parts in the divine economy, and from the point of view of divine reward and retribution, to exhibit them as perfectly adjusted one to the other. It was of the nature of apocalyptic thought and of the distinctively apocalyptic writings (for example, the writers of Enoch and 4 Ezra) to seek deliverance from this evil world in the next, to contrast the perfect heavenly order with the disorder of the present world, to visualize not the duration of human life but

[1] Cf. 3[4f.], 7[114].

its conclusion. But it was the function of the Rabbis, whose interest lay in the religious and moral implications of the Law, and who were thus in one aspect at least the successors of the teachers of practical wisdom, to present the present and the future as one orderly connected system, and so provide a conception that would serve as a foundation for ethical teaching and moral conduct in daily life.[1]

Rabbinic Judaism evolved from the old doctrine of the probationary and disciplinary purpose of certain sufferings the further idea that, besides the disciplinary value of adversity, sufferings and misfortunes are a divinely appointed means whereby the righteous man may *atone* for his sins here upon earth so that the judicial necessity for his receiving retribution for these sins in the hereafter is removed. The close connection which suffering and sin were deemed to have in the old Deuteronomist theory of reward is maintained. All men are sinners. The misfortunes of the righteous, whether disciplinary or not, are punishment, but they are a sign of grace and great mercy of God Who gives to those who love Him the opportunity of atonement. In the case of the wicked, their sufferings are merely punitive or retributive. And last, but not least in importance as an apologetic for the present condition of the world—the prosperity of the wicked gives no cause for dismay but rather is to be expected, for this prosperity is the reward for any good thing they may have done in this world, God in His great justice being at particular pains to give them their reward here in order that they may have no further claim for anything save destruction or punishment hereafter. Thus, we perceive that the Deuteronomist theory which in the Old Testament was rooted in a this-world conception of existence is now perfectly harmonized with that factor which threatened its destruction, the belief in a future life. The measure-for-measure aspect of strict justice is upheld but refined. But

[1] On the attitude of the Rabbis to Apocalyptic, cf. Herford, p. 215 f., *op. cit.*

whereas in former days the prosperity of the righteous was a
matter of satisfaction to faith and the sufferings of the righteous
were a subject of amazement and complaint, there was now
ground for considerable alarm if the righteous should grow
particularly prosperous or free from this world's troubles.
This prosperity might indicate secret wickedness, that a man
was, as the Midrashim or Jewish commentaries express it,
receiving or " had received (his) reward " (*qibbel sakar*), that
he " had received (his) world " (*qibbel 'olam*) ; in other words,
that he would have no claim for good in the world to come.
But since the pains of life, even if they be not accounted as
out-weighing life's pleasures, are at least not far to seek and
are seldom long absent from any one of us, we may believe
that the rabbinic doctrine had less to prejudice it in the world
of reality than had the former theory of reward.

Before reference is made to the passages in which the
rabbinic doctrine is contained or implied, it is well to note
that some of its features appear in the thought of the previous
century (1st cent. B.C.).   The idea of atonement is old, but the
idea of an individual's suffering, sickness, and pains of death
being a means of atonement for his own sins appears at first
examination at least to gain currency only at the end of the
first or in the second century A.D.[1] But in the Psalms of
Solomon we meet with the conception that fasting may atone
for sins that have been unwittingly committed : " The righteous
. . . maketh atonement for (sins of) ignorance by fasting and
afflicting his soul " (3[8f.]).   This atonement has the future
world in view (3[16]).   But already previously the author of
the Second Book of Maccabees had applied the notion of the
atoning value of punishment with reference to Israel and the
present world in a passage, the thought of which is closely
parallel with the rabbinic theory.   " I beseech the readers of
this book," he says " to reflect that our people were being
punished by way of chastening and not for their destruction.

---

[1] Cf. Charles, *Apoc.*, note on Sir. 18[20] and reference to Siphre 73b and 33a.

For, indeed, it is a mark of great kindness when the impious are not let alone for a long time, but punished at once. In the case of other nations, the Sovereign Lord in his forbearance refrains from punishing them till they have filled up their sins to the full, but in our case he has determined otherwise that his vengeance may not fall on us in after days when our sins have reached their height. Wherefore he never withdraweth his mercy from us ; and though he chasteneth his own people with calamity, he forsaketh them not " (6¹²⁻¹⁶). This view that God punishes His own people at once, that vengeance may not fall upon them in after days, that He has granted to His own favoured nation the great privilege of having their sin cancelled speedily through suffering before their sins accumulate, is the same as is taken up by the Rabbis and made to apply to the individual person and to the present and the future world.

The rabbinic theory, in the stress it lays upon the need of atonement, shows a deep consciousness of human sinfulness. This characteristic of later Judaism is sometimes ascribed to the national catastrophe which overtook Jerusalem in the year A.D. 70. The acuteness of the blow to faith, caused by the adversities of the righteous, was now allayed by the disaster bringing misery to every one and consequently passed into a deeper appreciation of the universality of sin. But long before this, as the Second Book of Maccabees shows, the example of the righteous martyrs of the Maccabean period had done much to impress the lesson that righteousness is no passport to prosperity. In the succeeding years, the commemoration of the martyrdoms of this period in synagogue sermons and lectures, a sample of which we have in the Fourth Book of Maccabees, must have had the effect of causing a complete change of outlook upon the subject of theodicy, upon the problem of the ways of God with man. The troubles in the days of Pompey had revived again the old heart-searching question concerning the afflictions of the just. The teaching of

Jesus that righteousness implied a cross, tribulation, and persecution, that is, that righteousness was the very path of suffering was no doubt not an acceptable truth, but cannot have been a novelty to the people of the time.

The first certain witness to the theory of rabbinic Judaism on reward and retribution, although he cannot have been the first exponent of it, is Rabbi Shemuel the Less (c. A.D. 90–130).[1] In the Jewish commentary on the Psalms (Midrash Tehillim) he explains the words of Ps. 94[15], " But judgment shall return unto righteousness and all the upright in heart shall be after it " as meaning " the reward of the righteous shall be after (that is, in the other world), the reward of the godless on the other hand shall be before their face (that is, already in this world)." Exemplifying this teaching of Shemuel we have a story concerning Eleazar ben Zadok. Roman medical men had rendered his father great services. The son, weighing the matter of the Gentile doctors' fee, says to his father : " Father, give them their fee in this world, that they may have no merit on your account in the next." [2] That sickness and other afflictions had in the case of the righteous atoning value, and that a state of outward well-being was regarded as a matter of anxious speculation as to a man's future destiny, is well illustrated by a tradition of Rabbi Aqiba (ob. A.D. 135). Around the death-bed of Eliezer ben Hyrkanos the pupils of Eliezer are standing and weep. But Rabbi Aqiba is smiling. When asked why he is smiling, he explains : " So often as I took note of our master, that his wine was never soured, his flax never blasted, his oil never rancid, his honey never fermented, I thought, perchance, God forbid, the master has already received his world : but now that I see him in pain, I rejoice " (San. 101a) After the time of Aqiba, who indeed Marmorstein thought was

---

[1] i.e. Of the second generation of Tannaim, those teachers who are mentioned in, or existed at the time of, the Mishna (Codification of Jewish Law, completed about the end of the second century A.D.).

[2] Midrash Ekha Rabbati on Lam. 1[5].   Rab. E. ben Zadok, c. A.D. 130.

the first representative of the theory, evidence of the rabbinic doctrine of reward accumulates.[1] Its generality may be inferred from the fact that in the fourth century we perceive an attempt to mitigate it in favour of the prosperous righteous. Raba (*ob.* A.D. 350) the Babylonian teacher (Hor. 10b) believed that it was possible that a righteous man could receive full reward in both worlds. " But woe to the wicked," he says, " with whom it goes as with the just in this world " (that is, badly : for since they are wicked they will also fare badly in the coming world). Raba, however, appears only to be desirous of stating that there may be exceptions to a general rule. He admits that for most of the just, life is hard.

A question, of minor importance compared with the fact of the growth of the rabbinic doctrine of reward, and of this doctrine bringing the Deuteronomist theory to what may seem to be a state of theological completion, remains to be answered : how long before the time of Shemuel the Less was the rabbinic teaching that we have been considering current ? It is not possible, of course, to ascribe for it any exact date, but from the Gospels and the letters of St. Paul we have evidence that it was known in the earlier part of the first century. If this be so we cannot account for its origin, as we might otherwise have had reason for doing, by the fact that the cessation of the temple sacrifices in A.D. 70 gave rise to the idea that personal sufferings were, for the righteous, a substitute for the ancient atoning temple rites now impossible of fulfilment. This idea, no doubt, did strengthen the rabbinic doctrine after A.D. 70. But, as we have seen, the religious thought and history of the first pre-Christian century had been in themselves a sufficient preparation.

In St. Matthew's gospel (6[2]) Jesus, rebuking those who were careful to make their almsgiving with publicity as " the

---

[1] For further examples see W. Wichmann, *Leidenstheologie, eine Form der Leidensdeutung im Spätjudentum*, 1930 ; also Strack and Billerbeck, *op. cit.* p. 390, 590 f. vol. i.

hypocrites do in the synagogues and in the streets," remarks,
" Verily I say to you, they have their reward " (ἀπέχουσιν τὸν
μισθὸν αὐτῶν). The literal translation : " They have their
reward away," reveals a striking expression. As Deissmann
(*Licht vom Osten*, p. 77 f.) has shown, the Greek papyri and
ostraca disclose that Jesus here employed a technical phrase
which appears on business receipts. Every hired labourer in
the Hellenistic age would understand Jesus' words as meaning
that the hypocrites who sought honour of men had been
" receipted," had received their wages, and had absolutely
no claim on anything more. Those who did their almsgivings
in secret would yet have reward of their Father. The Greek
words which Jesus in the gospel uses are the exact equivalent
of the terms (*gabbel sakar*) [1] which appear in the Midrash passages
which set forth the rabbinic theory. There can be little doubt
that Jesus had this teaching in mind.[2] Also the parable of
the rich man and poor Lazarus in St. Luke would appear to be
best interpreted in the light of the same teaching. The rich
man's appeal for mercy is answered in this wise : " Remember
that thou in thy lifetime receivedst thy good things and likewise
Lazarus evil things, but now he is comforted and thou art
tormented " (16[25]). This verse would then seem to imply
that the rich man had already, as the Rabbis expressed it,
" received his world," God having been at pains to gratify the
man's selfishness and to reward him in the fullest measure
for the odd scraps that had fallen to the poor man from his
table.

The writings of St. Paul afford at least two passages which,
though they are not typical of the Pauline teaching on the
subject of reward, recall the rabbinic doctrine. To the
Corinthians he says : " But when we are punished by the Lord,

[1] For use of this phrase both in the secular and religious sense, cf. Jastrow's
Talmud Dictionary.

[2] Billerbeck and Strack in their *Commentary on St. Matthew*, as explained
by Talmud and Midrash, bring examples of the rabbinic doctrine to illustrate
Matt. 6[2].

we are chastened by Him, so that we may not be condemned along with the world " (1 Cor. 11³²). The context speaks of weakness and sickness among the community as being the result of unworthy partaking of the Lord's Supper. It is the only place in the Pauline writings, G. P. Wetter says, where a misfortune befalling a Christian is regarded as a punishment.¹ But the thought is obvious—the punishment suffered in this life has atoning value and forestalls condemnation. Again, in the Second Epistle to the Thessalonians (1⁵), speaking of the persecutions the Christians have undergone, St. Paul describes their sufferings as a " token (ἔνδειγμα, i.e. indication ; German, Vorzeichen) of the just Judgment of God that ye may be accounted worthy of the kingdom of God." The apostle does not refer merely to the probationary value of sufferings, but means that God has sent these afflictions upon the Christians so that they may escape the Judgment,² with which He will judge the unrighteous. Having received opportunity for atonement, they have in the future the joyous expectation of reward only.

Wichmann (op. cit. p. 79) thinks that after the Tannait period the influence of the rabbinic doctrine in Judaism gradually waned. But this does not seem to be the case. We find it in full course in the fourth century ³ and a writing of the Middle Ages, the Darke Teshubah (Means of Repentance), dating from the thirteenth century or later, quoted by Gressmann in his treatise ⁴ on the Parable of Lazarus, shows that the rabbinic viewpoint was still effective as an apologetic. In defence of the law of compensation in relation to conduct this writing begins : " Our masters say : whose good works are many and his sins few, these few minor sins . . . are taken account of

¹ Op. cit. p. 61.

² See Volz, Jüdische Eschatologie, on this verse, p. 97.

³ Cf. Strack and Billerbeck, vol. i. p. 390, for currency of the doctrine c. A.D. 300 and later.

⁴ Abhandlungen d. königl. Preuss. Akad. d. Wiss. 1918 ; Phil.-Hist. Klasse " Vom reichen Mann und armen Lazarus."

in this æon, in order that in the other æon he may be compensated by God entirely (for his good works)."

Thus the Deuteronomist theory was gradually fashioned into something more stable and systematic. The school of Shammai had taught that the future world provides for purgatorial cleansing and atonement in the case of those who were neither righteous nor completely wicked. The specific feature of the rabbinic doctrine is the atoning value of present suffering. Principal Fairbairn states that " though the two evils (*i.e.* physical and moral evil) are different in fact and distinct in thought, yet unless physical evil have a moral reason and function, it can have no justifiable existence in a mora universe." [1] This was the premiss on which Jewish thought on reward and retribution was based. In reviewing the history of this thought, we may ask whether, besides the idea of the probationary and educative value of adversity—an aspect of the Deuteronomist theory which has gained most appreciation in theistic religion—suffering has not in the purpose of God a retributive and an atoning function. In its speculation on the subject Judaism struck the note of atonement. In second Isaiah, atonement for other peoples is made by Israel, the nation ; in the Fourth Book of Maccabees it is effected for the nation by the martyrs ; in the rabbinic doctrine it is effected, through suffering, by the individual himself. This is where Judaism and other religious systems differ most widely from Christianity, which does not think of atonement as effected by man's effort or suffering. The one great problem of the Old Testament and of later Judaism, Christianity met with its Christology.[2] The last specific trace in Christian literature of the rabbinic doctrine is in the Pseudo-Clementine Recognitions which Harnack places in the middle of the third century.[3]

---

[1] *The Philosophy of the Christian Religion*, p. 163.

[2] Cf. Strack and Billerbeck, p. 274 f. A suffering Messiah such as the N.T. taught was not a conception entertained by contemporary Judaism.

[3] See *Ante.-Nic. Lib.* bk. ix. ch. xiii.: " If any are evil, not so much in their mind as in their doings, and are not borne to sin under the incitement of pur-

Wichmann mentions as a curiosity and as a sort of interesting fossil a hymn in the Saxon hymn-book which expresses the wish that punishment may be received in this life rather than in the hereafter. Founded upon the same principle as the rabbinic doctrine, namely, that suffering cancels punishment, was the Buddhist Law of Karma, which necessitates the coming back to birth to work out the overplus of reward and punishment. This theory completely satisfies the condition that man must effect his own atonement. It is a striking fact that this path of thought was actually taken by the Jewish Qabbalists,[1] notably by Isaac Luria (1534–72) and by Manasse ben Israel (1604–57) in his philosophic religious work, *The Living Soul.* They had the old rabbinic doctrine to work upon and also the doctrine of the pre-existence of the soul as taught by the Wisdom of Solomon.

pose, upon them punishment is inflicted more speedily and more in the present life ; for everywhere and always God renders to every one according to his deeds, as He judges to be expedient. But those who practise wickedness of purpose . . . and take no thought of repentance . . . their punishment He refers to the future. For these men do not, like those of whom we spoke before, deserve to end the punishment of their crimes in the present life."

[1] See *Die Kabbalah* (" Introduction to Jewish Mysticism ") by Dr. Erich Bischoff, Leipzig, 1917, pp. 80 and 111 f., and also his volumes on *Die Elemente der Kabbalah*, Berlin, 1920, on the Qabbalist doctrine of transmigration (*Gilgul* of souls.

CHAPTER V

The Belief in a Future Life—Its Growth and Development in Israel

1

The belief in a future life in the form of the doctrine of the immortality of the soul comes to clear expression in Israelite religious thought in the first pre-Christian century. In the Second Book of Maccabees (*c.* 100 B.C.),[1] apart from extensive mention of a resurrection or restoration of bodily life to those who have died (7[9. 11. 14. 23. 29]), there is one allusion to the future state in terms of immortality—"These our brothers enduring a brief pain have now drunk[2] of everflowing life" (7[36]). In the same close connection with faith in divine justice and the doctrine of reward and retribution as in 2 Macc., we meet with a fuller statement of immortality in the Wisdom of Solomon (*c.* 30 B.C.). "They (the righteous) are in peace, for though in the sight of men they be punished, their hope is full of immortality" (3[3f.]). The righteous, though they die before their time, "shall be at rest" (4[7]), they "live for ever, and the Lord is their reward. . . . Therefore shall they receive a glorious kingdom, and a diadem of beauty from the Lord's hand" (5[15f.]). The possession of Wisdom gives the assurance of immortality (8[13]), and to know God's dominion is the root of immortality (15[3]). Though there are clear traces in the Wisdom of Solomon of the purely Jewish eschatological belief in a Messianic kingdom on earth,[3] either of an everlasting or

---

[1] *Re* date of 2 Macc.; cf. my *Origins of Hanukkah*, p. 16 f.
[2] See Charles, *Apoc., ad loc.*
[3] See Charles, *Apoc.*,vol. i. " Intro. to Sap.Sol."

temporary nature (cf. $3^{7f.}$, $4^{18f.}$, $5^{17f.}$), the author does not feel this to be inconsistent with an immortality immediately after death—which is a purely Greek idea. Richer and fuller are the references to immortality (athanasia) in a still later work, the Fourth Book of Maccabees (between 63 B.C. and c. A.D. 38). Here we read that the seven youths, martyred in the days of Antiochus Epiphanes, hastened to death by torture as if "running the road to immortality" (14^5), their God-fearing mother encouraging them thereto as if for the second time she were in travail with them in a birth "unto immortal life" (16^{13}). In the place of their ancestors these loyal sons of Abraham are gathered, "having received pure and immortal souls from God" (18^{23}). This immortality is "a divine inheritance" (18^3) and "the prize of victory in incorruption in everlasting life" (17^{12}), "the prize of virtue" (9^8). "Men dying for God live unto God" (16^{25}) and "stand beside the throne of God and live the blessed age." "A great struggle and peril of the soul awaits in eternal torment those who transgress the ordinance of God" (13^{15}; cf. 9^9). Thus not only the righteous but the unrighteous have an immortal life. The author of 4 Macc., whose thought is steeped in Stoic philosophy and adapts this to Judaism, does not accept the belief in a resurrection of the body. This belief which the author found so strongly expressed in the Second Book of Maccabees in connection with the story of the seven martyred brothers is, in conscious opposition, carefully expunged, and for it is substituted the view that the pious, at death, are received by God in heaven.[1] His thought is that man possesses or is an immortal soul, and thus the writer avoids the intellectual difficulties which result from a fusion of Jewish eschatological ideas with the Greek idea of the soul as a spiritual entity and sufficient unto itself and requiring no embodiment, difficulties with which St. Paul wrestles in 1 Cor. (15; cf. v.^{35}).[2] The three sources we

---

[1] See Schürer, *Gesch. d. jüd. Volk.*, Bd. ii. p. 642.
[2] Cf. *Theol. of N.T.*, Stevens, p. 475.

have been considering—2 Macc., Wisdom of Solomon, and 4 Macc.
—are non-Palestinian in their origin, and they exhibit the gradual
infiltration into Hebrew thought, in the course of a period of
perhaps a century, of the Hellenic teaching of immortality.
In all three, the doctrine is embedded in a context of belief
in God's justice and purpose to reward or punish, and pre-
supposes Greek speculation on the nature of the soul itself.
In the Wisdom of Solomon the soul is pre-existent, and the
body its merely temporary tenement.

As binding link between the sources mentioned and the
eschatological ideas of the Old Testament, we may regard some
of the conceptions we meet with in the older portions of the
First Book of Enoch. Here, in 1 Enoch 91–104 (105–64 B.C.),
the righteous departed go to a place where they are guarded
by holy angels, and where, till God makes an end of wickedness
and sin, they may have to remain a long time as in " a long
sleep " (100[5]). Then " they shall arise from their sleep "
(91[10]; cf. 92[3]). But this resurrection is not corporal—" the
spirits of you who have died in righteousness shall live " (103[4]).
These spirits " shine as the lights of heaven," " joy as the
angels of heaven," and " become companions of the hosts of
heaven " (104[2f.]). It has to be observed that this portion of
1 Enoch is the earliest witness to a belief in the resurrection of
the spirit only. But in the main the earliest sections of the
Book of Enoch, 1 En. 91[f.] and the apparently older chapters
12–36 in their description of national and personal destiny,
present a development of thought that more perceptibly connects
with Old Testament conceptions. Thus, 1 Enoch 12–36 teaches a
final judgment; an eternal Messianic kingdom established for
the nation, but in which the individual righteous person after
resurrection lives for a long time; and a Sheol, or underworld,
of four departments, in which righteous and wicked dwell in
an intermediate state, but where already they have foretaste
of their final destiny of joy or torment (22[8f.]). By the author
of chaps. 91–104, for whom heaven is the ultimate abode of

righteous souls departed, a Messianic kingdom and a Sheol are given a place in the picture of final events, but the kingdom is of a temporary nature, and Sheol (99^{11}) assumes the character of hell. Both these latter traits emerge here for the first time in the literature of Judaism. We must now, therefore, examine the main lines of thought which in the Old Testament lead up to the stage of reflection upon survival after death which 1 Enoch 12–36, 91–104, represents.

2

The popular conception of the " day of Jahve," older than the reference to it in Amos ($5^{18.\ 20}$) in the eighth century, cannot be properly described as eschatological. The term indicates the hope of the intervention or epiphany of the thunder-and-lightning-god Jahve in the day of battle on behalf of His people. In the storm he will rout his people's foes (cf. Judg. $4^{14f.}$, $5^{4f.}$; Ex. 14^{24} ; Josh. $10^{10f.}$; 1 Sam. 7^{10}, etc.). The term has its Assyrian analogies and the idea its Greek and Roman parallels.[1] But the " day of Jahve " had a religious and political content that was capable of inner transformation and of attracting to itself other conceptions of a like nature and potentiality. Foremost amongst these was the idea of judgment. For Amos the " day of Jahve " is one that will reveal Jahve as a God who judges in accordance with ethical principles and who will punish Israel. The judgment of the people by Jahve is depicted by Isaiah as a process that will smelt and purify them ($1^{25f.}$) when, as in the glorious (Davidic—Duhm) past, righteous governors will be appointed and Jerusalem be called " a citadel of justice." On that day idolatry shall cease ($2^{18f.}$). Jahve will descend in the storm and lay low trees and towers and towns (2^{13}). It is a day of doom on all human pride, and the majesty of Jahve alone will be completely manifested. As for Hosea, so also for Isaiah this judgment of God will be a

---

[1] See Hölscher, *Gesch. d. isr. u. jud. Rel.*, p. 105.

prelude to better national conditions. A purified and faithful remnant (*Shear jashub*) will constitute the new state. To the temple at Jerusalem the nations will come for instruction in social and political morality (2^3). Jahve will decide their disputes, and perfect peace will reign ($2^{1f.}$). In passages which Stade and Marti held to be from the hand of another and a later author than Isaiah, but which now are generally accepted as genuine,[1] namely, 9^{2-6}, 11^{1-10}, Isaiah foreshadows for the future of his people, after the breaking of the power of their oppressor (Assyria), the establishment by Jahve of a Davidic kingdom which will be of permanent duration and of righteous character ($9^{5. 6}$). The occupant of the throne, the prophet affirms, will be " a shoot from the stump of Jesse " (11^1), a second David upon whom the spirit of Jahve will rest, endowing him with a superhuman[2] insight and judgment. In this kingdom unjust and cruel men will appear, but will be destroyed. So also humble and helpless persons will have citizenship in it (11^4), but will have justice. Peace will reign in the animal world (cf. Hos. 2^{20}), the beasts of the field being friends with one another and with man ($11^{6f.}$). Like his predecessors Hosea and Isaiah, Jeremiah, who had sternly proclaimed the approaching destruction of the Jewish state and cultus, looked forward to a future earthly kingdom of Jahve. The pre-exilic prophets thus hand down to their successors in the post-exilic age, as heritage of political and religious thought, the ideas of a manifestation of Jahve in majesty in the coming days, a judgment upon Israel and the nations, a faithful elect remnant in Israel as nucleus of the new state, a future kingdom which will rely for its permanence upon conformity with Jahve's will.[3] Exalted as the description of the Messianic kingdom in the eleventh chapter of Isaiah is, it is purely of a national and terrestrial character.

---

[1] Cf. Duhm, *Comm.*, and Sellin, *Intro.*, p. 132.
[2] So Duhm, *ad loc.*
[3] Cf. Jeremiah *re* Jahve's covenant—new covenant.

The political and religious hopes of the period of the Exile brought a new creative influence in the development of Jewish thought upon the nation's future. There is now an approach to what can be more correctly described as eschatology or reflection upon the "last things." The kingdom of Jahve still continues to be conceived of as near at hand, as terrestrial, and in terms of Israel's hegemony. In contrast with the pre-exilic period which marked no particular or definite personage as Davidic king, the kingless post-exilic age could look to Cyrus as Messiah-deliverer or to Zerubbabel as Davidic ruler of the new era. But, on the other hand, the perspective or world-view becomes appreciably wider. The strengthening of the notion of monotheism through Israel's contact with the nations and of Jahve as universal ruler, which came to clearer expression in the prophetic utterances of Deutero-Isaiah, also has effect upon the eschatological picture. The sole world-Governor must bring the nations of the world to the recognition of His power and completely destroy all His foes.

The Messianic kingdom, as described by Ezekiel, presents us with a broadening out of the eschatological scheme. In spite of the fact that he regards this kingdom as at hand, he stamps the phrases "in the end of the days," "in the end of the years" (*b^eharith hajamim . . . hashanim*) as signifying the Messianic End-Time.[1] He describes this kingdom as preceded by a judgment on Israel and its foes. Then after it has been established it is attacked by Gog at the head of the hordes of the North and South who are destroyed and brought to nought by a second judgment. Ezekiel thus prepares the way for the later viewpoint of the Apocalypse of Baruch and 4 Ezra, according to which the Messianic blessedness is not the highest, and judgment which decides the final destiny of men takes place at the *end* of the Messianic age. This new feature in Ezekiel of a renewed attack upon the kingdom and of a *second* judgment is regarded by Stade as due to the author's perception of how

---

[1] See Stade, *Biblische Theol. d. A.T. on Ezekiel*, p. 295,

much must be accomplished in the world before Jahve's power
and holiness is made universally manifest.

The Book of Daniel (166–164 B.C.) provides us with the last
great schematic formulation of the Messianic idea in the Old
Testament. Throughout the centuries after Ezekiel this idea
had retained now a greater, now a lesser, degree of strength.
As in the Exile, so now the conditions of national emergency
awaked it to vigour. The persecution that befell the Jews
under Antiochus IV. Epiphanes called it to life, and the author
of the Book of Daniel to his task of inspiring his people with
encouragement and hope. In this work the national outlook
on Israel's future is retained, but adequately blended with the
universal. " The people of the saints of the Most High "—
that is, Israel—who in Daniel's imagery are represented by the
" one like unto a son of man," and thus contrasted in their
true humanity with the four cruel and bestial world-tyrannies,
are the governors in the everlasting kingdom of Jahve, but
they have as their willing subjects " all peoples, nations, and
tongues." But more important still is the introduction of
a transcendental element. The final judgment upon the four
world powers is thought of as given from heaven. Here appears
the Ancient of Days to sit in judgment. Here thrones are set.
In the clouds of heaven the " one like a son of man " is seen
coming to present himself before God ($7^{9f.}$). This transcendental setting of the judgment as also the suggestion of
its forensic character paves the way for those later apocalyptic
reflections upon human destiny where heaven is the provisional
or final repository of souls (cf. 1 Enoch 91–104 above), and
which thus make room for the Hellenic doctrine of immortality
immediately after death. But of far greater importance than
these features is that in Daniel there emerges for the first time
as a result of Hebrew eschatological thought the expression
of a belief in a resurrection of individual persons. From
aspirations of a national character there arises the belief that
in the case of *some* there will be a survival after death in the

mode of a return to physical life to share in the earthly everlasting kingdom of Jahve and His people :

" And many who sleep in the dust of earth   shall awake
Some to eternal life   others to eternal reproach . . .   (12²)
And the wise will shine with splendour   as the splendour of the
                                                                        firmament
And those who led many to righteousness   as the stars for
                                               ever and always." (12³)

Here in 12² the doctrine of a resurrection appears with hesitancy.
It is not of general application.   It embraces only the élite
(" many "), by whom is probably meant the leaders in the
religious resistance to Antiochus, and the most notorious of
those who, to their eternal reproach, supported the Seleucid
government.

The Book of Daniel, which exhibits marked dependency
upon Persian (Zoroastrian) conceptions in its reference to the
four world-periods, in its angelology, in its picture of the
destructive fire proceeding from before the throne of God, and
most probably in its description of Jahve as the Ancient of
Days (Ahuramazda or Zarvan [1]) may well be credited with
dependence for its doctrine of resurrection upon the same
source where this doctrine is characteristic.   Söderblom,[2]
who admits that Persian influence upon the teaching of a
resurrection in the Book of Daniel is not improbable, contends
that this influence is nevertheless not a borrowing pure and
simple, but a ripening of germs of thought already present.[3]
He, as does also Couard,[4] points to the hesitancy with which
the doctrine takes lodgment in Judaism.   In Mazdeism the
resurrection is of all the dead, while in Dan. 12² it is confined
to " some " (" many ").   But neither this hesitancy on the
part of Judaism to adopt the whole doctrine at first, nor the

[1] See below, p. 143.
[2] *La vie future d'après le mazdéisme*, p. 316.   Cf. Rankin, *Festival of
Hanukkah*, p. 175 f.
[3] See also Schürer, Bd. ii. p. 587.
[4] *Op. cit.* p. 63 above.

fact that the teaching of this particular mode of survival after death springs naturally, rationally, and cogently from Israel's Messianic hopes, militates in the least against the supposition of Mazdean influence. A borrower usually borrows just as much as he needs. That the borrowings by Judaism became in time more extensive is shown by Bousset (*Rel. d. Jud.*, p. 511), who points to the fact that Judaism develops the same inconsistencies in the eschatological scheme as are present in Iranian thought upon the same subject. The literature of the post-exilic period, particularly in regard to the intervention of Jahve in the End-Time, displays a marked receptivity for mythological [1] and religious elements of Chaldean-Iranian origin.

In the small book on the Last Things (Isa. 24–27), we have possibly evidence of an infiltration into Judaism, prior to Daniel, of the doctrine of a personal resurrection. Edward Meyer prefers, with Smend,[2] to assign this apocalypse to the time of the defeat of Persia by Alexander, and regards the time of the Maccabean uprising or the late Maccabean period (100 B.C.) to which Duhm assigns it, as altogether excluded by both the tone and the contents of the book. The date of the apocalypse, except that it is post-exilic, is uncertain, and the interpretation of the passage in question (chap. 26^{12-19}) is difficult. It may be translated thus :

Oh Jahve establish (*i.e.* by judgment) our peace,
For all that we have been able to do has been done for us by Thee.   (12)
Jahve, our God, lords other than Thee have been our masters ;
But only Thy name would we praise.   (13)
The dead do not live (again), the shades (in the underworld) do not rise again,
For the reason that Thou hast visited them with destruction
And caused their memory to perish.   (14)

---

[1] Cf. Hölscher, *Gesch. der isr. und jüd. Rel.*, p. 153, and Walter Baumgartner, *Das Buch Daniel*, 1926 : Giessen.

[2] E. Meyer, *Ursprung und Anfänge des Christentums*, Bd. ii. p. 177 f.   Cf. Smend, *Z.A.W.* iv., 1884, p. 205 f.

Increased hast Thou the nation, Jahve, increased the nation and got
  Thee honour ;
Thou hast extended all the borders of the land. (15)
They (*i.e.* the nation) sought Thee in distress
Thy chastenings were to them a powerful charm [so Duhm, text uncer-
  tain] (16)
As a woman in labour, about to bring forth, cries out in the throes of her
  pains
So were we before Thee, Jahve. (17)
We have been in the throes of labour (but it was) as if we brought forth
  wind :
We have not brought the land deliverance,
And world-inhabitants have not been born. (18)
(So) May [1] Thy dead live again, my corpses rise again.
Awake and shout, ye that dwell in the dust,
For the dew of (the heavenly) lights is Thy dew
And the land of shades [2] brings to birth. (19)

It is to be noted that the content of this passage goes in its
conception much beyond Ezekiel's (chap. 37) vision of the valley
of dry bones and of the dead rising again clothed with flesh,
for Ezekiel's vision is merely a picture of the nation's recovery.
Here, if we interpret rightly, Isa. 26[12f.] presents a picture
of the future that is hoped will become reality. The thought
is that, though the nation has been increased by natural means,
nothing has resulted for the nation's welfare and power. This
can be achieved only by supernatural means, namely, by Jahve
causing the dead to rise again by His reviving, through the
heavenly dew from the regions of light, the inhabitants of the
underworld, the *Rephaim*.[3] Even if this be merely a fantastic
hope or prayer, we cannot assert, as Meyer does, that it concerns
merely the nation as a whole and not the individual, since
it is impossible to conceive of the nation being increased in
this supernatural manner without there being a resurrection

---

[1] Best translated as a wish (Jussive) by Meyer and Hölscher. *My corpses*
is perhaps a gloss. See Duhm *ad loc.*
[2] Duhm, " The land brings forth shades " (Rephaim), but better sense is
given if we read with LXX *construct state* of word for *land*.
[3] *i.e.* the shades.

of individual persons. But what the passage does not entitle us to do is to interpret " Thy dead " (v.[19]) with Duhm,[1] as a reference to the pious, or particularly to the martyrs in the cause of Jahve, or to speak, as Sellin [2] does, of " a resurrection of the just." Here no thought is disclosed of the resurrection as reward or punishment as is presented in Daniel.

Ezekiel c. 37 and Isaiah c. 26[12f.], whether the latter be prior to Daniel or not, show how slowly and gently the idea of a resurrection percolated into the thought of Judaism. Jesus Sirach [3] hopes for a Messianic age of an unlimited duration for his people (36[16f.]), but therewith goes no hope of resurrection. He expounds the old Hebrew conception of Sheol, and of man's requital in the reputation that he leaves behind and in his descendants (44[8f.]). But in a period of little more than a century, from the composition of the Book of Daniel to the writing of the Wisdom of Solomon, both the doctrine of a resurrection and that teaching which was characteristic of Hellenist Judaism, namely, of a blessed immortal existence in heaven immediately after death for the souls of the righteous, have established themselves in Jewish speculation. In the Wisdom of Solomon the two doctrines stand side by side unreconciled. The belief in a restoration of some to life on earth had, in Judaism, its logical and ethical basis in the nation's Messianic hope. It vindicated the character of God, who would not exclude from the future kingdom of bliss and righteousness the righteous themselves who had departed before its coming, or those who had lost their lives in His cause. The Hellenist view had the same ethical basis, but had no real logical connection with the hope of an earthly Messianic kingdom. Both Judaism and Christianity recognized, as the author of the Wisdom of Solomon did not, and as the writer of 4 Maccabees does not appear to have considered, that the belief of Hellenized Judaism was inimical to their great Messianic expectation. On the Jewish side, Pharisaism, which held strongly to the faith in

---

[1] " Isaiah," *ad loc.*   [2] *Intro. to O.T. on Isaiah 24–27.*   [3] *Circa* 180 B.C.

a resurrection continued to teach (Josephus, *Ant.* xviii. 1, 3)
that souls at death went to the underworld, though there the
good were distinguished from the evil by their lot. Justin Martyr
(*Dial. with Trypho*, c. 80) denies the name of Christian to those
who say there is no resurrection and that the soul at death
at once is received into heaven. Also Irenæus (v. 31, 1–2)
condemns as heretical the view that " the inner man " on
dissolution of the body ascends to the heavenly regions.
Christianity had to defend itself against the gnosticism of the
first and second centuries which, influenced by Oriental religion
and Greek philosophy, denied the resurrection of the body.[1]
But the history of dogma in the Church (Greek) in the East
shows a depreciation of the old Christian biblical eschatology
even in respect of what was most valuable in it, the idea of
final judgment.[2] This development in the realm of dogma
was due to the disparate elements of Hellenic and Jewish
thought. Both Christianity (St. Paul,[3] Origen) and Judaism
did, however, make such accommodation as was possible for
these elements. Alongside the view that Jesus died, descended
to the underworld and rose from the grave, there was current
the view expressed in the narrative of St. Luke 23[43] of the
promise to the penitent thief that he would that day be with
Jesus in Paradise. That by the latter name a place in heaven
is meant seems most probable. The Hebrew equivalent of this
heavenly paradise of souls was " Gan Eden," the garden of Eden,
a term whose first literary witness in this sense is Rabban

---

[1] Harnack, *Dogmengeschichte*, p. 65 f.   [2] *Ibid.* p. 169.

[3] Cf. Bousset in *S.A.T.* on 2 Cor. 4[13]–5[10], p. 186. Paul states his belief in a
provisional and in a final judgment. The former takes place immediately at
death. The righteous person then has his home with the Lord, but in a discarnate condition. (This hope is not expressed either in 1 Thess. 4[13f.] nor in
1 Cor. 15 but for the first time in 2 Cor. 4[13f.].) Then follows the decision of the
general judgment in its different stages (1 Cor. 15[23f.]) when the righteous receive their new heavenly body which is already laid up for them in heaven—
the dead are then clothed with this, those not dead at the parousia are " clothed
upon " with the heavenly body. " Paul's view had not any appreciable
influence at first upon the Church at large," *ibid.* p. 187.

Jochanan ben Zakkai, who lived before the year A.D. 80, and
which becomes a current expression in rabbinic literature.[1] The
souls of the righteous immediately at death go to this heavenly
place. Also when the judgment, which in the older eschatological
scheme inaugurated the Messianic age, comes, as in the Apocalypse of Baruch and 4 Ezra, to be a final judgment placed at the
end of that age, the Messianic kingdom loses in importance
in contrast with the kingdom of heaven and the heavenly
bliss of the pious. Thus Palestinian Judaism made room for
the transcendental form of Hellenist belief in a continued
existence of the soul.

3

Having described the rise in Israel of the two forms of
belief in a future existence, we can now return to scan more
narrowly that period which lies between the date 164 B.C.,
when in Daniel 12[2] the doctrine of an individual resurrection
appears, and the date, *circa* 30 B.C., when in the Wisdom of
Solomon the Hellenist teaching has come to clear expression.
Between these two formulations of belief we saw that, particularly in 1 Enoch (chs. 91–104), *c.* 105–64 B.C., there were
developments of thought that might be considered as binding
links. To these may be added the view found in the Book of
Jubilees (before 105 B.C.) that in the Messianic age men live nigh
to a thousand years, beget children, to whom is allotted the same
generous span, and that on death " their bones shall rest in
the earth and their spirits shall have much joy and they shall
know that it is the Lord who . . . shows mercy . . . to all
that love Him " (23[31]). The author knows of no resurrection
of the body, or rather, as Dr. Charles (*Apoc.* ii. p. 9) remarks,
has abandoned all hope of this. The passage evidently means
that the spirits of the righteous rise to heaven to enjoy a blessed
immortality after death. But Dr. Charles's statement that " this

---

[1] Billerbeck and Strack, p. 265 in *Commentary on N.T.* from Talmud and
Midrash, vol. ii.

is the earliest attested instance of this expectation in the last two centuries B.C." is subject to qualification, and that in regard to the Old Testament itself.

In the Book of Daniel 12³, after mention of a bodily restoration of some to life and of some to shame, it is said of " the wise " (the *maskilim*) that " they will shine resplendent as the splendour of the firmament, and those that led many to righteousness as the stars for ever." These persons are apparently distinguished from those that rise again to *earthly* life by their being received into the *heavenly spheres*. They, the " pious loyalists," as Dr. Moffatt calls them, died in the religious persecution under Antiochus, the renowned martyrs of that time. They are more particularly described as having " led many to righteousness," pre-eminent teachers of the multitude (cf. 11³³ᶠ·) and examples of righteousness. Max Haller [1] therefore suggests that the author of Daniel, in describing their destiny, is thinking of such pattern figures of Hebrew legend as Enoch and Elijah who were taken to heaven. But the stories of Enoch and Elijah belong to the well-known class of primitive translation-myths. These heroes are translated *bodily* to heaven. But here, in Dan. 12³, as " the wise " have died, having succumbed to fire and sword (11³³ᶠ·), we can only think of their *spirits* as having ascended to the regions of light. In the meantime, until the time of the End and the setting up of the Messianic kingdom, we must assume that they have rested (cf. 12³³), like those others who are called again to life on earth, in the underworld or Sheol. We are therefore not presented with the doctrine, as in Jubilees 23³¹, that the souls of the righteous *who have passed through the Messianic age* ascend to heaven *immediately* after death. But common to both books, different as the Messianic conceptions of each are, is the doctrine of the ascent of the spirits of some *to heaven*. And significant as is the appearance, in Jewish literature of this date, of this thought of the ascent of the soul to heaven, proportionally important is the question whether we

---

[1] " Commentary on Daniel " in *S.A.T.*, p. 261

have here already in the earlier work, the Book of Daniel, trace
of Greek influence on Hebrew religion, or whether, as Gressmann
supposes,[1] contact has been effected with the beliefs of astral
religion which were current in the Hellenistic age. This question
also takes within its scope the still earlier reference in the Book
of Qoheleth (Ecclesiastes, 250–200 B.C.) [2] from which may be
inferred that the belief that the soul's ascent to heaven at death
had made sufficient advance in Judaism to make it worth while
to combat that belief. It is this form of belief in immortality
which Qoheleth, in rejecting all hope of a future life, rebuts. The
text, which the Massoretes ingeniously altered (cf. A.V.) but
which the Septuagint and other codices preserve, asks (3[21]) :
"Who knows if the spirit of man ascends upwards (h^a *olah*
l^ema*lah* ; Greek, *anabainei eis anō*) and the spirit of a beast
descends downwards to the earth ? " Here, then, we have the
first occurrence within Judaism of the idea of the ascent of the
soul to heaven, apparently immediately after death, without
intermediate resting in Sheol. Hertzberg, in his commentary
on Ecclesiastes,[3] states that, in the case of "the wise," the Book
of Daniel (12[3]) also announces this teaching of an *immediate*
passing to heaven, and drops the idea of an underworld. This
conclusion we have shown is not permissible. In Daniel, the
doctrine of an ascent of souls to heaven, limited in its application
to a certain class, is combined with and restricted by the writer's
Messianic conceptions and the traditional Jewish notion of
Sheol. As in his teaching of a resurrection, so here the author
has borrowed with restraint from the current ideas of non-
Jewish origin that were prevalent in the world of his time. On

---

[1] *Die hellenistische Gestirnreligion*, " Alten Orient," 5, 1925, p. 30. "With
astral religion was connected . . . an eschatology which vouchsafed the
believer a life in the world beyond as star amid the star-divinities. The oldest
witness to this belief is the Jewish *Apocalypse of Daniel*."

[2] E. Meyer, *Ursprung und Anfänge des Christentums*, Bd. ii., dates Ecclesiastes as from middle of third century B.C. Hertzberg (cf. note below), 200 B.C.

[3] Der Prediger (Qoheleth), 1932, in *Kommentar zum Alten Testament*,
herausgegeben von Dr. Sellin, see p. 95.

the other hand, Qoheleth, who spurns and criticizes his people's faith and hopes, can afford to state the popular notion of an individual future existence in its fullest form, in the form best suited for him to expose its futility.

When now we ask : Whence did this teaching of an ascent of the soul to heaven which we find in Judaism of this period come ? there are two directions to which we may look, either to Greece or to the Orient. Hertzberg, although he holds that the author of the Book of Ecclesiastes was a Palestinian Jew, and not, as has often been surmised, an Alexandrian, a Jew of the diaspora, as was the writer of the Wisdom of Solomon, where for the first time and so much later the Greek doctrine of immortality makes its appearance, thinks that already in Eccles. 3[21] there is evidence of Greek influence. Hertzberg, indeed, breaks with the views of the critical school which saw in Ecclesiastes a large deposit of Greek thought [1] and sets aside the view of Bertholet [2] that Qoheleth seeks to counter Greek philosophy, and of Margoliouth [3] that he seeks to introduce Greek philosophy, but he holds that Qoheleth was an open-minded man who imbibed the spirit of his age, and that age, Hertzberg affirms, was steeped in Greek philosophy. [4] For the rest, he would admit that the writer of Ecclesiastes was acquainted, though not at first hand, with the maxims of Theognis, and in a general way with Babylonian and Egyptian literature and ideas. Hertzberg's careful analysis of Ecclesiastes may exactly describe the character of that work, but the question remains whether in the tenet represented by chap. 3[21] we have to regard as origin of the idea therein contained the particular element of Hellenic as against Oriental thought. The Hellenistic age in Palestine reflected in the realm of religion a religious syncretism. The phrase, Hellenistic age, is apt to give a preponderance in the mind

[1] Cf. Siegfried, *e.g. Stoic and Epicurean Thought*; Pfleiderer, *Heraclitus' philosophy*.

[2] Berthotel, *Kulturgesch. Israels*, p. 223.

[3] *Exp.* 1911, p. 463.

[4] Page 59, " *von der griechischen Philosophie durchtränkt.*"

to the concept Hellenic or Greek. But, as Bousset points out, "the religion of the Hellenistic age was in short (*schlechthin*) the Chaldean astral religion permeated with Iranian elements."[1] A true perspective is not won by thinking merely of Greek influence on the East. What is remarkable is the reverse process. From the days of Alexander the Great, whose campaigns disestablished the priestly colleges of the Euphrates, the influence of the Babylonian stellar religion grew apace in the Greek world, the soil of which had been prepared by the philosophies of Plato and Aristotle, who assigned high honour to the heavenly bodies."[2]

Two leading tenets of this astral religion were that the Sun (the "Highest God," Theos Hypsistos) and, under Him, moon and stars exercised influence on earth and on man, determining the destiny of man and of everything ; and that the soul of man, partaking of the fiery nature of the stars, had come from the heights of heaven and thither amid the stars ascended after death. Another doctrine concerned the period of the world's course and the divisions of time, the year, day, and hour as determined by the stars and as applying to all existing things.[3] This is the plane of conceptions upon which Qoheleth's thought moves, his observing of all things done "under the sun," his teaching that all things have their time and that man's fate is determined. The doctrine that man's soul ascends to heaven at death is a dogma of astral religion that he rejects in the interest of his own Jewish dogma which denied a future personal existence. The influence of astral religion was, on the whole, uplifting. It gave in an age of inquiry and cosmopolitan outlook a scientific basis to the belief in providence and world-order, and promoted an exalted hope and faith in man's future in a world beyond.[4] Qoheleth accepted its fatalism, discarding its

[1] *Religion des Judentums*, p. 522 f.
[2] Angus, *The Religious Quests of the Græco-Roman Empire*, p. 257.
[3] Cf. Hölscher, *Gesch. der isr. und jüd. Rel.*, p. 165.
[4] Cf. Gressmann, *Die hellenistische Gestirnreligion*, p. 31.

hope, and this is the primary source of his scepticism apart
from any possible contact with the spirit of Greek melancholy
or acquaintance with the spirit of world-tiredness in the Babylonian and Egyptian Wisdom literature.   The author's " *carpe
diem* " outlook has its root in this scepticism and its parallel in
the maxims of the Babylonian [1] and Egyptian " wise." [2]

More discriminating than Hertzberg's notion of the Hellenistic age in the East as steeped in Greek philosophy is the view
that while Greek culture had effect upon art and architecture,
upon trade and military affairs, and was responsible for the building of theatres, baths, and gymnasiums, leaving its mark in
democratic institutions and, in a certain degree, upon religious
rites and practices,[3] its influence did not, till the Roman period,
penetrate beyond the surface of Oriental life.   To quote Dr.
Hölscher—" any deeper spiritual influence on the part of Greece
in the third and second centuries B.C. upon the educated upper
class in the Oriental cities, let alone upon the mass of the people,
can hardly be considered." [4]   In respect, then, of the idea of the
ascent of the soul to heaven, even if, as against Anz, Bousset,
Reitzenstein, and Cumont, who derive the doctrine from Chaldean
and/or Iranian belief,[5] we were to adopt the view of Dieterich

---

[1] Cf. Meissner, *Babylonien und Assyrien*, Bd. ii. p. 143 ; p. 431.

[2] Cf. Paul Humbert, *Recherches sur les sources Égyptiennes de la littérature
sapentiale d'Israel*, p. 110 f.

[3] Cf. my *Festival of Hanukkah re* festival commonly called " The feast of
the Dedication," and cf. the witness of Hekataeos of Abdera (*c.* 290 B.C.) *re*
change of Jewish customs under Persian and Macedonian sovereignties.

[4] Hölscher, p. 161.

[5] Anz, *Zur Frage nach dem Ursprung des Gnostizismus*, Leipzig, 1897.
Bousset, *Relig. des Jud.* and in *Himmelreise der Seele* (*Arch. f. Religions-
wiss.*, iv. pp. 136 f., 229 f. Reitzenstein, *Das iranische Erlösungsmysterium*.
Cumont, *After-life in Roman Paganism.* Dieterich, *Liturgy of Mithras.*
J. Kroll, *Lehren d. Hermes Trismegistos.*

The theology of ancient Babylonia had no teaching of an ascent of the
soul to heaven. Its underworld was, like Sheol, " a land of no return." But
its deities were, or became through priestly systematizing, astral divinities.
The seven towers leading to the upper tower of the Temple of Babel represented the seven planets, the seven Planet-gods. Wilhelm Anz in his book
(1897) tracing the doctrine of the ascent of the soul in Gnosticism (and Manda-

and Kroll that the idea is essentially Greek, we would not be entitled to suppose, so far as Judaism of the age of Qoheleth and Daniel is concerned, that Hellenic influence was primarily operative. This is made clear when we consider the history of the sect of the Pythagoreans. This sect having removed Elysium from the underworld to the moon, identifying the Blessed Islands with the sun and the moon, were, according to Cumont,[1] the first to promulgate the doctrine of celestial immortality in Greece and Southern Italy. Now, in the syncretic religious world of Alexandria, in the time of the Ptolemies, Pythagoreanism undergoes a revival. But already, we are informed, their doctrine of immortality had been brought " into alignment with astrology " under the influence of Babylonia and Egypt.[2] Thus even if Qoheleth be regarded as an Alexandrian Jew who had become acquainted with the teaching of this sect, or with this teaching as held by other Greeks who had acquired it from this sect, we should still be unable to infer that the chief source of the idea in chap. 3[21] was not Oriental astral religion.[3]

The passage in the Book of Daniel (12[3]) concerning " the wise " who " will shine resplendent as the splendour of the firmament and those that led many to righteousness as the stars

ism) to its origin, shows this doctrine is the result of the mingling of Persian belief in the ascent of the souls of the righteous (over the Mount Hara) to Paradise, and the final blessedness of souls, with the astral conceptions of Chaldea, see pp. 61, 83–88. Anz's special concern with the seven planets (through which, in Gnosticism, souls ascend to the upper regions), and his argument concerning these—the planets were regarded by Parsism as creations of the evil spirit—do not detract from the main conclusion regarding the source of the main doctrine of the ascent of the soul. In the belief that Ahuramazda created the fixed stars and the zodiacal signs Parsism itself had an astral element. Cf. Gressmann, *Die hellenistische Gestirnreligion*, p. 9.

[1] *After-life*, pp. 97, 194.

[2] Angus, p. 299.

[3] Gressmann (*die hellen. Gestirnrel.*, p. 7) speaks of a probable reaction of Greek thought (Pythagoras and Plato) as influenced by Oriental thought upon Babylonia even in the pre-Hellenistic age. The point therefore at issue is whether in respect of the idea of the ascent of the soul, the probability of this being derived from Greek thought fructifying Chaldean religion is greater than the latter being fructified by contact with Iran.

for ever and aye," strengthens our conclusions regarding the direction from which the doctrine of the ascent of the soul came to Judaism. The religion of Iran (Zoroastrianism) had quickened and assimilated the old Babylonian astrological conceptions. Already before the days of Eudemos, a pupil of Aristotle, who reports on the subject, it had overcome its dualistic theology that taught of an eternal struggle between the god of goodness and light, Ahuramazda, and the god of evil and darkness, Ahriman, by postulating a neutral principle to which these divinities were subordinate and which was called *Zarvan akarana* or " Endless Time." This development due to the urge of reason itself to rest is a Monism, must also be regarded as the result of contact with astral religion and its idea of world-order. Zarvan was regarded as a divinity of Eternity (or Time) and of Light and equated with the Chaldean Bel or Lord of the Heavens as also with Kronos-Helios, the God Saturn—and the Sun—an equation which according to Reitzenstein was common to the whole Semitic area in the Hellenistic age.[1] But though Iranian dualism was modified by this process of assimilation of astral religion, its ethical power remained and was carried both into Judaism and into Christianity. Between the two powers of good and evil, darkness and light that waged eternal wars, stood man, and man was forced to the campaign to take his part. The reign of Ahriman, or darkness, would have an end and a new æon or age would begin. Participation in the light was the main element in Iranian soteriology.[2] Light was the divine essence, the nature of the inner man, whose soul was a particle of the light ($\mu o \hat{\iota} \rho \alpha \ \tau o \hat{\upsilon} \ \varphi \omega \tau \acute{o} \varsigma$) or, simply, light itself ($\varphi \tilde{\omega} \varsigma$).[3] Light was the portion of the blessed. Along with the dualistic form of thought which made an impression on Judaism, and which appears as early as 200 B.C. in the Book of the Testaments of

---

[1] Reitzenstein, *Das iran. Erlösungsmysterium*, p. 177, note 3, and p. 188. Also cf. Cumont's article " Kronos " in *Pauly-Wissowa-Kroll's Encyclo.*

[2] Cf. Angus, *Religious Quests*, etc., p. 297.

[3] Reitzenstein, *Ir. Erlösungsmyst.*, p. 135 f.

the XII Patriarchs,[1] with its contrasts, God and Beliar, Spirit
of truth and Spirit of untruth, darkness and light, there enters
also concepts of light which are no mere metaphor or symbol.
We may compare with the language of Daniel regarding the
destiny of " the wise," the expressions with which First Enoch
describes the future blessedness of the righteous—" but now ye
shall shine as the lights of heaven " (104[2]) ; " and all the righteous
and elect before Him shall be strong (shine) as fiery lights "
(39[7]) ; " and they shall see those that were born in darkness
led into darkness, while the righteous shall be resplendent "
(118[14], cf. 1[8], 38[2.4], 50[1], 58[3-6], 92[4]). The similarity of the language
here employed with that used in Dan. 12[3] is striking—indeed it
is the same language and refers to the same class " the elect."
As in Jewish apocalyptic the term " life " departs from the
Old Testament idea of the *summum bonum*, and signifies a
blessed immortal existence in heaven,[2] so the expression " light "
undergoes a like change. Reitzenstein speaks of this theology
of light (*Lichttheologie*) which we see in its beginnings in Daniel
and Enoch (cf. Isa. 26[19]), and from which, later, Gnosticism drew,
as having in its more stereotyped form, penetrated Judaism
first from Iran.[3]

That the conception of an ascent of the souls of " the wise "
to heaven is not of Hellenic origin is supported by the fact that
the other predominant elements in the religious thought of the
writer of Daniel are, so far as they are not Jewish, of Chaldean-
Iranian derivation. Besides those features of Persian teaching
which we have already mentioned (the resurrection of the body,
the angelology, the destructive fire in the Judgment), besides
the Chaldean-Persian idea of world-periods, there is the astral
geography which the book employs. The symbolism behind
the picture of the two-horned ram (8[20f.]) which represents the

---

[1] See Eduard Meyer, *Ursprung und Anfänge des Christentums*, Bd. ii., *re*
date, p. 44 ; *re* dualism in Judaism and Christianity, p. 80 f.

[2] Cf. Gunkel in Kautzsch, *Apokryphen* , iv. Ezra, p. 129.

[3] Reitzenstein, *Die hellenistischen Mysterienreligionen*, p. 292.

kingdoms of Media and Persia, and the he-goat which represents the kingdom of Greece, that is the kingdom of Alexander and of the Seleucids (Syria), has been traced by Burkitt[1] to the astral view of the world that was current in the Persian period. At this time the chief lands of the world, from the frontiers of India to Italy, were brought into connection with the twelve signs of the zodiac. In this world-map the Ram was Persia ; Capricorn (Daniel's he-goat) was Syria.

The whole surrounding field of ideas in the Book of Daniel is unfavourable to the view that the doctrine of the soul's ascent to heaven is of Greek origin. Thus, during that period extending from the time of Qoheleth (*circa* 250) to the appearance of the Wisdom books, Wisdom of Solomon and 4 Maccabees, we have, in the development within Israel of belief in resurrection and immortality, to take into account three sources of influence : Persian religion, Chaldean-Iranian astral religion, and, later, Hellenic thought.

The Canaanite Adonis-myth, that is, the nature-myth of the dying and rising god (see below, p. 180 f.), was known to Israel in early pre-exilic times. Baudissin and Sellin believe that the Jewish doctrine of resurrection derives from this.[2] But while the god Adonis, like Osiris in Egypt, was conceived of as dying and then appearing on earth again in the new vegetation of spring, the after-life of the Adonis-worshipper does not appear to have been represented as involving a reappearance on earth. Not only in Egyptian Osiris-worship and presumably in Phœnician Adonis-worship,[3] but also in Iranian belief the true worshipper entered at death a region of bliss, receiving (Jasna 51[7, 17]) a perfect body. But this is quite another thing from the Jewish and Iranian teaching of a final resurrection and final judgment. In Iranian religion and in Judaism we have the same phenomenon of opposition to the nature-divinities[4] and the same idea of a revivification of the physical body to life on earth. The eschatological picture and other elements in the Book of Daniel where the doctrine appears point to Iran. The absence of all sacramentalism in Judaism points away from the nature-religions as having influenced Judaism in its teaching of a future life.

[1] Cumont, *La Plus Ancienne Géographie Astrologique*, Klio. ix., 1909, 273.

[2] W. Baudissin, *Adonis und Esmun*, 1911 ; Sellin, *Auferstehung und ewiges Leben*, p. 232 f., *Neue Kirchl. Zeitschrift*, Heft 5, 1919.

[3] Cf. p. 188 f. below.   [4] Cf. Meyer, *op. cit.* p. 60

CHAPTER VI

THE BELIEF IN A FUTURE LIFE—THE QUESTION OF ITS APPEARANCE IN JOB AND THE "JOB-PSALMS" (Ps. 73 and 49)

1

HAVING traced the development of the ideas of resurrection, the ascent of the soul to heaven and of immortality immediately after death, we now can inquire whether there emerged in the Old Testament, apart from the eschatological conceptions of a judgment and Messianic age which fostered these ideas, the belief that the communion with God which the righteous experienced here on earth would continue beyond the grave. This inquiry is not here concerned with the traces of an early primitive belief in a totem-ancestor who was regarded as living still, somewhere, or with the worship of ancestors who were believed to exist somewhere and were propitiated with sacrifices, or with the evidence afforded by the practice of the art of necromancy. This very early stage of belief will be touched upon later so far as it serves our purpose. The stage of thought with which we are concerned is that at which the belief in an underworld or Sheol is prevalent, the departed being regarded as having no real existence, but as mere shades or shadows in a land of gloom and forgetfulness where man can no longer praise God. The question before us is : whether before the Messianic hope acquires those transcendent features which we perceive it has in the Book of Daniel, Hebrew reflection upon God's nature, His justice and His regard for the righteous had broken with the Sheol-conception and attained a theological belief, however vague, in the soul's endurance in an after-life ? The conditions for the forming of such a belief were certainly present. There was the impression made upon Israel's national life by personalities such as that of Jeremiah. Wellhausen[1] remarks that in him we have not merely a picture of the prophet as mediator between God and the nation, but one of an intimate religious private relationship with God. Here the outpourings of the soul to God are not merely the utterances of exalted moments. The height to which consciousness of communion with God could attain, apparently not at all embarrassed by the restriction of life's interest to the present life, is signally demonstrated by what we must simply describe as this teacher's *conversations with God*. It has been suggested[2] that this inner experience of a personal relationship with the Divine, as exemplified by Jeremiah, prepared the way for the writers of such psalms as Ps. 39 and 73 in which some have discerned the note of the hope of immortality. But this view tends, unjustly, to regard the expression of piety as we have it in Jeremiah as something unique, whereas it must have been more general. It is sufficient for us to note that the literary expression of the religious and personal experience of communion with God, joined with the deepening conception of the unconditional righteousness of God, was capable of becoming the basis and starting-point for a doctrine of immortality. Further, as an effective force working in the same direction, must have been the ever increasing urge of personal faith to seek clarity upon the subject of reward and retribution as God's response to man's conduct. The orthodox Deuteronomist standpoint might hold the field, as in fact it did for the mass of the people, and find utterance in the full conviction of Ps. 37, but orthodoxy provokes criticism. The problem of suffering, the oppression of the faithful, the prosperity of " the scoffers," the lawless—this awaited the solution which was ultimately found for it, namely, the belief in a future life. We are thus led to the examination of those

[1] *Isr. u. jüd. Gesch.*, p. 143.
[2] Cf. Torge, *Seelenglaube und Unsterblichkeitshoffnung im A.T.*, 1909, p. 219 f.

passages for which the strongest claim has been made that such
an attitude of belief has been attained. This refers especially
to three passages, all in the Wisdom literature, Job 19[25-27] ;
Ps. 73[23-26], and Ps. 49[16] which Gunkel calls the " Job-Psalms."
Almost every phrase of Job 19[25f.] presents difficulties of
interpretation, and the verse which is most decisive for our
understanding of the thought (v.[26]) suggests textual corruption.
We therefore give a translation by a modern scholar who accepts
the text practically without emendation and defends most
adequately the conservative viewpoint that here is uttered the
hope of a survival beyond the grave. Eduard König[1] renders
the verses thus :

And I for my part know : my Redeemer lives
And, as He that remains at the last, will appear upon (the) dust ;   (25)
And after loss of my skin which has been torn to this state,
And even deprived of my flesh, I shall see God.   (v. 26)
And I shall see Him to my salvation ;
And my eyes will behold Him and indeed not as One estranged to me,
Him for whom my inward parts within my breast have pined away (27)

The commentary which König supplies to this is, that the
Redeemer (Goel) is Job's Saviour from calumny and misunderstanding—God, who as the One who endures to the last, will
appear upon the earth, an earth reduced to dust at the time of
the world-judgment, when even the stars in heaven will be
dissolved (Isa. 34[4] ; cf. Pr. 8[26]). Job, König says, does not
think of God as appearing in the midst of the world's course,
nor at the grave of Job (Duhm) nor over his body now become
dust. Job is confident that after his flesh, ragged and torn with
leprosy, has been discarded and he is dead, God will vindicate
him and his discarnate spirit will know it. This is also the
interpretation of v.[26] which Duhm and G. F. Moore offer.
König and others who agree with him point out that although
in the rest of the Book of Job the view prevails that the dead
do not return from the underworld, the hero of the poem,

[1] *Das Buch Hiob.*, p. 192.

wrestling with his problem, grows in spiritual insight and in his travail of soul reaches a height of certainty, but for a moment and not sustained, that death will not break his communion with God. The hope is not of resurrection, but, according to König, of immortality, there being no reflection upon the mode in which Job will see God.

Many attempts have been made to solve the difficulties of the Hebrew text of Job 19[25f.] by suggesting emendations from which, assuming textual corruption to have taken place, these corruptions may have sprung. An example of such a restored text is that made by Bertholet [1] who understands " the dust " to mean Job's grave :

But I know the avenger of my blood is alive
And will at the last take His stand over the dust ;   (25)
The witness of my innocence will be with me ('Ed niqīoni itti)
And Him that frees me from guilt shall I see for myself (u-meshari
    ehezeh li)   (26)
And with my own eyes shall I behold it and no stranger—
Though my inward parts dissolve within me.   (27)

It is probable that there will never be complete agreement on the exegesis of the passage before us. The argument that the Sheol belief represents the general outlook of the Book of Job upon man's destiny will always be liable to be overcome by the thought that perchance the author allows his hero, in an ecstasy of anguish and of feeling, to break with this conception of man's common lot. As Duhm [2] remarks : " An observant reader will be inclined to suspect from the purposefulness with which the sorrowful view of death as the end of all is repeated, that there is a suppressed and secret hope ever seeking to spring up and affirm that the issue of life may be quite otherwise." If, therefore, we give due weight to this consideration and admit the words of v.[25] as genuine and as signifying that God will appear

---

[1] *Biblische Theol. d. A.T.*, 1911, p. 113 f. Baumgärtel reconstructs v. 26 thus : And then will my witness ('edi) raise me up (*jizqoph 'othi*) /and as my messenger of joy (*u-mebassari*) will I see God. See also Duhm's proposal in Peake's *Century Bible* (Job).   [2] *Kommentar*, p. 52.

on earth to vindicate Job ; and if further we admit that v.[27] certainly affirms that Job will then see God ; then there are four possible interpretations. After Job's death God appears in the world-judgment and Job as revenant immortal spirit sees Him vindicate his cause and bring his accusers to judgment ; or God appears at the tomb of Job, in an interval of the world's ordinary course, to vindicate and judge and Job's discarnate and immortal spirit beholds Him ; or after Job dies and before his spirit departs to Sheol, the place of the dead, he will perceive God in action on earth as Vindicator and Judge ; or, finally, that before he dies, even though he is sinking in unconsciousness and " his reins be dissolved within him," Job hopes and believes he will be vouchsafed a sight of his complete justification and of God Himself performing it.

The two last explanations where the thought of immortality is not introduced at all have on the whole most to recommend them from the point of view of the theme and conceptions of the rest of the book. " If the author of Job had really represented his hero as reaching such a depth of faith and insight as to hope in a future life, it is inexplicable why no use is made of this attainment in knowledge as a solution of the problem of the book." A flash of vision that lit up the world beyond with the hope of immortality and afterwards disappeared like a shooting star, all too soon, into darkness, would be a dramatic trait corresponding to the psychological state of Job, suffering and in mental anguish grasping at any straw of hope. But the *author* of the book of Job was under no such stress or tension ; his resources of imagination are abundant ; he has given careful shape and form to his work ; he is not writing in a hurry ; and yet the thought, that with a later generation would have weighed heavy in the scales of argument, is left without evaluation in those considerations which he leaves us as the answer to his theme. But regard must be paid to the scheme of the thought of the Book of Job. Both Job and his friends stand upon the dogma of reward and retribution with its reference to this present life. The last part of the Folk-tale, the epilogue of the book, which records the return of Job's earthly prosperity, may seem to be an artistic blunder and even to surrender territory in the realm of truth that had been bravely contested in the foregoing discussions. Its cruder outlook is apparent, and to modern feeling strikes almost the note of caricature. But in the epilogue the faith in the doctrine of reward and retribution is only a more antique and less sophisticated expression of the same Deuteronomist doctrine which is common to the rest of the book whether in its present form or in the dimensions to which Baumgärtel reduces the original dialogue of Job. The problem of the book concerns not suffering in general but Job's individual suffering in the light of his clear conscience and of a life lived in close communion with God, and it arises within and remains within the limits of a doctrine which, however modified, is itself limited to man's earthly experience. It is as under this dogma of reward that Job demands his " rights." As conceived under this dogma his " rights " have been taken away, and these can only be restored by his being rehabilitated before the eyes of men and acknowledged as innocent. The great value of the book is that it represents an attempt to wrestle with this question of providence in an aspect most perplexing to faith, by remaining, in spite of the Prologue, in the sphere of the visible and present world and does not seek a way out by drafting a blank cheque upon the Bank of the Future. In the history of religion the Book of Job is of outstanding importance as testifying to the high degree of faith (or waiting-upon God) and the reality of that consciousness of communion with God that could exist within the limitations of a belief which had not attained to a doctrine of an after-life. This accounts for the proneness to read into expressions of Hebrew piety thoughts and hopes which are not there.

Of the two explanations of Job 19$^{25f.}$ which we distinguished as preferable, it remains to observe that that which regards Job as imagining himself as having died but as yet not entered into the realm of Sheol is consistent with the Sheol-belief in the rest of the book and has the merit, if this be a merit, of being able to retain, unemended, the suspect v.[26]. P. Humbert (*op. cit.* p. 85 f.) makes out a very good case for the view that Job expresses the hope that he will receive an attestation of the divine justice after he has died. He compares the verse "I know that my Avenger lives and will stand at last over dust" with the thought and words of the Egyptian "Dialogue of one tired of life," where the Tired of life, addressing his own soul says: "Be kind enough, thou my soul and my brother, to be my survivor [? this word is mutilated in the text] who will sacrifice and remain near my bier on the day of burial to prepare for me the couch of the realm of the dead."[1] The Tired of life reflects that it is necessary for his peace in the other world that some one should pronounce over his body the customary prayers and sacred rites. He has no surviving relative or friend. He beseeches his own soul to take the part of the survivor. Humbert points to the striking similarity of the Hebrew words "stand over dust" (qum 'al 'aphar) with the Egyptian "hold (keep, remain) near the bier," of the Hebrew term "the last" (*acharon*, survivor, successor) with the Egyptian term which though mutilated can only have some such equivalent meaning. The Dialogue also contains the expression "he who is on the earth." The parallelism of thought and expression is striking. Job, too, feels himself forsaken of his friends and counts on God to render after his death an ultimate homage of justice, to establish his innocence. Humbert thinks that the author of Job knew the Dialogue and appreciated its thought in his own dialogue. Alternatively, he suggests that at least the rôle of survivors in respect of duties to the dead, as practised in Egypt, was known to him. The Egyptian text certainly supplies an excellent commentary on the debated Job passage. But even if we grant this, there would appear to be no more contained in this passage in Job than the thought that before his soul retired to Sheol,

---

[1] Cf. Erman, *Lit. d. Aegypt.*, p. 124 f.

the land of everlasting gloom and forgetfulness, Job might for
an all sufficient moment see his justification wrought by God.
According to Pedersen (*Israel*, p. 180 f.) the current Hebrew
conception was that as long as the body is a body, the soul
was closely connected with it ; that which is done to the body
is done to the soul, so that when the worms gnaw the dead
body the soul feels it (Job 14[22]).   If the body is not laid in the
grave, it is anxious and rushes about restlessly.   But these conceptions and even that the dead could peep and mutter (Isa. 8[19],
29[4]) in a state of lifeless exhaustion did not amount to a belief
in immortality.   Thus the theory that Job hopes to see his
vindication after he has died need imply no more than the
experience which the grateful dead had when their unburied
bodies were at last committed to the dust.   The question or
wish expressed in the fourteenth chapter of Job (14[13f.]; cf. v.[15])
concerning the dead being able to live again shows that the author
was well aware, as otherwise we know he must have been, of
the belief in survival after death, but it also shows that he never
entertained this belief or conceived of the possibility of any
person ever escaping Sheol.   There is no return from Sheol : otherwise Job would be willing, could he be *preserved* [1] (*tsaphan*)
from the devitalizing powers of shadow-land and could he be
concealed from the forces of destruction, to remain there till
God's wrath would be over and God call him back and establish
his right or pardon his sin.   But to be preserved in Sheol !
That in itself was hopeless and impossible.   The other view which
represents Job as assured that though on the verge of death,
about to succumb but still alive, he would behold God as
Vindicator on earth (where, on all the views submitted, his
accusers are to await the appearance of the deity), makes what
appears to be the best sense of the words in v.[27c] and which
present a picture of fast-ebbing life.

[1] Baumgärtel, *op. cit.* p. 65, thinks that Sheol in Job 14[13] is a metaphor only
=Misery (Elend).   But he rightly points out that the emphasis should be on
the words " preserved " (protected) and " concealed."

2

Of similar content with the poem of Job is Psalm 73. In an inner conflict of faith, caused by the patent contrast between his own misfortune and the prosperity of the worldly and ir-religious, the writer describes how he was almost reduced to faithlessness. The claim that in this psalm the hope of immortal-ity finds expression is based on the vv.[16-18] where the writer draws a first conclusion regarding the fate of the wicked and on v.[23f.] where he draws another conclusion as to " the chief good " in life. The first group of verses are :

> And I thought to know this :
> It was troublesome in mine eyes   (16)
> Till I came into the holy-places of El (God) [1]
> (And) considered the end of them (*i.e.* of the wicked)   (17)
> That on slippery ground Thou settest them,
> Causest them fall to ruin.   (18)

The later group of verses continue :

> But I remain constantly with Thee,
> Thou holdest my right hand,   (23)
> Thou guidest me with Thy counsel,
> And to honour Thou wilt bring (take) me.   (24)
> Whom have I in heaven but Thee ?
> And besides Thee I desire nothing on earth.   (25)
> Though my flesh and my heart should fail,
> Yet God is [the strength of my heart and] my portion for ever.(26)

In this poem both Duhm[2] and Bertholet[2] take "the holy-places " or " sanctuaries of El " to indicate small esoteric circles or coteries of the pious who, when the doctrine of immortality

---

[1] Cheyne (*Psalms*) and Gunkel (*Ausgewählte Psalmen*) think " Miqdeshe El " (sanctuaries of El) is error for mishpete el =judgments of God. But the more difficult reading is to be preferred. For the same reason Staerk's transla-tion " mysteries " = " God's wonderful wisdom in His government of the world " (Psalms, *S.A.T.*, p. 227) is to be rejected as not doing justice to the concrete term. It was in these sanctuaries that God's wonderful wisdom came to the author.

[2] Cf. Duhm, *Comm. on Psalm*. Bertholet in *Bib. Theol d. A.T.*, p. 120.

was yet rejected by Jewish orthodoxy, believed and propagated this doctrine. They regard these " holy-places of El " to be the equivalent of, or to have relationship to, " the mysteries of God " (μυστήρια τοῦ θιοῦ) mentioned in the Wisdom of Solomon (2²²), a writing that reflects very strongly the influence of Greek thought. Further, rendering v.²⁴ᵇ as " and to glory Thou will take me " they understand this to mean a *taking* of The soul to God's heavenly glory or glory of His presence, and find support for this in the fact that the verb " take " (laqach) is employed to describe the translation of Enoch and Elijah to heaven in the accounts of Gen. 5²⁴ and the Book of Kings (2 Kings, 2¹⁰). Enoch walked with God and God *took* him. Now whatever " the sanctuaries of El " may have been, it is very probable that the poem intends by them circles or associations of godly Jews : but the result of the psalmist's attendance at these meetings is quite clearly stated to be that there came the conviction to him as a new light of knowledge that the end of the ungodly was ruin. They were on slippery places, though in their prosperity their path seemed so sure. God's retribution could seem to tarry, but it could come very suddenly and in manifold ways. If there is any mystery about this, it is the mystery of life and of the manner in which God works His retributory justice finally and skilfully out. There is not the least idea or notion of immortality perceptible here. It is remarkable also that the Greek translator who might be credited with some feeling and ability to find an equivalent for the phrase " sanctuaries of El," does not employ the term *mysteria* or even *thiasos*, but renders quite literally with the phrase *hagiasterion tou theou*.

While our interpretation of the verses which we have considered appears to be the only one of which the actual text permits, it does not exclude the possibility that this singular expression " sanctuaries of El," which certainly does not refer to the temple, does owe something of its colour and content to the author's Greek surroundings. Psalm 73 is placed by Briggs

in the Greek period, and he also holds the psalm to teach the
doctrine of a life beyond the grave. The connection which
Duhm and others perceive between the " sanctuaries of El "
and " the mysteries of God " mentioned in the Wisdom of
Solomon (2^{22}), is rendered very strong by the fact that each of
these expressions occurs where the doctrine of retribution is
being discussed, and the contrast between the prosperous
wicked and the suffering or unfortunate righteous man is drawn.
In the passage in the Wisdom of Solomon ($2^{10f.}$), the ungodly
are represented as scoffing at the weak and righteous man in
his adversity, and as conspiring against him to bring him to a
shameful death.

> Thus reasoned they, being far astray,   (21)
> For their wickedness blinded them,
> And they knew not the mysteries of God,   (22)
> Neither hoped they for the wages of holiness.
> Nor did they judge that there is a prize for blameless souls,
> Because God created man for incorruption,   (23)
> And made him an image of his own proper being.

The author here intends by the " mysteries of God " the
knowledge or faith that suffering is not necessarily punishment,
but is often a trial of faith which will be rewarded with immortality.[1]   That his language in v.[22] is borrowed from the
non-Jewish religious world of his day, in particular from the
mystery-cults of the Hellenistic age there can be no doubt at
all.   The vocabulary of this Greek-speaking Jew who lived
shortly before the beginning of the Christian era displays a
marked, though necessarily merely popular, knowledge of
the Greek (Dionysian) mysteries.   In his descriptions of ancient
Canaanite worship ($12^{3f.}$) and of idolatry in general ($14^{22f.}$),
the picture he draws of secret mysteries (14^{23}) and of merry
madness (14^{28}), ritual murder of children and adulteries, is largely
coloured by his acquaintance with the mystery cult of his age.
Such were the calumnies popular at the time in the non-Jewish

Cf. Charles, *Apoc.*, *ad loc.*

world among the uninitiated, who were hostile to the mysteries of Dionysus. The author of the Wisdom of Solomon, as Johannes Leipoldt [1] puts it, " plucks the blossoms of rhetoric of the opponents of Dionysus " in his polemic against heathendom. The phrase " mysteries of God " as appearing in such a book as the Wisdom of Solomon, impregnated as this is with Greek conceptions, shows a very direct dependence of orthodox Judaism upon the speech and thought of the Greek world. For the author it possesses already, as it must have possessed for his fellow religionists, an inherent religious contrast with the mystery cults of that world which he attacks. If this be so, it is nowise unlikely that the " sanctuaries of El " of the Ps. 73, composed earlier in the same period, may present the same contrast in Judaism with the Greek religious communities or θίασοι of its time. As early as the reign of Ptolemy IV. Philopator (221–204 B.C.), special privileges were given by this king to the Jews in Egypt who entered into the communion of those initiated into the mysteries (3 Macc. 2[29f.]) and this refers to the rites of Dionysus, with whom he sought to equate the Jewish Jahve. The first and second book of Maccabees show also that before the revolt of Judas (164 B.C.) the Jews in Palestine came under the same propaganda in favour of Dionysian rites. Knowledge, therefore, of what these rites taught, as distinguished from what they were, must have been widespread among Jews of the Hellenistic age. But although the mystery cults offered to their initiates among other things a solution of the dark riddle of death, and while knowledge of this is apparently reflected in the passage quoted from the Wisdom of Solomon, there is no ground for the deduction that in Ps. 73 the secret knowledge which the psalmist gained in the " sanctuaries of El " had any reference to a doctrine of immortality. A much nearer parallel, when regard is taken as to what the author of Ps. 73 himself tells us he learned concerning divine retribution in these sanctuaries or associations, is supplied by a writer who

[1] " Dionysus," p. 18 (Angelos-Beiheft, 1931).

reports on the Orphic mysteries which were a Reformed or
Protestant form of Dionysian worship. Andocides [1] (De mysteriis
31) in a speech addressing initiates says : " you have been
initiated and have seen the ' sacra ' of the two deities, in order
that you may punish the impious and preserve (σώζητε) such
as commit no injustice." Here the doctrine taught in the Orphic
community or fellowship of the pious is of an ordinary religious
or moral kind regarding the Gods' interest in the punishment
of the wicked and the preservation of the righteous. But inasmuch as these communities did seek immortality, we must
inquire whether in Ps. 73, apart from the verses examined,
which speak of " the holy places of El," a doctrine of a future
life is taught as many scholars hold.

We mentioned that in the group of verses (23–26) some
translate verse 24b which we render "and to honour Thou wilt
bring (or take) me " as "and to glory Thou wilt take me " and
understand the verse as an assurance of the transference of the
soul after death to heaven. Further, it is argued [2] that the word
take is a technical term signifying the taking-up or receiving of
the soul by God to Himself since the word has this meaning in
the Enoch and Elijah stories. But neither the translation of
the Hebrew word *kabod* by " glory " nor the understanding of
the word *take* (laqach) in the sense of taking-up to heaven is
justified by the context of the psalm.

The idea that God will cause the impious to come eventually
to ruin (v.[18]) has its exact parallel in the thought that God
will *bring* the righteous man to honour. The poetic device of
Hebrew " parallelism," as observed in the line that precedes
line 24b, and which expresses the thought that God will *guide*
the righteous man with counsel and advice (24a), is more satisfactorily met with the plainer idea that He will also bring him
to honour than by the sudden introduction of the notion of a
transference after death to heaven. In those struggles of faith
which emerge in Judaism with the growth of reflection upon the

---

[1] Fourth century B.C.   [2] So Staerk, *S.A.T.*, on Ps. 73 and 49.

dogma of reward and retribution, the righteous and God-fearing, on the basis of this belief, incurred when they fell on misfortune the suspicion of secret sin. Fortune cannot easily be mended but reputation in the eyes of men was all important. Honour, not to be too ideally conceived of, must be established and retrieved. This comes to poignant utterance in the cry of Job :

> Of my honour (k^{e}bodi) has He stripped me
> And has torn the crown from my head.   (19[9])

Apart from the passages Gen. 5[24], 2 Kings 2[10] where the text makes it as clear as day that the taking of Enoch and Elijah was a taking-up to heaven, the best evidence of the word *take* ever being used in this sense again in the Old Testament is supplied by the familiar verse, Isaiah 53[8], and that evidence is neither certain nor particularly good. Here, if we interpret with Duhm, it is said of the suffering servant of God : " from oppression and from judgment he was taken (away)." [1.] This might mean, as Duhm holds, that the servant was taken after death to God's presence. On the other hand it may signify no more than that the sufferer was released or removed by death. Others think that the words " was taken " in Isaiah 53[8] intend the same as they do in Isaiah 52[5], namely " was put to death," and render the former passage : " he was put to death through oppression and through judgment." But the sense of the passage does not seem to require more than the thought that " the servant " was either released by death or was delivered up to death. When Jeremiah (15[15]) appeals to Jahve : " take me not away in thy long-suffering (towards my persecutors)" he means " do not deliver me up or reject me," or as in the Authorized Version, " Do not remove me." But if the significance of the debated line in Psalm 73 be " and to honour thou

---

[1] A.V. " He was taken from prison and from judgment," see Skinner (Cambridge Bible) *ad loc.*, Duhm renders " Aus Druck und Gericht ist er entrafft." Torrey (The Second Isaiah) translates : " From dominion and rule he was plucked down " since (p. 419) the words " taken from judgment " can only mean . . . he was taken away from exercising judgment."

wilt bring (or take) me," we have only the ordinary use of the
verb *laqach* to take or bring as used in such a sentence as Num.
23[11. 14]—" Balak said to Balaam . . . I *took* thee to curse my
enemies . . . and Balak *took* him to the field of Zophim."

But alongside the reference to Enoch and Elijah and the
ambiguous passage Isaiah 53[8] the advocates of a technical use
of the word *laqach* place an expression of hope in Psalm 49 (v.[16])
which, at first sight, appears to support their plea, namely,
" God will ransom me from the power of Sheol for He will take
me." But does this verse, which Briggs and Staerk, on good
grounds from the point of view of sequence of thought declare
to be a later marginal gloss, mean that *after* death God will
rescue the supplicant from the underworld and take him to
Himself ? Two considerations inhibit us from thinking so. The
first is the fact that the language of prayer for help in the time
of disease and danger both in Hebrew and Babylonian literature
is characteristically couched in terms of petition for deliverance
from Sheol which is a mere metaphor for deliverance from dire
distress or the present danger of death.[1] The second consideration is—and this is conclusive—that both this mode of
language and the use of the word *take* in the sense of *deliver*
appear in the eighteenth psalm and are combined in a way that
makes the meaning of both unmistakable. This psalm, which
is a hymn of thanksgiving for the deliverance of a king from his
enemies, describes the danger as it appeared to him : " the
(breakers) of death encompassed me/the torrents of Belial fell
upon me/cords of Sheol came round me/snares of Death came
to meet me " (18[5-6]). But from this peril of destruction Jahve
was at hand to rescue : " He sends from on high, He *takes* me/
He draws me out of many waters/He delivers me from my strong
enemy " (18[16f.] ; Heb. 18[17f.]). From this we see that the expression *take* in Psalms 18 and 49 has the same value and
significance. The author of Psalm 49 describes Sheol as the place
where all men must go after death, " the wise " and "the brutish"

---

[1] Cf. Hölscher, *Gesch. d. isr. und jüd. Rel.*, p. 150 also Gunkel (Psalms).

alike. None can escape. There they remain for ever and neve
see the light of day again. None can " buy off," or ransom
himself from his destiny. If verse 16 is from the hand of the
author of the Psalm it means exactly the same, as the context
shows, as our prayers express when they present the petition :
" from all accident, disease, and death O Lord deliver us."
If the verse be from the hand of a later glossator it still must be
judged as within the context of the thought of the Psalm
where it is found. To assume, as Briggs does, that the gloss
contains the contrast between a paradise or " Gan Eden " to
which the souls of the righteous go and the " pit " (or Abaddon)
of Sheol, is not only to read into the words that which is not
there, but to assume a lateness of date for the gloss that is not
at all probable. The Psalms contain assurances of God's power
and protection and justice, outpourings of the heart and its
emotions, expressions of communion with God which have
constituted them as a book of hymns and prayers that have
retained their powers and appeal throughout the ages, but,
nevertheless, the Psalms are not the writings in the Old
Testament where we would be justified in first searching for
intimations of immortality. As the official hymn-book of public
worship this is the very book from which there would be carefully excluded any doctrine that ran counter to the traditional
sentiment of the mass of the people or in particular of the
temple-priesthood.[1] The Psalm-book, with the exception of
about half a dozen Maccabean psalms, was complete by the
time the belief in a future life *for some* makes its hestitating

[1] " The priests were the aristocrats who held their powers and their
authority (much curtailed, it is true, at the beginning of the Christian era)
from their descent and the prestige of the sacred rites which only they had
the right to perform. The Rabbis were laymen whose reputation among the
people sprung from their knowledge of the Law and the rigour of their piety. At
the beginning of our era they had monopolised almost entirely the interpretation of the Law—up till now the proper domain of the priests " (Adophe Lods
in *Revue de l'Histoire des Religions*, 1923, Tome 88, n. 1-3, Juillet-Octobre,
p. 121). The completion of the Psalm-Book is long anterior to the evolution
here described.

appearance in the apocalyptic vision of Daniel (164 B.C.). No
doubt the doctrine thereafter, spread rapidly among the pious,
as we see from the Book of Jubilees and 2 Maccabees, but the
official hymn-book was in the control of a conservative priestly
class. In our thought, the idea of immortality is the com-
plement to the idea of communion with God. Among the
Hebrews we perceive a fact that is remarkable and of signal
importance in the history of religion, namely, that for many
centuries this complementary relationship of those ideas did
not exist and yet the latter idea represented a reality of the sub-
limest kind. This is vital to our understanding of many Psalms,
and especially of the Book of Job and of Psalm 73. Of this
psalm, Gunkel remarks [1] that " the introduction of the thought
of immortality would alter completely the perspective of the picture which the author has drawn since the whole problem he is
wrestling with acquires its difficulty from the fact that for him life
here is the only one he knows." We may add that to disregard
this is to take away from the beauty of the climax of the poem
where communion with God is stated to be the highest value in
life and where the idea is disclosed that virtue is its own reward.

Baudissin (op cit. p. 396 f.), who makes a careful study of
those poetic pieces in the Old Testament which have been held
by many to express the hope of an after-life, shows that from the
earliest times in Semitic thought sickness and trouble were regarded as a coming under the power of death and Sheol. In
Babylonia the title " He who makes the dead alive " is given to
Marduk and other deities in contexts where at least as a rule—
for in theory the god is able to do all things—a raising from the
bed of sickness must be understood. In the Old Testament in
certain cases the dead are awakened to life by prophets (1 Kings
17[22], 2 Kings 4[35], 8[1. 5], 13[21]). But this occurs immediately after
death, before the journey to Sheol is complete, is extraordinary
and exceptional in nature, and has nothing to do with belief in
a future life.

---

[1] Gunkel, Ps. 73 in " Ausgewählte Psalmen."

CHAPTER VII

AN INQUIRY INTO THE REASON OF THE LATENESS OF THE
DEVELOPMENT IN ISRAEL OF A BELIEF IN A FUTURE
LIFE. (RESISTANCE TO THE IDEA IN PRE-EXILIC ISRAEL)

THOUGH the doctrine of a future life makes what seems to be a
strikingly late appearance in the history of Hebrew religion,
only two late passages in the Old Testament yielding indubitable
witness to it (Dan. 12[2, 3]; Isa. 26[19]),[1] it is certain that the
Israelites must have been early acquainted with the fact that
such a belief existed and was elsewhere firmly held and cherished.

In Egypt in remote antiquity, as shown by the oldest form
of funerary literature, the pyramid texts, it was believed that
the dead awoke to real renewed life in full possession of their
body and mind.[2] Already in the time of the Old Kingdom
the ethical conception of a judgment of the dead is found,
although, apparently, only in the period of the Middle Kingdom
did this doctrine acquire definite form and general recognition.[3]
Since the Middle Kingdom extends from about the year 2000 B.C.
to c. 1580 B.C., we see that before Israel appears in the light
of history a belief and teaching concerning a Hereafter had
attained high development in a people with whom the Hebrew
race was to be brought into close contact. The Egyptian
writings of the New Kingdom (from 1555 B.C. onwards) are full
of loan words borrowed from the inhabitants of Canaan, from

---

[1] Isa. 25 promises the destruction of death itself *for the Messianic era of the
future*; v.[8] appears to be a gloss of later date.
[2] Erman, *A Handbook of Egyptian Religion*, p. 97. Cf. *Book of the Dead*, chap.
68.
[3] *Ibid.* p. 101. R. Anthes, *Lebensregeln und Lebensweisheit der alten
Ägypter*, pp. 16 f., 24, 30. Cf. *Book of the Dead*, chap. 125.

which intercourse with Palestine Erman concludes that there must have also been a literary influence on Canaan from the side of Egypt.[1] In the settled times of the Hebrew monarchy, in the reign of Solomon, the connection with Egypt through marriage alliance and commercial enterprise was intimate. From then onwards, if not earlier, the features of Egyptian religious thought concerning the destiny of man, the more strange they may have appeared, must have penetrated into the realm of Hebrew knowledge and become the subject of reflection.

Now in those sections of the Book of Proverbs which represent the beginning of the Hebrew Wisdom-literature where the international currency of thought is most manifest in the Old Testament writings, there is as clear indication as we can expect in such matters both that the articles of Egyptian faith regarding the Hereafter were known, and that such a belief was regarded as beyond the power of Jahvism to accept. The sections to which we refer are chaps. 10–29 (30), which recent criticism places in the pre-exilic period, indeed even in eighth and seventh centuries.[2] In these chapters the old Hebrew belief in Sheol as the end of all stands firm, except perhaps for the single remark that " Sheol and Abaddon are before Jahve " (15[11]), which seems to imply that Jahve takes some sort of cognizance of the realm of the underworld. But that the authors knew of the Egyptian belief of the judgment of the dead and transferred the rôle of Thoth, the god of wisdom, who *weighs the hearts* of men, to Jahve is evident. The judgment of the dead and the weighing of hearts by Thoth is a familiar scene in Egyptian pictorial representations. A pair of scales is portrayed as hung upon a balance. In the left scale there is the script-sign for the word " heart," in the right a feather,

---

[1] Erman, *Die Literatur der Ägypter*, p. 5 f.

[2] See Sellin, *Intro.*, and Gressmann, *Israel's Spruchweisheit*, p. 34 f. and *Z.A.W.* 1924, " Die neugefundene Lehre des Amenemope, etc., p. 286. Sellin places the beginning of the composition of Prov. 10–22 in time of Solomon, and nucleus of Prov. 25–29 in time of Hezekiah (722–699), Prov. 22[17]–24[34] between 608–586.

the sign of Maat, the goddess of justice and truth. How heavy the feather weighs is shown by the sinking scale that holds it. The god Anubis at the balance-stand observes results. The god Thoth notes them on his tablet. A fabulous dog-like monster, who devours the wicked, awaits the verdict that acquits or condemns. Thrice we are reminded by the pre-exilic Hebrew collectors of maxims that it is Jahve who weighs the hearts (16^2, the spirits ; 21^2, 24^{12}) of men. In the Book of Proverbs the portion that is distinguished as the third collection (22^{17}–24^{34}) contains a large section (22^{17}–23^{11}), the maxims of which are almost wholly paralleled by sayings from the Egyptian Wisdom-book known as " The Teaching of Amen-em-ope." Outside this section, which is obviously dependent on the Egyptian work,[1] but inside the same third (III.) collection, the description of God as " He that weigheth the heart " occurs in verse 24^{12}. It is true that the exact expression, " weigh the hearts," does not appear in Amen-em-ope. But, nevertheless, we may conclude that the writer depends either upon Amen-em-ope or some other Egyptian prototype. To Amen-em-ope the *idea* of Thoth weighing hearts is familiar (XVI. xvii. 22–xviii. 3 ; XXIV. xxiv. 4, 5 ; cf. II. iv. 19) ; an allusion to Thoth's well-known functions being contained in the saying : " The ape (*i.e.* symbol of the god Thoth) sitteth at the balance/ His heart being the plummet (XVI. xvii. 22–xviii. 3)." Moreover, the verse in Proverbs, which directly precedes the verse we are considering, has every mark of being a paraphrase of a maxim of Amen-em-ope. The latter's warning not to persecute the desperate, " Cry not ' Crime ' at a man/Hide the manner of (a fugitive's) flight " [2] has its parallel in the Hebrew, "Deliver them that are carried away to death/And those who are tottering to slaughter hide " (24^{11}). That the

---

[1] Cf. H. O. Lange, *Das Weisheitsbuch des Amenemope* (Copenhagen), 1925, pp. 13, 14. Gressmann, *op. cit. Z.A.W.*, dates Amen-em-ope's work, *c.* 1000 B.C. (cf. *Israel's Spr.*, pp. 35, 43). Griffith (1926), *Journal of Egypt. Arch.*, dates present form of Amen-em-ope 600 B.C.; original form *c.* 750 B.C. Erman and Sethe place Amen. *c.* 1000 B.C.   [2] Cf. Amen. VIII., xi. 6, 7.

description of Jahve as weighing hearts is a judicious borrowing from the Egyptian is made all the more certain when we also note that the maxim (21²), "Every way of a man is right in his own eyes/but Jahve weigheth the hearts," is followed by a verse about justice as more acceptable than sacrifice that is practically identical with a saying of the Egyptian wisdom-book, "The Teaching for Meri-ka-re" (c. 2000 B.C.) : "Righteousness of the heart is more acceptable to God than the sacrifice of an ox offered by an unrighteous man" (cf. Prov. 21³).[1] The same conclusion may possibly be made in regard to Prov. 16² ("Jahve weigheth the spirits"), for the very next verse (16³), "Commit thy works unto Jahve," occurs also in Egyptian form in the work of Amen-em-ope (XXI. xxii. 7, and elsewhere), who advises his pupil, "Place thyself in the arms of God." To these literary considerations, which strengthen the view that the Hebrew conception of Jahve as weighing the hearts of the living was based upon the Egyptian model picture of Thoth weighing the hearts of the departed in the judgment of the dead, may be added the further observation that the Hebrew word *takan* (weigh), is never used except in Proverbs in reference to the heart or spirit.[2] We have thus again, in view of the Egyptian influence on the Book of Proverbs to which we have pointed, another indication that the Hebrew sage is dependent on a non-Hebraic pattern of thought. But impressive as the debt to Egypt is, particularly to the teaching of Amen-em-ope,[3] in the second (10¹–22¹⁶), the third (22¹⁷–24³⁴), and fourth collection (25¹–29²⁷) of Hebrew maxims it is a striking fact that Amen-em-ope's doctrine of a Hereafter [4] and of future

---

[1] Cf. Erman, *Literatur*, p. 118.

[2] Cf. Oesterley, "Book of Proverbs" (*Westminster Commentary*) on Prov. 24¹².

[3] See Oesterley, *ibid.* pp. xxxvii f., liii f., 11 f.

[4] Cf. Amen. XI. 4, 5; XXIV. 19. 20. For archæological evidence of Egyptian influence in Canaan, cf. Dr. S. A. Cook, *The Religion of Ancient Palestine, etc.* ("Schweich Lectures, 1925"), 1930. Macalister, *Excavations of Gezer*, 1912. Cf. A. Lods, *Israel*, 1932, p. 68 "the interpenetration of Egypt and Canaan extended to the field of religion."

reward finds no echo, that this belief could not in the pre-exilic age be evaluated in Hebrew thought, and that nothing but an innocuous fragment, the phrase, " He that weighs the hearts," remains as witness of contact with a theology that could rise to the lofty conception of a judgment of the dead.

We have now to inquire into the reason of the belated appearance of a doctrine of a future life among the Hebrews, a belated appearance all the more remarkable on account of the certainty that such a belief was known to them as existing and might have been appreciated for its ethical and religious value. To put the question into another form : why did Israel resist the belief in a Hereafter in favour of the gloomy conception of an underworld where man could not praise Jahve ? Moreover, inasmuch as there are traces in primitive Hebrew thought of a survival of the spirit after death, how do we account for the fact that the Sheol conception became the normal belief of the Old Testament regarding the state of the departed ?

Dr. Oesterley, in *Hebrew Religion : its Origin and Development* (pp. 317 f., 326 f.), after comment upon the traces of primitive belief (ancestor-worship, sacrifices to the dead, food in tombs, necromancy) to which we have referred, regards all of these, including necromancy, as preceding the belief in Sheol. Oesterley states that he is thus led to believe " that the Hebrews came into contact for the first time with the Sheol conception after the settlement in Canaan, but that for a long time it meant nothing to them. Then, after the champions of Jahve-worship were at last able to assert themselves under the leadership of Elijah, it became more and more realized that the practices and superstitions of the older belief, connected as it was with ancestor-worship and necromancy, was incompatible with Jahve-worship. The polemic against the older belief continued to gain force until the rise of the great prophets of the eighth century, when it became definitely a mark of disloyalty to Jahve and the Sheol conception became firmly

established as the official belief." According to Oesterley, the
fear of necromancy, against which in later times there appears
legal enactments, is the reason why "the Sheol conception
arose among the Hebrews." Now primitive conceptions of
a continued existence of the spirits of the dead, in so far as
they were connected with the cult of the dead,[1] or with necromancy, the art of raising or communicating with the dead,
were certainly felt to be inimical to the cult of Jahve. But that
the fear of necromacy, as hostile to Jahve-worship, established
the Sheol conception and caused it to become the normal view
of the Hereafter, does not survive nearer examination. The
Sheol belief, which Oesterley thinks was taken over by the
Hebrews from the Canaanites, who inherited it from the
Babylonians, had ample room for necromancy. From what
we know of the Babylonian religious beliefs, here was the least
likely quarter to which those who feared necromancy would
resort for help. Here necromancy was an organized pro-
fession. Among the various kinds of priests who told the
future there were special priests, the *sha'ilu*, or askers, for the
interpretation of dreams, and the *mushelu-etimme*, or necro-
mancers, for bespeaking of the dead. They belonged to the
great guild of seers (Baru). Their patron was the sun-god
(Shamash) who brought everything to light. Their activities,
according to Meissner, are traceable up to the times of Sargon
the First [2]—that is, 2800 B.C.[3] If, among the Babylonians, as
Oesterley holds, we can distinguish (cf. p. 321 f.) between
earlier beliefs regarding a Hereafter and a later Sheol belief,
the change in no wise seems to have interfered with the practice
of necromancy. The association of necromancy with the
underworld appears in Babylonia to have been of the closest
kind and to go back to a remote period. In the Gilgamesh

---

[1] Cf. Bertholet, *Die israelitischen Vorstellungen vom Zustand nach dem
Tode*, p. 14; and see Deut. 14[1f.].

[2] *Babylonien und Assyrien*, Bd. ii. p. 66.

[3] S. Winckler, *Vorderasiatische Geschichte*. Gressmann, *Texte u. Bilder* (1909,
p. 79), c. 2600.

Epic, it is Nergal, the god of the underworld, who arranges that Gilgamesh may speak with his dead friend Enkidu, and Enkidu comes up through an opening in the earth, " like a breath of wind," and the friends embrace each other. The material of the Gilgamesh poem goes back to the Sumerian period.[1] It is impossible, therefore, to see how Jahvism could have thought to counter necromancy by the adoption of the belief in Sheol.

That the Sheol conception, by which Jahvism is supposed to have sought to overcome necromancy and primitive belief in the activity of the spirits of the dead, is, in contrast with these primitive beliefs, of later origin, Oesterley thinks may be shown by both the Sheol idea itself and by literary evidence. As to the idea of Sheol ; in Babylonian thought the underworld is described as a city of the dead, surrounded by seven walls and with seven gates with bolts and bars. In the Old Testament, Hezekiah speaks of the gates of Sheol (Isa. 38^{10}), and the Book of Job mentions the bars (17^{16} ; cf. Ps. 38^{17}, 9^{13}, 107^{18}). Such a description of the habitation of the dead, it is justly argued, would not be used by nomads unfamiliar with cities. But while this is true, the probable influence of Babylonia here only affects the form of the conception of Sheol and not the conception itself. Descriptions of the resort of the dead have always been subject to development and expansion. The concept of an underworld might still in Israel be old and primitive. Again, it is submitted, that in pre-prophetic times the Sheol belief is never mentioned, that the earliest references to it are in the prophetic literature of the eighth century,[2] and that the story of Saul and the witch of Endor (1 Sam. $28^{3f.}$) " clearly reflects the earlier traditional belief." [3] But against this it may be urged that, in the absence of any considerable

---

[1] Cf. Gressmann, *Altorientalische Texte zum A.T.*, 1926, pp. 150 f., 185.

[2] 1 Kings $2^{6. 9}$ being a Deuteronomic addition ; 1 Sam. 2^6 in Song of Hannah, *i.e.* a late insertion.

[3] That is, presumably, communication, *at the grave or tomb*, with the dead.

remains of Hebrew mythology, it is exactly in the prophetic, and not in the historical, records that we would expect any mention of Sheol. It is noteworthy that when prophecy begins we hear of Sheol at once, and not as if it were a novelty. The idea may have been acquired from the Canaanites, but there is no evidence of this. The notices of Sheol in Gen. 37[35], 42[38], 44[29, 31], and Num. 16[30, 33] all probably belong to the Jahvistic source [1] (so Kautzsch [2]) and are thus much older than the eighth-century prophets. The story of Saul and the witch of Endor takes us to a still earlier period. It is true that here there is no mention of Sheol. All we are informed of is that Samuel appears as an old man clothed with a mantle, and that the woman saw him as " a god (Elohim) coming up out of the earth." But the scene is not at the tomb of Samuel, who had been buried in his house at Rama where, on the ground of the earlier primitive beliefs Oesterley speaks of, we might have expected an attempt at communication. The scene is at Endor. It is rather the Sheol belief to which the narrative points. But had the scene been laid at Rama, would the belief concerned have been materially different ? Pedersen [3] appears to be right in his judgment that to the ancient Israelite " the ideas of the grave and Sheol cannot be separated. Every one who dies goes to Sheol, just as he, if everything happens in the normal way, is put into the grave. . . . Jacob now speaks of going into the grave (Gen. 47[30]), now of going to Sheol (Gen. 37[35]). The dead are at the same time in the grave and in Sheol, not in two different places " (cf. Num. 16[30, 33]).

If this close relationship, without any special connection,[4] of grave and Sheol represent Hebrew thought on the subject of the domain of the dead, it possesses, apart from the evidence of the early sources, all the marks of being an extremely primitive

---

[1] Sellin, *Intro. c.* 950. Sellin regards Gen. 37 as mixed with the Elohistic source (*c.* 800) and Num. 16 as mixed with Elohist and Priestly sources.

[2] " Religion of Israel," *H.B.D.*

[3] *Israel : its Life and Culture*, p. 461 ; cf. p. 473.

[4] *Ibid.* p. 473.

notion untouched by rational reflection. We must, therefore, beware of separating the idea of Sheol from supposed earlier and more primitive conceptions of the state of the dead, merely on the ground of apparent inconsistency between the emotion-less state of Sheol and the idea of an occasional activity of the spirits of the dead at the place of burial. The Hades of Homer, where the dead dwelt as half-conscious and pale phantoms, was the counterpart of the Hebrew Sheol. But, nevertheless, the dead can be conceived of as partaking of an offering made at the place of sepulture. At the funeral pyre of Patroclus, for example, Achilleus drew—

" Wine from a golden jar and, sprinkling, moistened the ground,
Ever invoking the soul of the unhappy Patroclus " (*Iliad*, xxiii. 218 f.).

Though Israel's religious belief retained for long vestiges of the cult of the dead and conceived of the dead as profiting by offerings [1] (cf. Deut. 26[14]) this does not imply that this early practice was prior to the Sheol belief. The two concepts, as in early Greek thought, were doubtless held together. It is only later reflection which causes inconsistencies in belief to become patent. As Hölscher, speaking of the prehistoric development of Hebrew religion, remarks : " The two ideas of the dwelling of the soul in the grave and in Sheol stand side by side in Hebrew thought unreconciled." [2] That the Hebrews did not necessarily take over the notion from the Canaanites is indicated by the fact that the ancient Arabs also believed in an underworld which they named *Sha'ub*.[3] If, following a necessity of the modern mind, we seek to analyse ideas which in ancient Hebrew thought we find undifferentiated, we may regard the Sheol conception as originating in a nature-mythology which contrasted the upper world of light with the lower regions of darkness

[1] See A. Bertholet, *Die israelitischen Vorstellungen vom Zustand nach dem Tode*, p. 21.
[2] *Gesch. der isr. und jüd. Religion*, p. 46, notes 3 and 4.
[3] *Ibid.* note 2.

which began where the sun sank.[1] We may suppose that in some remote period the notion of the grave as man's last resting-place and this cosmology were assimilated, Sheol thus acquiring the description of the " pit " (*Bor*), and being described in terms appropriate to the grave (cf. Isa. 14[11]).

We now turn to consider briefly the reaction of Hebrew thought in its development to the Sheol idea it anciently possessed. Far from the Sheol idea being adopted as a weapon against necromancy and the cult of the dead, we find that Jahvism, doubtless because of a connection of the Sheol idea with these practices, exerted its power to sterilize the idea of Sheol. Sheol was not adopted, but gradually *adapted* to exclude all contact with the spirits or the realm of the dead. And this adaptation only comes clearly to view in the post-exilic period.

While in the Babylonian religion the realm of the dead is a place of melancholy and torpor, as Enkidu's report to Gilgamesh illustrates : " Were I to tell you the Law (of the place) that I have seen/so must you sit down and weep/. . . in the dust he (*i.e.* the dead) crouches down," yet within the same poem there is indication of a certain liveliness within the underworld, for Enkidu tells that they who were killed by the sword lie on couches and drink pure water ; those slain in battle have their fathers and mothers and wives attending them ; while those dead who received no burial " find no rest in the earth," but their spirits wander about and eat the food-remains that are cast on the street.[2] There were thus distinctions in the underworld. Also, though it is by no means certain, it is probable, according to Meissner, that the Babylonians also had the idea of a judgment of the dead.[3] The planet

---

[1] Cf. the Egyptian conception of the nightly journey of Re (the Sun-god) through the underworld, " He (Re) hears the prayers of those that lie in their coffins, he cures their pains and drives away their sorrows. He restores breath to their nostrils." Cf. Erman, *A Handbook of Egyptian Religion*, p. 11.

[2] *Gilgamesch Epos* p. 185 f. Gressmann, *Altorient. Texte zum A.T.*

[3] *Babylonien, etc.*, p. 146 f. Gilgamesh (*K.B.* vi. 1, 266, 1 f.) is called " Judge of the Anunnaki " (*i.e.* gods of the underworld).

Mars is called the star " of the judgment of the dead," and tomb inscriptions in Susa [1] in Babylonian speech which contain the idea support the assumption that in the neighbouring Babylonia a similar conception had been formed.   But while in Babylonian mythology the goddess Ishtar descends to the underworld to seek for Tammuz, and Erishkigal, the goddess of the realm of the dead, accepts an invitation to a heavenly banquet with the gods of the upper regions ; while also on occasion necromancy can for a brief space recall the spirits of the dead, and even " an awakening of the dead and their return to life was theoretically possible " ; [2] the official belief held that the underworld was a " land of no return " (*irsit lâ târi*), " the dark house," where dust and clay were food, and where " dust lay on door and bolt." [3]   " When the gods created man they decreed death for man and retained life in their own hand." [4]   When an inscription [5] of King Assurbanipal in the seventh century B.C. narrates that " the rules of making offerings to the dead, and libations to the ghosts of the kings my ancestors, which had not been practised, I reintroduced.   I did well unto God and man, to dead and living," this information, all the more that it concerns kings, speaks for there having been a tendency to relapse into the more rigid view of the state of the dead rather than to develop those germs of thought that were favourable to conceiving of a real existence beyond the grave.

But whatever be the tendency discernible in Babylonian thought up to the seventh century, it is clear that in Hebrew religion the movement of thought, as seen within the Old Testament, was towards the *attenuation* of the Sheol conception. In Ezek. 32[18f.] a picture of Sheol receiving the defeated army

---

[1] One of these tomb inscriptions reads, " I will hear the judgment and will grasp thy (the god's) foot" ; cf. *ibid.* p. 147.

[2] Bruno Meissner, *Babylonien und Assyrien*, Bd. i. p. 149 ; cf. p. 145.

[3] *Keilinschriftliche Bibliothek* VI. i. 80, 4 f.

[4] *Mitteilungen d. Vorderasiatischen Gesellschaft*, vii. 8 ; iii. 3 f.

[5] See *Cambridge Ancient History*, iii. 127 (1925).

of Egypt among the slain warriors of other nations, who also
in their day had been a terror in the land of the living, possibly
distinguishes " the pit " as a place less sufferable than other
places within Sheol.   The Babylonian idea of the nether region,
which admitted general distinctions among the dead, may,
as Torge suggests,[1] have influenced Ezekiel's description.   The
same is probably true also of the taunt-song (Isa. 14), written
at the close of the Exile, which prophesies the descent to the
underworld of the fallen king of Babylon, and which emphasizes
the indignity of the king's body being left unburied.   But
comparatively elaborate as are the descriptions in Ezek. 32
and Isa. 14, this must not deceive us, as it has deceived some,
into thinking that here begins a tendency towards the quickening
or enlivening of Sheol, for the animation in Sheol is only apparent
and due to rhetoric and poetry being unable to express the
misery of Sheol and the humbling of fallen pomp except in
lively colours.   Ezekiel's Sheol is, to quote Duhm,[2] only " a
collection of graveyards."   In Isa. 14, those who dwell in the
underworld and greet the arrival of the Babylonian king with
mocking are as those who are " stirred " or " roused " from
sleep.   They say :

> " Sheol from beneath is stirred for thee
> To greet thy coming,
> Rousing all the shades (Rephaim) for thee . . .
> Thou also hast become weak as we."   14[9, 10].

Their characteristic is weakness.   The term *Rephaim*, in the
sense of " weak ones " or " flaccid ones," describes the state
of all the dead and is thus applied only from the time of the
Exile, in our passage probably for the first time.[3]

As time goes on, the process of emptying the concept of the
underworld becomes more marked.   In the Book of Job, as

---

[1] *Seelenglaube und Unsterblichkeitshoffnung im A.T.*, p. 94.

[2] *Kommentar on Isa.* 14.

[3] Cf. Kautzsch, *H.B.D.*, extra vol. p. 669.

Adophe Lods [1] observes, the underworld becomes more pale and mournful than it had been in earlier times. According to Qoheleth, the dead know nothing (9[5]), and " there is no pursuit, no plan, no knowledge or intelligence within Sheol " (9[10]). That this is not merely Israel's sceptic speaking, but is in accord with a general movement of thought, is nowhere clearer than in that writing where Israel's Messianic hope gives birth to the thought that some *élite* shall rise to life to share in the Messianic kingdom. For the Book of Daniel, Sheol is the " land of dust " (*admath-'aphar*, 12[2]) where the dead " sleep," and where apparently the mass of men, the non-elect, continue to repose without experiencing either joy or suffering.

We may now ask : When did this tendency which we have traced from the time of the Exile and which is echoed by various psalms (6[5], 30[9], 83[4f.] ; cf. Isa. 38[18f.]) begin ? In early times the soul or spirit of man could be thought of as hovering near the grave or as having demonic power after death, and on occasion necromancy could summon one who had departed life. That such popular conceptions were long in disappearing may be perceived from Jeremiah's picture of the long since departed ancestress of the race, Rachel, weeping for her children. The first strain of thought antagonistic to these notions of the condition of the dead and of the constitution of man is found where we might be led to expect it, in the Jahvistic source. In the Jahvistic account of creation (Gen. 2[4f.]), which reflects, according to Gunkel,[2] the agricultural stage of Hebrew history, man is viewed as consisting of two parts, earth substance and breath of life given by God (2[7]). The breath of life is regarded as an impersonal element [3] which God breathes into man. When (3[19]) man dies this breath departs and man returns to the earth as he was. This teaching in its formulation discloses quite another line of thought than the less rigid ancient view

---

[1] " *Revue de l'histoire des Religions*," lxxxiii. Nos. 1–3, 1923, July-Oct., p. 122, in review of Kreglinger's " La Religion d'Israel."

[2] *S.A.T.*, Genesis,   [3] Hölscher, *op. cit.* p. 16,

that the soul or life of man was the blood dispersed throughout all the body.   The doctrine that the spirit (*ruach*) is an impersonal principle of life which is lent by God to man and beast and withdrawn by God at death is adopted by Ps. 104[29f.] and is resorted to by Qoheleth, where consequently the Sheol conception, already emptied of all real content, becomes little more than an atrophied vestigial appendage.   Had the early Jahvistic tradition of Gen. 2[4f.], with its view of man's constitution and of his fate at death, been accepted by Hebrew religion of the time, it would have entirely destroyed primitive notions of the soul being able to inhabit rocks or trees or to disturb the peace of the living,[1] and would have abolished the old Sheol belief.   It appears to have had no immediate effect ; [2] the Sheol belief remains.   But the Jahvistic account of Gen. 2[4f.] provides the link between the time it represents and the Mono-Jahvism which gained ascendency and forbade in its own interests all practices associated with the cult of the dead and necromancy associated with Sheol.   To the influence of this Mono-Jahvism we must ascribe the reduction of the underworld to a place of " weak ones " or *rephaim*.   The dichotomous or dualistic theory of Gen. 2[4f.] is the beginning of the process and of the conflict of conceptions the process discloses.   This theory, says Kautzsch, in his work, *The Religion of Israel*,[3] plainly belongs to Jahvism, while the other idea, namely, that an indefinable somewhat of the personality descends to Sheol is a relic of pre-Jahvistic or ex-Jahvistic influences.   Whether Kautzsch is right when he attributes the tenacity of the Sheol

---

[1] Pedersen (*Israel: Its Life and Culture*, p. 97 f., see especially note to p. 180) holds that all along Hebrew psychology identifies body and soul and that at death it is the soul that dies ; but Pedersen makes the mistake of regarding Hebrew psychological ideas as having been homogeneous.   Even Pedersen himself acknowledges in the last two paragraphs in his chapter on " The Soul " that the soul could appear on earth and interfere with the living. Cf. Hölscher, *op. cit.* p. 14 f. and Kautzsch *H.B.D.* who says " almost all accounts of so-called Biblical psychology are vitiated . . . by attempting to read into Scripture a finished system of its own."

[2] Hölscher, p. 16, " bleibt . . . ohne Echo."   [3] *H.B.D.*, p. 668.

belief throughout the centuries to man's inability to accept the idea of the complete annihilation of a living personality, even if he has to content himself with a sorry substitute for a real continuation of life, is, however, questionable. To argue as Kautzsch does (p. 669) is to transfer ideas and feelings that have grown up in a civilization moulded in its thought by the idea of immortality into conditions of time and thought in no way thus moulded or fertilized. The facts we have to envizage are that the hope of immortality, of continued personal life, was known, but did not take root ; Sheol, except by the desperate and suffering who cursed their birth, was not ever imagined to be a desirable place ; [1] the *summum bonum* or life's chief good regarded as " fullness of days," honour and prosperity together with continuance in posterity, possesses a subtlety and satisfaction that escapes the modern power of appreciation. And, finally, we must weigh this consideration—that when in Isa. 26 and Dan. 12 the notion of a life after death does arise, the form which this expectation of the continuance of personality takes is of a return to earth, to the phenomenal world of things that can be touched and seen. The only exception to this is the hope which Daniel expresses that some will shine as stars. The Sheol belief persisted *in spite of* the fact that with this belief necromancy had been most closely connected. For the reason of the opposition which we see that Jahvism as early as the J narrative in Gen. 2 offers to any ideas that might have fructified the hope of a continued existence after death and for the cause of its resistance to the idea of an After-life, we must search for a clue in the nature of Jahve Himself and in the concept of deity therein implied.

The first principal cause of the retarded development and late appearance in Hebrew religion of a doctrine of personal existence after death was the tenacious endurance of the conception of the nature of Jahve as a sky- or heaven-god. To

---

[1] Hence suicide among Babylonians is seldom and hedonistic tendencies prevalent ; cf. Meissner, *op. cit.* vol. i. p. 424 ; vol. ii. p. 420 f.

demonstrate this, the history of the coming and growth of the
belief in a future life as this belief appears in Greece, offers the
best means of comparison and proof.   Here the vehicle of the
doctrine, long before it becomes the tenet of philosophers,
was the religious mysteries connected with the earth- and
underworld-divinities, the deities of vegetation and fertility.
The belief in immortality did not arise from philosophic speculation.   The concept involved in Greece, as in Phœnicia[1] and
Egypt, was a religious one, namely, the power of man to identify
himself with the fertility god, or, through communion with the
god, become divine or immune from death.   This concept,
associated with the worship of the earth- or vegetation-deities
was the power which overcame the old Hades idea in Greece,
and in Greece the opposition to the progress of the new thought
came from the Greek conception of Zeus as Heaven-god.

We must first observe the very close parallel that can be
drawn between the Hebrew Jahve and the Hellenic Zeus.
Jahve, like the gods of Semitic paganism, Baal Lebanon and
Baal Peor, is a god of the mountain.[2]   From Mount Sinai
He utters His voice.   He becomes established in Mount Zion.
His thunderous voice proclaims His coming to judgment
(Amos 1[2]).   He is a sky- or heaven-god who reveals Himself
in the lightning, the thunder, and the thick cloud, " a voice
of the trumpet exceeding loud " upon Sinai (Ex. 19[16], 20[18]).
He appears in the cloud that fills Solomon's temple (1 Kings 8[12])
when the ark is brought in.   Even to the latest periods [3] the
phenomena of thunder and lightning supply the similitudes for
Jahve's manifestations.   He is the God who sends the rain.
The blowing of trumpets, mentioned in the Mishna (Ta'an III. 2 f.)
as practised on occasions of disaster and drought, has as its
origin the belief that through sympathetic magic and imitation

---

[1] See p. 193 note 3.

[2] E. Meyer, *Ursprung, etc.*, p. 96 ; cf. *Die Israeliten und ihre Nachbarstämme*,
p. 3 f., thinks that the most primitive idea of Jahve was that he was a fire-
demon (at Sinai, burning-bush).

[3] Cf. Stade, *Biblische Theol. d. A.T.*, p. 42.

of Jahve's thunderous voice man can compel rain from heaven. As sky-god Jahve acquires the title " Elyon " (Most High) for, as Cumont [1] states, this does not mean that the god holds highest rank, but that he lives in the starry heavens. In the course of time also, among Hellenized Jews, he gains the name " Hypsistos " (Highest) in the same sense, although pagans thought, on that account, that the Jews considered the heavens as their god, an error no doubt encouraged by the term " Shamayim " (Heavens) being applied to God by later Judaism which, through reverence, shunned mention of the divine name itself. We see thus the character of Jahve as heaven-god maintaining itself from the earliest time down to the latest.

When now we turn to Zeus, we perceive the same features. As heaven-god almost everywhere in Greece he is worshipped on mountains. He is, therefore, called *epakrios*, the one who dwells on summits and hilltops. He is called " the highest " (Hypatos, Hypsistos) as signifying both rank and place in the heavenly regions.[2] " The undoubted Lord of the heavens is Zeus," says Zielinski,[3] . . . " His character is not in the least degree derived from his significance as a god of nature." Zeus is " the cloud-gatherer " and " caster of thunderbolts." Sacrifice to Zeus is made by fire, the true tribute to the gods of the heavens, and the gift ascends in the smoke and steam of the burnt-offerings. In the Orient, Zeus becomes the representative of Belsemin (Lord of the heavens). Therefore, in his policy of bringing religious uniformity into his kingdom, Antiochus IV. Epiphanes renames the temple of Jahve in Jerusalem the temple of Zeus. Celsus, the opponent of Origen (cont. Cels. 5, 43), can even regard Jahve and Zeus as identical. The common element in both deities which drew them together was their essential nature as heaven-gods. It was this element in Zeus which constituted a conservative antagonism to those cult-practices through

---

[1] Article, " Hypsistos " in Pauly-Wissowa, *Encyclo.*
[2] Cf. Leopold von Schroeder, *Arische Religion*, Bd. i. 1923, p. 453 ; cf. Herodotus I., 131.   [3] Zielinski, *Religion of Ancient Greece*, p. 26.

which was introduced the belief in a personal existence after
death.

We must now describe how the doctrine of a life after death
became a tenet of Greek religion.   The Eleusinian and Dionysian
mysteries, those of Samothrace, the Orphic mysteries which
are a later wave of the Dionysian from Thrace, but a reformed
or protestant [1] version of them, are not of Hellenic origin, but
go back to the pre-Greek period.[2] In the sixth and fifth
centuries B.C. in Athens the mystery religions had a strong
hold,[3] but their progress must have been slow and protracted
up till then.   The word "mysteries" already in antiquity,
as Kern believes, had the meaning of secret practices, and this
secret character, he explains, was due to the circumstance
that, when the Greeks entered the Balkan peninsula as conquerors, the old indigenous cults had to maintain themselves
by secrecy, and the rites had to be performed under the darkness
of night.   The Greek conquerors brought their own gods, the
heaven-divinities.   The old gods of the conquered race were,
however, earth- and underworld-deities, and the mysteries and
rites connected with them proclaimed the teaching of a rebirth
and an after-life.   In this struggle between the two kinds of
divinities the old deities gradually asserted their strength.[4]
It is this struggle which is of supreme interest when we compare
with it a similar phenomenon in the history of the religion of
Israel.

In the Eleusinian mysteries the goddess who is worshipped
is Demeter or Mother-Earth, who shares that honour with her
daughter Kora, who is queen of the underworld.   The mother
is the representative of the ripening grain, and her daughter
of the kernels from which the grain of the coming year will

---

[1] Cf. Orphism, J. R. Watmough, 1934.   [2] Cf. Kern (as below), pp. 4, 5.

[3] Cf. Otto Kern, *Die griechischen Mysterien der klassischen Zeit.*, Berlin,
1927, p. 21. Zielinski, *op. cit.* p. 150, says Dionysus conquers all Greece in the
eighth and seventh centuries B.C.

[4] See Watmough, *op. cit.* p. 29 f. " The Orphics broke away completely
from the cult of the Olympian pantheon."

spring forth. As the grain cast into a furrow of the earth dies to rise again to life, so the souls of the initiated who die and are buried will revive in a new birth.[1] The myth which reflected this teaching was that Kora was carried away by the king of the underworld ; her mother, after long and painful searching,[2] discovers the place of her daughter's abode and gains from her daughter's husband the concession that Kora may spend two-thirds of the year with her mother, while for the other third she remains with her lord of the underworld. In the mystery cults the idea of the underworld is not one of gloom and mourning. The god of the underworld who robs Demeter of her daughter is not called Hades but Pluto—that is, *Plutodotes*, the bestower of wealth. The uninitiated, indeed, lived as pale phantoms, without suffering or pain, in the jaws of Hades when death claimed them, but those who were " stamped with the seal of Eleusis " (*Zielinski*, p. 149) Kora would take by the hand and lead into a realm of happiness below.[3] In contrast with the Homeric Hades, the language of the chthonic cults in regard to the nether world is euphemistic.

We learn of the *dromena*, or cultic rites, of the mystery religions from scattered literary fragments and from representations on vases and from dedicatory reliefs. These rites were of a sacramental character. The vases and reliefs, which evidently depict what the initiated in the Eleusinian mysteries *saw*, show Demeter sitting upon a cista mystica (*cistē*) or round

[1] Cf. The Egyptian festival of " Harrowing the Earth " in the seed-time where mourning for Osiris (identified with the corn) takes place. Mourning for the death of the seed takes place before the joy because of the new crop. Cf. Ps. 126[5] " Who sow in tears, reap in joy," etc. See Gressmann,*Tod und Auferstehung des Osiris*, p. 20. Also *Plutarch De Iside*, 70.

[2] Cf. The Search of Isis (later equated with Demeter) for Osiris, Gressmann, *op. cit.* p. 6 f.

[3] The Orphics were " the first to *moralise* Hades, separating it into penal Tartarus and the blissful Elysium " (Angus, *Religious Quests*, p. 298). The later Orphics regarded the upper world of light as the kingdom of souls (cf. Rhode, *Psyche*, pp. 343, 356 f.). For the Pythagoreans, who were pupils of the Orphics, the stars and planets, especially the sun and moon, were the home of elect souls.

chest of wicker-work, and beside her stands her daughter, "the maiden," holding a torch or two torches. Otto Kern in his work, *The Greek Mysteries of the Classical Period*,[1] describes the mystery rites and their significance thus : "From many representations that refer to the cult of Dionysus we perceive in the midst of a chest that contains all sorts of fruit, the *phallos* (or male pudendum) as token of the never-dying power of nature which ever generates anew. In the Eleusinian chest (*ciste*) lay the counterpart, an imitation of the womb of the mother (the female pudendum), contact with which brought to the initiate the pledge of a new life. Rebirth is thus expressed in a symbolic act in a tangible manner, in accordance with ancient belief and rite." How this contact with the image of the female organ was effected by the initiate is a matter of speculation. Kern suggests an act of masturbation. Alfred Korte [2] supposes that the initiate drew the image gently over his body. But, in any case, there is no doubt about the act itself, for Clement of Alexandria, expressing his moral indignation at the mysteries, refers to the Eleusinian sacramental formula, "I fasted, I drank the mixed-drink, I took from the chest (*cistē*), worked therewith (ἐργασάμενος), put it then in the basket (*kalathos*), and out of the basket into the chest " (*Protr.* II. 21, 2). From Clements' words we can read the meaning of the rite. The handling of the organ of fertility was a pledge of divine sonship. This, with the drinking of the wine, was the central act, and preparation for the sacrament was fasting. Through the sacrament the worshipper became an *Epoptes*, that is, *one who has seen*. The torches which Kora carries in the representations symbolize the purification which the Epopt must undergo ; the ear of corn shown with the images of Demeter and Kora signify the new life which Mother-Earth and Kora bring forth from the deeps of their realms. The myrtle wreath which he

[1] Page 10.
[2] " Zu den Eleusinischen Mysterien," *Arch. für Relig.-Wiss.*, Bd. xviii. 1915, p. 121

who was initiated in the mysteries wore was a sign of his dedication to the divinity. The immunity of the worshipper from
death, as now being through the *ritus* a son of Kora, is expressed
in the sentence, "I came under the member of the mistress,
the queen of the underworld." [1]

Now the mystery religions which opened up the underworld
and dispelled its gloom by the teaching of a rebirth and
immortality through the means of adoption by, or union with,
the deities of vegetation and fertility met with the opposition
of the heaven-gods. The thought of the blue heaven which
arches far above man is remote to the mysteries where hopes
are concentrated upon the earth, which in spring brings forth
new life and in the depths of which strange powers that man
fears lie hid. The marvel of life, its waxing, waning, and re-
emergence constituted for the Ægean region the ancient
elements of religious thought. This was not destroyed by the
religion of the heavenly Zeus, but was opposed by him and
restrained.[2] The mystery religions, therefore, took upon them,
in self-defence, also the outward precautions of secrecy. The
process of opposition is more plainly seen when we take regard
to the Greek god Apollo. Apollo is by nature a god of light,
a heaven-divinity. At Delphi, his seat, he had already suppressed an earth-goddess. When, however, the Dionysian
worship made headway in Greece, Apollo was forced to make
concessions to the powerful vegetation god and to share Delphi
with him, assimilating many of the characteristics of Dionysus.
How complete the victory of the latter was is evident from the
fact that as becomes a fertility divinity who dies to rise again,
the grave of Dionysus was shown at Delphi. But the battle
had been intense. According to Zielinski (p. 152) it was the
repression of the primitive religion of Dionysus which occasioned
the new wave of it from Thrace under the name of Orphism.

---

[1] *Orphicorum fragmenta collegit*, Otto Kern, 1922, p. 107. Cf. J. Leipoldt,
Dionysus (Angelos-Beiheft, 3, 1931), p. 22, who translates "Ich glitt unter den
Schoss der Herrin, etc."   [2] Kern, *Die griech. Myst.*, p. 6.

The sharpness of the conflict may also be noted when we view
the association of Dionysus with Zeus. The religions of Zeus
and Dionysus had also to blend. A mythology arises which,
relating the struggle between Zeus and the Titans and the death
of Dionysus-Zagreus, records the birth of a second Dionysus
as son of Zeus and Semele. This second Dionysus becomes even
more powerful than Zeus. But that this sacred legend reconciling the two divinities did not find easy acceptance is shown
in the Bacchæ of Euripides (in the 4th cent.) where Pen-
theus, attacking the worshippers of Dionysus, states that
Dionysus is not a son of Zeus, but that his mother Semele had
only alleged this, and that therefore Zeus had struck her and
her child with lightning-fire (Bacc. 242 f.). Opposition to the
Dionysian religion was, of course, based on its orgies, its excesses,
its appeal to women, and on suppositions, of the uninitiated, as
to its immoralities. But behind this hostility was the conflict
between the two types of gods. That both kinds of opposition
mingled is seen from a terracotta relief which portrays a kneeling
maiden, a worshipper of Dionysus, uncovering a corn-sieve in
which are fruits and a phallos. Behind her approaches a satyr.
Before her hovers the figure of a winged Olympian goddess
who would turn away in horror and escape, although the
kneeling girl seeks to hold the goddess fast, catching at her
robe.[1] Even after Greece had accepted the mystery religions
and their teaching, and was well acquainted with, if not wholly
reconciled [2] to the notion of a dying and reviving god, a notion
which comprehended deity, plants, and man in a like experience,
echoes of the warfare between the heavenly and the chthonic
divinities are still heard. Xenophanes, a pre-Socratic phil-
osopher, criticises the Egyptians for bewailing the death of
Osiris, on the ground that if Osiris were a god he could not die.

[1] H. v. Rohden und H. Winnefeld, *Architektonische römische Tonreliefs der
Kaiserzeit*, 1911, p. 52.   Cf. Johannes Leipoldt, *Sterbende und auferstehende
Götter*, 1932, p. 71.

[2] J. Leipoldt, *op. cit.*, pp. 5, 25, says that for Greek piety the thought that
Kora, Dionysus, Orpheus, and other deities die, falls into the background.

Several centuries later, Callimachos of Cyrene ridicules the Cretans for building a tomb of Zeus in Crete ; and still later this protest is taken up by Pseudo-Epimenides : " A tomb they built for thee, O holy and high One ; the Cretans, liars, evil beasts, and lazy bellies ; thou art not dead, thou art alive and remaineth for ever ; for in thee we live and move and have our being." [1] The indiscretion which the Cretans committed in subjecting Zeus himself to the conceptions to which that deity was hostile, shows the completeness of the triumph of the earth- and underworld-divinities who had introduced the doctrine of immortality to the Greeks. It is now a far cry to the time when Poseidon, the god of the ocean, had to tell Zeus to mind his own business, to keep to his realm of the skies and clouds, attend to his own sons and daughters, and leave him, as king of the ocean, and Hades, the king of the underworld, to manage their affairs in their own distinctive realms (*Iliad*, xv. 184–199).

Although Jahvism in the pre-exilic age, and in the centuries after the exile up to the Hellenistic period, did not come into contact with the Greek mysteries, early Israel was well-acquainted with the idea of dying and reviving divinities, a conception prevalent in its surroundings, and which either contained or was capable of developing into the belief that man himself could survive the event of death. It is our task to show that it was the character of Jahve as heaven-god which countered that idea and postponed that belief.

In the Old Testament there is evidence of the penetration of the practices of the Adonis festival into Israel, and that consequently Israel could not have been unconversant with the Adonis myth and the intention of this Phœnician cult. The myth has two forms : the first narrates that Astarte, the equivalent of the Greek Aphrodite, entrusted the child Adonis to the goddess of the underworld. Astarte had placed the

---

[1] *Commentaries of Isho'dad of Merv*, edited and translated by Margaret Dunlop Gibson, vol. iv. (*Horæ Semiticæ*, x. 1913).

child in a box. The goddess of the underworld opens the box and is so pleased with him that she desires to keep him for herself. The judgment of heaven is invoked by the two deities, and it is decided that Adonis remain part of the year with Astarte above, and part of the year with her rival, below the earth. In the second form of the myth, which possibly has been influenced by the Egyptian Osiris legend, Adonis is a youth, beloved of Astarte. While hunting one day he receives fatal wounds from a boar (or a bear) and dies in the arms of the mourning Astarte.[1] The Adonis myth is clearly a nature-myth reflecting the growth and decay of vegetation and man's prayer for the reappearance of the plants and fruits of the earth. There was, as Theocritus [2] tells us, and as we might naturally expect, much joyousness in the festival of Adonis, but the celebration culminated in mourning the death of the god, and this mourning became the most notable feature of the ritual. The intention of the cult of Adonis was to cause the deity to beget or bring new fertility to the world, that is, to effect the resurrection of the god from death to new life. " Adonis-gardens " were prepared by the female celebrants. Adonis-images were also made. These " gardens " were pots or vessels filled with earth sown with seeds that quickly sprouted into shoots and plants and wilted again in the summer heat. At the end of the festival both gardens and images were thrown into rivers and streams, this action being, as Sir James Frazer describes,[3] a charm to obtain refreshing rain for the wheat and barley of the coming year. The vegetable-form of the god, represented by the gardens, and the human form, portrayed

---

[1] Another variation of this myth, evidently derived from the Egyptian Osiris myth (see below), is that Adonis was drowned. Probably the Sumerian tradition that Tammuz, with whom Adonis is equated, was drowned in " the river " (*i.e.* Tigris or Euphrates) comes from the Adonis myth. For the link between the Egyptian Osiris myth and the Tammuz-Adonis myth, see Hooke's essay, p. 82 f., in *Myth and Ritual.*

[2] " Adoniazousai," cf. Gressmann in *Expositor*, 1925, ix. vol. viii. " The Mysteries of Adonis and the Feast of Tabernacles."

[3] *Adonis, Attis, Osiris*, p. 194 f.

by the images, were cast upon the waters that the bread of man might in the future be secure. The *dromena* of the festival, as we may gather from Theocritus, were the erecting of booths in the courts or on the roofs of the houses,[1] the placing of images of Adonis and Astarte in each booth as representation of "the sacred marriage," the setting of the Adonis-garden near the booth, the singing and rejoicing, and, finally, the mourning of the women who took their "gardens" and images and cast them in the streams, calling out, "Come back again." Gressmann (*op. cit.*) concludes from the rites and intention of the festival of Adonis that the Hebrew Feast of Booths, held after the fruits of the earth had been gathered in, is derived from the Adonis festival celebrated by the Canaanites.[2]   The

[1] Cf. Ezek. 8[14] ; Plut. Nicias 13.

[2] In "*Myth and Ritual* (Essays by Blackman, Gadd, Hollis, Hooke, James, Oesterley, Robinson, Oxford Univ. Press, 1933) the thesis is presented that Canaanite and Hebrew myth and ritual are traceable to a "pattern" myth and ritual which existed in Egypt and Babylon (p. xviii), and was associated there with an annual (New Year) festival. The "pattern" contained the following elements : a dramatic representation (a) of the death and resurrection of the god ; (b) of the myth of creation ; (c) of the ritual combat in which the god conquers his enemies ; (d) of the sacred marriage ; and (e) a triumphal procession of the deified reigning king who played the part of the god, who was followed by a train of lesser deities (cf. p. 8). The Hebrew festivals exhibit portions of this "pattern" which as it spread in Canaan underwent disintegration and adaptation. In particular the three festivals, Unleavened Bread, Weeks, and Booths represent the breaking up of the myth and ritual of the Babylonian *Akitu* festival held at the New Year (in Nisan and Tishri). See essay by Oesterley, pp. 112, 145. With this thesis of the essayists Gressman's view that the Hebrew Booths is derived from the Canaanite Adonis festival is not irreconcilable ; for the Canaanite Adonis festival may quite well go back to the Egyptian-Babylonian pattern and yet be the first source from which the Hebrew festival of Ingathering or Booths derives. Indeed, this is the most probable supposition. The Hebrews would first come into contact with those fragments of the "pattern" which the Canaanite had adopted. Oesterley appears to attempt to work too much of "the pattern" into Booths, *e.g.* the ritual combat. Booths may, with the passing of time, have undergone more elaboration in accordance with the pattern, but his comparison of the booth of Marduk with a supposed booth of Jahve at Jerusalem has not the same naturalness and spontaneity as a comparison of the Adonis booths and the booths at the Hebrew festival of Ingathering. The simplicity of the Canaanite festival of Ingathering as seen in Judg. 21[19f.]

cycle of events extending from the first of the month of Tishri, and including the festival of Booths (15–22 Tishri) was signalized by both mourning (fasting) and rejoicing. Even to very late times the Jews were, it would seem, sensible of the fact that the ritual of " the water drawing " from the pool of Siloam, and the water-libation at the altar at the Feast of Booths was in intention a rain-charm, for the Talmud explains the reason of this libation as being, " that the rains of the year may be blessed to you." [1] Both Gressmann and Oesterley (*op. cit.*) regard the booths in the festival of Booths as having their original significance in the representation of " the sacred marriage " of the god and goddess of fertility, and connect with this the rite of " sacred prostitution," which even the rising standard of Hebrew ethical and religious thought had difficulty in eradicating.

The question now presents itself whether, in the Adonis cult, besides the idea of the decay and reappearance of vegetation and the rites that promoted fertility there was any thought of the drama of the dying and reviving god being a symbol of man's dying and surviving death ? Although the living are in general less occupied with the thought of their own mortality than with endeavours to promote their present prosperity, and although the Adonis festival thus bears the stamp and broad significance of a nature festival, there is evidence that it also bore in the minds of the celebrants the conception of personal immortality. The Adonis festival which Theocritus describes as having taken place in Alexandria in 273 B.C., that is, more than a century before the doctrine of an After-life appears in the Book of Daniel, was, at the expense

would seem to supply more nearly the model of the Hebrew festival of Booths as held at least in the earliest period. Also the " booth " of Marduk at the *Akitu* festival does not offer so close a parallel to the practices at the Hebrew festival as the booths of Adonis on the roofs and in the courts present.

[1] Rosh-hashana, 16a. To be noted also, is the close connection in later Judaism between the prayer for rain and the prayer to God " who awakens the dead." Cf. Bousset, *Rel. d. Jud.*, p. 370.

of Queen Arsinoe, celebrated with special pomp as a thanks-giving, because her departed mother Berenice " had been received among the goddesses." Here we note the same euphemistic language regarding the dead as Kern points to in the chthonic religion of the Greek mysteries. The Adonis festival in Alexandria in Egypt may, no doubt, have been influenced by the Osiris worship with its pronounced teaching of a future life, but that influence must have already penetrated the home of the Adonis worhip, Phœnicia, from a very early period. That feature of the Adonis-myth, which reports that Adonis was drowned, and which is discernible in the Alexandrian festival where the image of the god is cast into the sea, is generally recognized as being an importation from the Osiris myth. The Phœnician Adonis myth related that Adonis was killed by a boar. It was Osiris who was drowned ; and when, in Plutarch's account [1] of the Egyptian myth, it is told that Osiris' body was borne by the sea to Byblos in Phœnicia, we seem here to have some indication of there having been contact between the two myths and rituals. But the relations between Phœnicia and Egypt are extremely old, and therefore we cannot suppose that any of the rites of Adonis as practised at Alexandria in 273 B.C., or the concept of the divine drama of death and resurrection reflecting man's hope of blessedness beyond were recently acquired features. The Greek vases from Attica, with representations of the Adonis ritual, are from tombs of the fifth and fourth centuries B.C.[2] This may not be conclusive evidence of the belief in immortality attaching to the Adonis worship, but it has certainly much confirmative value. Even, however, if we were to assume that this belief did not attach originally to the Adonis worship, the probability is that this attachment was very early effected by the medium of Egypt and the Osiris myth.

---

[1] *Die Iside,* 12–20.
[2] Friedrich Hauser, *Adoniazousai (Jahreshefte des oestreichischen arch. Institut. in Wien* xii. 1909), p. 90 f.   Cf. Leipoldt, *op. cit.* p. 19.

Now, in addition to those resemblances in ritual and motive which cause Gressmann to conclude that the Hebrew Festival of Booths is a derivative of the Canaanite Adonis festival, two passages in the Old Testament are of importance to our inquiry into Israel's knowledge of the cult of Adonis and its meaning. The prophet Isaiah in the eighth century makes open reference to the " Adonis gardens," their significance as symbolizing the perishing of vegetation, and to the ritual mourning. Addressing Israel (17[10f.]) he says :

> " For thou hast forgotten the god of thy help,
> And the rock of thy strength hast not kept in mind ;
> Therefore though thou plant plants of Adonis,[1]
> And sow it with the slips of a strange (God),
>
> .   .   .   .
>
> (Yet) vanished is the harvest in the day of sickness
> And doleful pain."

From the context it is clear that North Israel (Ephraim) had made league with the Syrians against Assyria. Isaiah condemns the political alliance, and at the same time Israel's disloyalty to Jahve in taking over the cult-form of a foreign god. The passage reveals such marks of the Adonis festival as its celebration at the end of harvest, and the part played in it by women. Israel is addressed by the feminine " thou." How indefinite Israel's religious boundaries are at this time and later is shown by their variation in accordance with political circumstances.

But more illuminating even than the poem of Isaiah is the description, in the sixth chapter of Hosea, of Israel, after her desertion, of Jahve, returning to her own lord and master for help and healing. Professor Hempel [2] sees in this utterance of Hosea a reference to the Adonis worship, and certainly this interpretation sheds a light upon the thought of the passage which otherwise would contain only pale and general conceptions. Hosea describes Ephraim and Judah as saying :

[1] Cf. Duhm's *Kommentar, ad loc.* p. 107.
[2] *Gebet und Frömmigkeit im A.T.*, 1922, p. 24 f. So also Baudissin and Sellin, *op. cit.* p. 145 above.

" Come and let us return unto Jahve !
For he has torn us and he will heal us,
He has struck us and he will bind us up.
After two days he will revive us
And on the third day he will raise us
To live under his care.

.   .   .   .   .   .

He will come to us like rain
Like the late rain that waters the earth " (6$^{1\text{-}3}$).

The expressions " bind us up," " revive us," " raise us," are in
the Hosean passage vivid metaphors of general welfare, but
they suggest that their real context and background is one of
ideas, rites, and beliefs where the metaphorical is altogether
absent.   The expressions " after two days," " on the third
day," are not satisfactorily explained as a speech-idiom
intending a round number or a short time, or as having their
origin in a supposed popular belief that the soul hovers over
the grave for three days before leaving the dead body.[1]   When
we know that the old Egyptian tradition concerning Osiris
was that he died on the 17th Athyr and rose again on the
19th, on the third day,[2] it is far more probable that we have in
Hosea another trace of the Egyptian influence upon the Adonis
myth.   If this conclusion be justified, we are presented by this
Hebrew document of the eighth century B.C. with testimony
of the conception of a future life attaching to the Adonis-worship
and ritual.   In the oracle of Isaiah we observe the *ritus* of the
worship ; in Hosea its meaning and significance.

It now behoves us to examine more closely the nature and
principle of the resistance which Jahvism offered to those
deities of vegetation through whom was opened up a way of
approach to a doctrine of personal immortality.   Though

---

[1] Cf. Midrash Rabba, Gen. 50^{19} ; Lev. 15^{1} for this belief.   Cf. Bousset
(*Rel. d. Jud.*, 3rd ed., p. 297 note ^{1}), who points out that this belief has only
late witness.

[2] In Rome the death of the Phrygian deity Attis was celebrated on 22nd
March and his resurrection on 25th March.   Cf. Hepding, *Attis, seine Mythen
und sein Kult*, 1903, pp. 149 f., 167 f.

Jahvism in the pre-exilic period had occupied at times no higher
level than that of the local *Baals* or divinities of the land of
Canaan, although, like every living religion, it had borrowed
from its environment, particularly in festival rites, the victory
of Jahve over the Baals, as Hölscher (*op. cit.* 70) expresses it,
is the content of Israel's pre-exilic history. The local Baals
were, in general, deities who presided over the fertility and
gifts of the earth. The conflict of Jahvism with them has its
great memorial in the story of Elijah and the destruction of
the prophets of Baal. The fertility Baal cannot consume by
fire the sacrifice upon the altar which his priests have prepared,
but at the prayer of Elijah fire from heaven consumes the offering
on the altar of Jahve. " The fire of Jahve fell (from heaven
LXX) and consumed the offering " (1 Kings 18[38]). It was a
victory of the heaven-god, the old lightning-god, over the earth
deities, and the point of the story is that it is Jahve and not
the earth deity who dispels the drought and sends the rain to
the famished land. The dances which the worshippers of Baal
performed round their altar belong to the ritual of the fertility
gods, but in the contest with Jahve these rites are of no avail.
More than a century later than the period of Elijah, namely,
in the days of Hosea, we gain a view of the relationship of
Jahvism and Baalism quite uncoloured by legendary features.
The challenge which Elijah offered in behalf of Jahvism is still
taken up by Baalism. From Hosea we learn that the Israelites,
whose interests were now agricultural, had a very natural
attraction to the fertility deities and their cults, and, therefore,
had approximated the Jahve-cult to the cults of the various
Baals.[1] From the words which the prophet puts into the mouth
of the apostate people we discern that the question at issue
with them, which they tried to remove by a religious syncretism,
concerned Jahve's nature as heaven-God. The people say :
" I will follow after my lovers (that is, the Baals) who give me
my bread and water, my wool, flax, oil, and drink " (2[7] in Heb.).

---

[1] See Nowack, *Amos and Hosea*, Strassburg, 1908, p. 35.

The Baals had their particular sphere, the earth and its fruits, and performed their important business. Just as in the Elijah story it is Jahve who sends the rain to renew the vegetation, an office which in any case belonged to him as heaven-god, so Hosea affirms that the fruits of the earth are Jahve's gift. But the attachment of Jahve to nature could never become the same as that of the fertility deities, especially of those gods who died and rose again. When Hosea does describe Jahve as a fertility god, he does so through a series of gradations : " And it shall come to pass on that day, says Jahve, I will bespeak the heavens, the heavens shall bespeak the earth, the earth shall bespeak the grain, the new wine, and the oil, and they shall bespeak Jezreel (*i.e.* Israel)." [1] The character of Jahve as heaven-god is accentuated by the prophetic ethics and by the idea of him as the guide of Israel's history. He is enthroned in heavenly majesty in Isaiah's vision (chap. 6), in all respects the same as in that later description of him as " the high and uplifted One, who sits (enthroned) for ever " (Isa. 57[15f.]). The prophetic polemic against the Jahve-cultus could neither abolish this nor prevent it from assimilating rites of the Baal-worship, but the prophets conserved the ancient conception of Jahve as heaven-divinity which they moralized, spiritualized, and deepened.[2] The gap between Jahve and the chthonic god Adonis became as wide, if not wider, than ever, and thus a doctrine of a future life based upon the conception that the divine drama of dying and rising prefigured human destiny, or that man identified with or in union with the [3] deity could partake of the divine experience, had no chance of development. Such fertility rites

---

[1] From Dr. Moffatt trans. with slight emendation, *e.g.* " Jahve " " bespeak " (for answer). Cf. Gressmann, *ad loc.* in *S.A.T.* " *besprechen.*"

[2] Cf. Jer. 23[24] " Do I (Jahve) not fill heaven and earth ? "—a protest against a too local view of Jahve as heaven-god.

[3] Cf. W. W. Baudissin, " Gottschauen " (*Archiv. für Religionswissenschaft*, Bd. xviii. 1915, p. 232, note 1), says, that when the union of man with God is stated to be the aim of Oriental religions (so Norden in *Agnostos Theos.*, p. 97), this generalization is misleading. " Where, on Semitic soil—*e.g.* Syrian-Phœnician—this aim is adumbrated in the cultic practices, such as in the

as Jahvism adopted had reference to him solely as heaven-god, who caused increase by sending sunshine and rain.

A comparison of Jahvism with the religion of Babylonia is instructive. Here Tammuz and Ishtar are the counterpart of Adonis and Astarte. Tammuz, sometimes in our sources hardly distinguishable from Adonis, is a god who dies and rises again. Ishtar, goddess of love and fertility, descends into the underworld presumably in order to seek for him. Tammuz represents the decline of natural growth in midsummer; there is mourning for his disappearance to the underworld; his reappearance or waking comes in the forces of spring. But noteworthy of the worship of Tammuz is, as Johannes Leipoldt states, "the worshippers of Tammuz limited themselves to the worship of nature; all other peoples who honour a god who dies and rises to life, connect the experience of the god in some way or other with human destiny and not merely with nature." [1] Leipoldt gives no reason for this very significant break in the development of Babylonian thought. But we may discover the reason in that trait of Babylonian religion which Jastrow describes as "the hostility existing between the upper and lower pantheon," [2] between the gods of the world above and the divinities of the subterranean region. This differentiation Jastrow ascribes to the systematizing of the pantheon by the priests, who were zealous in defining the rank and functions of the gods, and as leading in consequence to the view that the deities of the upper sphere "exercised control of the living only, who upon death passed out of their supervision." Here the parallel with the religion of the Old Testament is very close—the old conception

---

imitation of the fertilizing power of the deity, these cult-forms appear to derive from Asia Minor, namely, from the Cybele and Attis worship. . . . These cult-forms, however, penetrated Syro-Phœnicia from very early times, probably through the medium of the Hittites. . . . In Egypt in other forms the same aim of establishing identity of man with the divinity appears. The thought is altogether absent from the Hebrews and Arabs."

[1] *Op. cit.* p. 28.

[2] " Religion of Babylonia," *H.B.D.*, p. 575; p. 544, Ex. volume.

of Jahve as heaven-god being strengthened and spiritualized by the prophets, and Jahve's interest being confined to the living. In Jahvism also, the festival of Booths remains purely on the level of a nature festival.

In Babylonia the conditions, apart from the circumstances that we have just observed, were otherwise not unfavourable to the evolving of a mystery-cult. As in Egypt the Sun-god was conceived of as travelling through the night the lower regions and lighting up the caverns of the dead, so the Babylonian underworld is visited by the solar deities, Tammuz, Nergal, and Bel-Marduk. Nergal, who appears to symbolize the wasting sun of noon, enters, equipped with the powers of pestilence, the realm of Erishkigal, forces her to submit to him, marries her, and thus becomes king of the dead. But this mythology only deepens the impression of wretchedness that pertains to the Babylonian conception of the place of the departed. Even Ishtar, "the lady of the earth," who, though an astral deity (Venus, Sirius), appears to have been primarily an earth-goddess, is afflicted on her descent to the world below with sufferings, indignities, and diseases. However, as the Adapa and Gilgamesh myths show, there were questionings as to the possibility of man escaping death and attaining immortality. Meissner, therefore, thinks that these myths may possibly have played a part as festival-roll in mystery celebrations where the idea of a future life came to expression, although the literary sources which we have at present bear no evidence of this.[1] If this hypothesis be ever justified through new knowledge, it would prove that the effects of the priestly systematization of the pantheon had at length been overcome. But though certain conditions for a mystery cult were present in Babylonian religion, it would seem that they never came to development nor overthrew the official teaching of the underworld as a land of no return and of gloom.

In the Old Testament, in the Jahvistic account of creation, the power of becoming immortal is put beyond the reach of man.

[1] *Op. cit.* Bd. ii., p. 187; cf. pp. 139, 196.

The tree of life, a significant vegetable symbol of the means to that power, is forever placed beyond his grasp. This accords with the Babylonian belief that the gods have retained life in their own power. Jahvism was not able to suppress the Sheol conception out of which through the acceptance of chthonic divinities there emerged in Greece, Egypt, and Phœnicia the belief in immortality. But it rendered that belief sterile and innocuous, and met the idea of a future life which attached to the notion of dying and reviving gods, deities of the earth and underworld, by holding firmly to the conception of Jahve as heaven-divinity. Psalm 115 might be regarded as the triumph song of Jahve's resistance, and at the same time as a theological statement of this aspect of Hebrew thought. The nations say : " Where is their God ? " The answer is : " Our God is in heaven." Jahve is all powerful, blesses, and increases his people. It is the gods of the nations who are powerless.

> "The heavens, the heavens belong to Jahve
> But the earth he has assigned to men.
> The dead cannot praise Jah
> Nor any who sink to the silent land" (v. [16f.]).

Professor Pettazzoni,[1] in his study of the development of monotheism, concludes that " there is an essential identity of character in the sole gods of the different monotheistic religions inasmuch as they have all been originally heaven-gods," and that in many polytheistic religions where there are monotheistic currents of thought, as for example, in Babylonia, where the first god of the first triad is Anu the sky-god, the supreme divinity is of this class and type. Our inquiry into the retarded development and late appearance of a doctrine of a future life in Israel has brought into the field of vision this same feature of Jahve's nature[2] as a concept which contained not only the

[1] " La formation du monothéisme," p. 204. Cf. p. 209 in *Revue de l'histoire des religions*, 1923, Nov.-Dec. tome 88, nr. 3.

[2] The recently discovered Ras Shamra tablets (Virolleaud, in *Syria*, vol. xii. pl. iii., 1931, pp. 193-194) witness to the presence in Canaanite religion in early

power to promote, but likewise to check and delay, the growth of theological belief.

times of the concept of a struggle between the chief gods El and Baal and between El's son Mot and Baal's son Aleyn.   We hear of Baal's death and resurrection and of the deaths and rising again of Mot and Aleyn.   It does not clearly appear, however, that this early Canaanite (Phœnician) mythology regarded these conflicts as being between heaven-gods and earth-gods.   For Aleyn and Mott (see J. W. Jack, *The Ras Shamra Tablets*, 1935, p. 13 f.) are both deities of vegetation, and El, though a solar god, and Baal a god of thunder, seem each to combine the characteristics of a sky- and earth-divinity.

CHAPTER VIII

Post-Exilic Monotheism and the Idea of Immortality

1

A SECOND cause of the late development within the religion of Israel of a doctrine of an after-life is to be found in the relationship which Jahve, the god of post-exilic Hebrew monotheism, holds to Nature or matter. This cause is subsidiary, since it evolves from the conception of Jahve as heaven-god, but, as it possesses distinctive power and effects of its own, it requires to be regarded independently. From the time of second Isaiah, monotheism comes to clear expression, and consequently only now could the thought of Jahve as Creator and Controller of the world have effective result in Hebrew religion. The idea of Jahve as Creator had long before been taken over by Israel from Babylonian mythology,[1] but only now does it become a tenet consciously possessed and a religious dogma of Judaism. But with the conception of Jahve as Maker and sole Ruler of the universe there enters the consciousness of His transcendence, not only in relation to men who now feel more acutely their sinfulness and distance from the divinity, but in relation to Nature itself. Hence, intermediaries arise, angels and Wisdom (Pr. 8[22f.]) as divine agents to fill the gap between the deity and the world of men and the world of matter. In the hymn on Wisdom, in the first section of the Book of Proverbs, though God is the Creator and Wisdom is created and subordinate, God from the beginning has worked through Wisdom, His instrument.[2] God as Creator is thus exalted above His world. The danger of Jahve becoming identified with Nature is made

---

[1] Cf. Stade, *Bib-Theol. d. A.T.*, p. 304.   [2] Cf. Oesterley, *Prov.*, p. 61 f.

more remote and thus the road, by which the doctrine of immortality came to neighbouring peoples through the drama of Nature's decay and growth being regarded as representing the death and resurrection of a god, was closed and rendered for ever impassable. To reach the goal of belief in an after-life, Israel was forced to go by another and a longer route.

In spite of Jahve's transcendence, we have to note that with the idea of Jahve as Creator and sole Author of life, from the time of the Exile onwards, there is a higher appreciation of the grandeur, beauty, and wonder of Nature. After, as well as before the Exile, Jahve's power is seen in the abnormal and catastrophic, and before as well as after that time He manifests Himself in Nature's silent operations. But in the period we are now considering, in second Isaiah, the Book of Job, and in certain of the Psalms, the idea of the manifestation of God's purpose and power in the material world seems to grow stronger. In Psalm 139 which, on account of style and speech, must be regarded as a relatively late composition, Jahve's omniscience and omnipresence come to classical expression: " My very thoughts Thou readest from afar " (v.[2]), " where could I go from Thy spirit, where could I flee from Thy presence ? " These reflections, as Gunkel remarks,[1] are foreign to Israel's early conceptions of Jahve's power. Also Psalm 104, the singularly powerful hymn on God's majesty and might, who makes the clouds His chariot and is the providence who provides for all His creatures their food in due season, must, even if it bases upon the Egyptian sun-hymn of the period of Amenophis IV., belong to our period, since it shows traces of a knowledge of the later account of Creation (Gen. 1) in the Priestly Code.[2] In second Isaiah (40) the Creator's omnipotence, the idea of the order, adjustment, and proportion in Nature as deriving from an infinite Intelligence which does not overlook a single star, is expressed with a boldness of conception that has nothing equal

---

[1] *Ausgewählte Psalmen*, p. 267 f; cf. Jer. 17[10], 23[24].
[2] Cf. Gunkel, *op. cit.* p. 214.

to it in earlier literature.[1] To Jahve's power there is nothing
comparable ; the great material masses and expanses of the
world are, as it were, in the hollow of the Creator's hand. Progress, also, in man's outlook upon Nature is perceived in the
Book of Job. In the Divine Speeches (chap. 38f.) Nature is looked
upon for the first time objectively, not merely as subserving
man's purposes and uses. God has not given man sway (cf. Ps. 8 ;
Gen. 2[46f.]) over all things He has made, putting all things under
man's feet, for so much in heaven and earth lies beyond man's
horizon, power, and use. The author of the Divine Speeches is
not filled with that subjective melancholy which mourns the
flower that is born to blush unseen, nor concludes that, therefore,
it wastes its sweetness. God's purpose, too, is fulfilled where no
man lives, there in the uninhabited deserts where the green-
sward gladdens the lonely wastes (Job 38[26f.]). The instincts of
animals, the variety of Nature's resources, the mystery in things
above and below, are all parts of a divine design, only the smallest
part of which is comprehended by man. But what man does
see, the poet concludes, must produce in him wonder, reverence,
and humility (42[3]).

Only with the explicit monotheism that comes with second
Isaiah could the idea of Jahve as Creator come to its own in the
realm of doctrine. In the literature reviewed, justice is done
to the Creator-God as all-powerful, all-knowing, and all-present,
and to the order and design in Nature. What is important to
observe is that the older conception, though it was by no means
the only or the oldest conception, of Jahve as related to Nature
as a workman or artist is related to His work (Gen. 2[46f.]) now
becomes a *theological* idea. In second Isaiah all things are
doubtless accomplished in Nature by the mere volition of Jahve,
but whether the author employs the verbs " do " ('asah),
" form " (jazar) or " create " (bara) in describing the deity's
action, he is always thinking of Jahve organizing material that
already exists.[2] In the story of Creation in the Priestly Code

[1] Cf. Skinner, Isa. 40 [4f.] in Cambridge Bible, p. 6.   [2] Stade, *op. cit.* p. 305 f.

(Gen. 1), the idea that God is the author of all things is indicated but is not carried through : God is the fashioner of world-stuff already at hand. In the Book of Job, too, particularly in the Divine Speeches (38$^{f.}$), Jahve is never represented as more than the Shaper of the world and the fashioning of the individual beings is *done* ('asah) by Him. It is only in later Judaism that the complete idea of an absolute Creation appears, and accordingly the Book of Jubilees (chap. 2) and 4 Ezra (6^{38}) silently correct the Genesis account.

A second effect of the working out of the monotheistic idea after the Exile, was that although this period eschewed the cruder anthropomorphisms of the earlier periods, yet the anthropomorphic conception of deity which philosophic thought in its progress tends to shed, finding some expression like the Greek τὸ Θεῖον, was retained in service, thus heightening the personality of Jahve above the world-substance. His individuality was thus insured against being merged in the cosmic processes, and protected against the more or less pantheistic character of the Nature deities.[1] The vegetation rites of the fertility Baals, with whom for five centuries,[2] from, say, 1350–850 B.C., Jahve had been in close association, assimilating their qualities, had become rooted in Israel's festival practices. These continued in popular thought to have the magical power of promoting growth. But now, over against the concept of *transcendent animation* [3] which signifies the power of a god to indwell a certain element and yet to be independent of it, there was placed the more rigid teaching of a transcendent *Artifex*, of sharply individual personality, differentiated from all His works. The old Jahve of the desert had indwelt the lightning, the cloud, and the storm ; had gone into battle with the ark ; could, as fertility-Baal, have an appropriate symbol in the bull-image which Jeroboam I. erected in north Israel. Even in the post-

---

[1] Cf. Meyer, *Ursprung*, etc., Bd. ii. p. 22.

[2] Hölscher, *op. cit.* p. 89. Cf. p. 70.

[3] A phrase used by the anthropologist Marett. Cf. Zielinski, *op. cit.* p. 62.

exilic age these conceptions of Jahve's operation in Nature did not easily die out, if indeed they ever did die out. Even if the author of Trito-Isaiah (537-520 ?) be addressing, as Duhm thinks, Israelites in Samaria, he is by no means exerting himself to attack a mere religious idiosyncrasy on the part of a section of his race when he writes scathingly of a certain fertility rite, akin to the " sacred marriage."

> " And behind the door and the posts hast thou set up thy Phallus-
>   image
>   And for its sake thou hast opened out and ascended and made broad
>   thy bed ;
>   And hast purchased for thyself such as thou lovest to lie with "
>   (57).[1]

Without doubt it was not until from the old relationship of the nation to Jahve there emerged the congregation of Israel or Jewish Church under the leadership of Nehemiah and Ezra (c. 458–420 B.C.) which subjected life and worship to a religious orthodoxy, that the nature rites of Israel were defined in scope, refined in character, and subordinated to a new theological interpretation. Traces of this occurring bring us to a third phase of Hebrew monotheistic thought.

Together with the monotheism latent in the pre-exilic prophets, but only becoming explicit in second Isaiah there was closely associated the belief, which also had its roots in the earlier period, that Jahve was the controller and director of the history of all peoples. In second Isaiah this thought likewise finds its clearest and most impressive literary monument. Israel stands in the centre of world-history. The chosen people is called to be the light of the nations. Its political history under this view has been, and is, the history of religion *par excellence*. The post-exilic period stands under the sign of this religious-historical outlook upon Israel and the world. It is in this period, stretching

---

[1] For translation, see Duhm's *Kommentar* and notes, *ad loc.* Cf. Moffatt's translation.

from second Isaiah to the great *dénouement* of history described in the eschatological picture in Daniel, that the words of Emil Brunner prove abundantly true : " In the Old Testament the Creator is not spoken of . . . as in Aristotle, as if He were to be known from the works of Nature, but as the Lord of His people through the discipline of history and the revealed prophetic word . . . The knowledge which we acquire of the Creator does not belong to the *theologia naturalis* but to the *theologia revelata*." [1] In the light of this powerful theological conception with its religious-historical bias, and in view of that natural theology which was fruitful elsewhere in promoting belief in immortality, it is instructive to observe a process that was neither begun in this time nor completed, but which was now revived. The old nature festivals are after the Priestly Code appears, all with the exception of the Feast of Weeks which later was made commemorative of the Giving of the Law on Sinai, transplanted from their original ground and soil, namely, mother-earth itself, and given historical interpretation. Passover was the spring-festival of the pastoral period when a victim from the herd was sacrificed in atonement for the family. Early it became commemorative of the freedom from Egypt.[2] The feast of Unleavened Bread which had marked the beginning of the Barley-harvest had also early been explained as commemorating the bread eaten in haste in the flight from Egypt.[3] Now at length Booths, a festival celebrated after the ingathering of the vintage and olives, is subjected to the same historical scheme and now commemorates the bowers in which the Hebrews dwelt in the desert.[4] The artificiality of all this is apparent, but the new interpretation was by no means due to mere pedantry or merely in the interests of a theology of redemption, but was due, as we may discern, to purposeful reflection. The purpose was, namely, to suppress the old Nature religion of Israel, and

---

[1] " Die Bedeutung des Alten Testaments für unseren Glauben," *Zwischen den Zeiten*, p. 37, 1930, Heft i.

[2] Ex. 12^{27} (J).   [3] Ex. 12^{39} (J).   [4] Lev. 23$^{40f.}$ (P).

to place in its stead festivals of a purely commemorative character.[1]

New interpretation does not easily affect ritual *dromena*, which are by nature conservative and continue to bear the traces of their origin. But at the time most suitable for effecting changes, namely, in the days of Ezra and Nehemiah, changes evidently were made in the chief [2] festival, the feast of Booths, which apparently stood most in need of modifying. In chapters viii–ix of Nehemiah we see the leaders of the Jewish Church at their constructive and destructive work. Of the festival of Booths that was celebrated on the occasion of the reading of the new Law-code (Tishri 432 B.C., Aug.-Sept.), it is said, in what is perhaps the Chronicler's additional note[3] (8^{17}): "for since the days of Josuah, the son of Nun, unto that day had not the children of Israel done so." " *Done so* " can only mean, if the note has historical value at all, that the children of Israel had not celebrated the festival hitherto *in this manner* (kēn). The chapters reveal a very tentative and almost maladroit attempt to explain the joy of the festival as recording the joy of receiving the Law,[4] for on the reading of the Law, we are told, the people had been depressed and had wept. It was now thought advisable to raise their spirits and that they should make merry "because they had understood the meaning of what they had heard" (8^{12}). Further, two days after the festival of Booths, which lasts from the 15th to the 22nd of the month of Tishri, a fast is proclaimed for the 24th, that the people in mourning might confess their own and the nation's

---

[1] Cf. Pedersen, " Passahfest und Passahlegende " (*Z.A.W.*, 1934, Heft 3, p. 167). " Not any more the world of animals and plants was celebrated (in Passover-Unleavened Bread) but the history of the people." Cf. George Buchanan Gray, *Sacrifice in the O.T.*, p. 298, " The most interesting feature of their (the festivals') history is the increasing and at last the dominating historical character of them."

[2] Booths was " The Feast " *par excellence*. Cf. 1 Kings $8^{2.65}$. Cf. Josephus (Ant. viii. 4, 1.).   [3] Cf. *S.A.T.*, Hans Schmidt, *ad loc.*

[4] Cf. above. Later but not in O.T. Pentecost Weeks was so interpreted of the receiving of the Law on Sinai.

sins and when " the seed of Israel separated themselves from all foreigners " (9²). Now, when we reflect upon the character of the festival of Booths as a nature festival, its certainly Canaanite origin, its resemblance with, if not actually derivation from, the Adonis festival, we discern the purpose of this latter prescription. The joy-making at the time the fruits had been gathered in is as far as possible spiritualized, namely, by the idea that it is on account of the gift of the Law. Indeed, founding doubtless on the attempt here made, the 23rd of Tishri becomes in later days the feast of *Simchath Torah*, the feast of the " Joy of the Law." [1] In light of this it appears more than probable that the mourning on the 24th of the month had as its intention— for the cycle of festivals in Tishri is one whole—the purpose of spiritualizing the mourning for the decay of natural growth and turning this rite into a bewailing of sins. In rendering the old rite innocuous, all *separation from all of non-Hebrew origin* would be efficacious. If the 24th of Tishri was, as is believed by some,[2] only meant to be a fast for the one particular occasion in the year 432 B.C., the great fast, the Day of Atonement on the 10th of the month, which does not seem at this time to have gained the importance and prominence which it acquired later [3] was a still better device from the point of view of the process of spiritualizing and moralizing the old nature religion. By placing the Hebrew mourning custom *prior* to the period of rejoicing,[4] it separated still further the Jewish festival rites from those that were recognized to be of non-Hebrew origin. It obliterated the traces of the festival's ancestry so far as that was possible. When we remember that the mourning in the Adonis festival had ended with the cry " Come back again," and thus with the expression of a belief in the resurrection of

[1] See my *Origins of the Festival of Hanukkah* (T. & T. Clark), 1930, p. 167.

[2] Cf. Hans Schmidt, " Das Judentum," *S.A.T.*, p. 174.

[3] Cf. Hans Schmidt, *op. cit.* p. 174 and George Buchanan Gray, *op. cit.* p. 306 f.

[4] Cf. Gressmann, *Expositor*, 1925, p. 416 f. " The Mysteries of Adonis and The Feast of Tabernacles."

the god, we may perceive that it was against no mere ritual as such that the zeal of the reformers was directed. The Chronicler by his remark that since the days of Joshua the festival had not been thus celebrated, evidently means what may have been actually the case, namely, that the festival was restored to that simple character which it held in the days of the Judges (cf. Jud. 21[19]) when the festival was taken over from the Canaanites, when it was still controlled by the concept of Jahve as god of the desert-period, and before it had assimilated the fuller ritual of the fertility cults. If up to the time of Ezra and Nehemiah the sacred prostitutes,[1] male and female, associated with the Booths and the drama of the sacred marriage had not been banished from the festival they certainly were banished now. So far as the theory of the meaning of the festivals was concerned the old nature religion came to a definite end. In accordance with the superimposed historical interpretation they became part of Jahve's redemptive scheme. The statement of Oehler is appropriate to this result : " What makes the festivals festivals is not any human selection of them that connected them with the process of nature, but the institution of them by the God of the Covenant, who thereby recalls to remembrance the great facts of the redemption of His people, and on the other hand that their earthly existence depends on Him as the Giver of all natural blessings." [2]

The One Personal God of world-history who had revealed Himself to His people in their political experience and in the Law and through Israel to the whole world—this thought bound together the older political-religious conceptions of a Day of Jahve, a Day of Judgment upon the enemies of Israel, a Day that will punish and purify Israel, the world-sovereignty of a purified remnant, that is, the true Israel. The final development of this within the Old Testament is the great eschatological

---

[1] Sacred Prostitution attacked in Deut. 23[17], *re* connection with sacred marriage. Cf. *Myth and Ritual*, pp. 73, 85.

[2] " Feste der Alten Hebräer," Herzog *Real. Ency.*

drama of the Book of Daniel with its prophecy of the resurrection of some *élite* righteous who will share in the eternal kingdom of the new age.   The doctrine of a future life is thus developed from the historical and political line of thought.   The politics of the age of Daniel in the historical situation brought about by the persecution under Antiochus IV. bring the doctrine to hesitating expression.   In Judaism there emerge no sacraments [1] in which natural elements become " sensible " signs of a real application of a supernatural gift of grace : there is no immortalizing of man through ritual which already effects this object in the present life (*Diesseitsmystik*) as in the Greek mysteries or which effects it in the future (*Jenseitsmystik*) as in the mysteries of Adonis and Osiris.   This concept arose from the natural theology which Jahvism suppressed.   Consistently therewith, in the Hebrew literature, for all its deep appreciation of the religious significance of nature, particularly in the Psalms, there is no development of a doctrine of divine immanence in nature.   The thought may be actually in individual utterances [2] or may be read into them, but the Book of Wisdom of Solomon (7^{22}) sums up in a phrase the whole spirit and tendency of previous thought regarding the relationship of God to nature, when it calls the intermediary Wisdom " the artificer of all things." [3]   The belief in divine immanence in nature which Christian thought arrived at arose from the specific doctrine of the incarnation and it was by this route as Illingworth says in his Essay on " Divine Immanence " that natural religion came to its culmination in the Christian Creed.   Moreover, it was on account of Christianity laying equal stress on the two ideas, the transcendence and immanence of God, that it was enabled to " appropriate and utilize both Neoplatonic and Stoic (pantheistic) thought, but with a

---

[1] Cf. Bousset, *Rel. d. Jud.*, p. 199.

[2] As, for example, Sirach 43^{27} where, speaking of nature, Sirach says, " He (God) is all " which, as Box and Oesterley (Charles, *Apoc.* i. *ad loc.*) remark, " sounds very Hellenistic." Sirach qualifies v. [27] by stressing the transcendence of God : " For greater is He than all His works " (v. [28]).

[3] *Technitis pantōn.*   Cf. Prov. 8^{22}.

tenderer appreciation of nature that is distinctively its own " [1] (p. vii. p. 35). This ability of Christianity to develop ideas that belonged to the old nature religion is perceived in respect of no less a doctrine than that of immortality itself. The belief in a resurrection was inherited from Judaism : but when it comes to the task of making this teaching intelligible to Greeks, S. Paul supports his arguments by developing the thought " that which thou sowest is not quickened except it die " (1 Cor. 15[36]) ; also the author of the Fourth Gospel (12[24]), on the occasion of the visit of the Greeks (proselytes) who would see Jesus, reports Jesus as saying to them with reference to His impending death : " Except a grain of wheat fall into the ground and die, it abideth alone, but, if it die it bringeth forth much fruit." The language of St. Paul and the Fourth Gospel provides no mere current comparison of natural and spiritual laws, but, as both the subject under discussion and the persons addressed may indicate, has its forceful quality in the bringing forward of a commonplace of religious thought for centuries familiar on the soil of the mystery religions.

The Jewish Church, which from the days of Ezra and Nehemiah had overcome the menace of natural theology, was in a still stronger position when from a theology of history and revelation, helped by the spread of Iranian belief, it developed its own doctrine of an after-life. Less than a generation before the author of the Book of Daniel wrote, Jesus Sirach (180 B.C.) felt so secure in his Jewish orthodox belief in Sheol as a land of shadows, where no reproach would be made regarding this life, that he could employ an idea inherent in the Egyptian mysteries of Osiris without fear of misunderstanding. Of the Judges and the Twelve Prophets he says (46[12], 49[10]) " may their bones flourish again out of their place," a phrase which means no more than " may their memory ever be green." This strikingly

---

[1] With what Illingworth says of Christianity, cf. Zielinski, *op. cit.* p. 184, " Greek religion was in its foundations a religion of nature : thanks to this primary quality it entered entirely into the Stoic system."

un-Hebraic phrase of Sirach has been explained by the supposition of its referring to " an old-world superstition " or to
an ancient Semitic practice of pouring water on graves which
suggests the desire to cause growth.[1] But the extant pictorial
representation of the dead Osiris [2] sprouting into corn and the
practice of placing corn-mummies in the graves of the departed
that the dead may go through the drama of the dying and rising
god, present a much more likely context of the idea in the days
of Sirach.

Acquaintance with the Greek mysteries in the days after
Alexander the Great, in the period of the Seleucids and Ptolemies,
came too late to overthrow the now consolidated defences of
Judaism.   But it penetrated these defences.   Even " the
pious," as the expression " sanctuaries of El " of which we have
spoken (Ps. 73) seems to show, could, without harm, borrow
something from the mystery cults, even if it were only the idea
of forming religious fraternities.   But in this period of religious
syncretism, which the enforced policy of religious uniformity
under Antiochus IV. Epiphanes (175–163), did more eventually
to retard than to foster, Hellenized Jews were foremost in support
of this policy of the Syrian government.   The second Book of
Maccabees (6[7], 14[33]) tells of the Dionysian festivals which the
Jews witnessed and evidently took part in.   The author of that
book does not feel any restraint in applying the Dionysian term
" thyrsi," to the branches or wands used in celebration of the
Jewish festival which appears at this time under the name of
Hanukkah (commonly called " Dedication," St. John 10[22]).   In
Egypt Ptolemy IV. (221–204) in the third century B.C., a strong
patron of the Dionysian mysteries, instituted propaganda
among his Jewish subjects to induce them to become initiates
(cf. 3 Macc. 2[29f.]).   The Hellenistic Jew who is the writer of the

---

[1] Cf. Charles, *Apoc.*, *ad loc.* note on 49[10].

[2] Cf. Picture (nr. 1 appendix to J. Leipoldt's *Sterbende und Auferstehende
Götter*) of "the Sprouting Osiris."   On Sirach 46[12], see Gressmann, *Tod und
Auferstehung des Osiris*, p. 9.

Wisdom of Solomon subjects the ideas of the mystery religions to criticism (14$^{15f.}$), and contrasts the "mysteries of God" (2^{22}, 6^{22}) which brought "knowledge to clear light."

That Jews in considerable numbers assimilated in this period their ancient faith to the attractive religious forms of the mysteries or old nature religions, is shown by the fact that in 139 B.C. the Roman Praetor Hispalus expelled from Rome Jews who were worshippers of Jupiter-Sabazius, that is, of Jahve and of the Thraco-Phrygian Dionysus.[1] But, however wide such syncretism may have been, it left unimpaired the Jewish Church which at the very time of the expulsion of the renegade Jews from Rome, became, under Simon the Hasmonean, again supreme, strong, and intolerant. As late as the third century A.D. Sabazius-worshipping Jews are in Rome. Of their number were the Sabazius priest Vincentius and his wife the priestess Vibia, whose memorial tomb depicts scenes of the felicities of the other-world of the mystery religion. But significant, as it is eloquent, is the fact that they found sepulture *not* among the Jews but in a Christian catacomb.[2]

2

To the two causes responsible for the belief in an after-life appearing late in Hebrew religious thought, causes which are inherent in the particular conception of the deity, Jahve, we must add a third. The form and strength of the Hebrew idea of reward and retribution as being the first principle of divine justice and government retarded the development of a belief in the world beyond. The idea that it is the will and attribute of a just God to reward goodness and to punish evil-doing might seem to be a prime factor urging thought to the belief in a future

---

[1] Valerius Maximus, i. 3. 2.   Cf. Cumont " Hypsistos " in Pauly-Wissowa-Kroll *Ency*.   Cf. Reitzenstein, *Die hellenistischen Mysterien-Religionen*, p. 107.

[2] See Gressmann, *Die orientalischen Religionen im hellenistisch-römischen Zeitalter*, p. 123.

existence, since as it must become obvious that there is no adequate redress for life's injustices in this world, God's justice and will to reward and punish can only be maintained by a doctrine of another life when redress can become possible. Renan, for example, held that the advent in Israel of a belief in a resurrection was due much more to the necessity of upholding belief in reward and retribution than to any influence from Greece or Persia. This is in part true. Borrowing is usually never made except in need. We have, however, to observe the remarkable fact that the religion of Israel with a highly developed ethic and a dogmatic teaching in regard to retribution staved off the day of need of a belief in a future life to a late stage of its history. We cannot suppose, as we have shown, that Israel had come into no vital contact with the belief in an after-life either as a religious tenet held by others or through cult-practices. We have, therefore, to consider why it was that Israel's moral and theological conceptions operated so slowly and reluctantly, even, as it seems, obstructively, in respect of the development of a teaching of immortality.

The truth of Kant's statement [1] that " immortality, being inseparably connected with the moral law, is a postulate of pure practical reason " is quite unaffected by any proof from the history of religion that the ideas of immortality and moral responsibility are by no means inseparable. But alongside the philosophic statement may be placed two facts—first, as Sir James Frazer discloses in his study of the beliefs of primitive races in Australia and Polynesia,[2] there are peoples who believe in an after-life where the destiny of souls is quite independent of moral responsibility or the idea of retribution. Second, the history of the religion of Israel presents us with a high ethic and a strong sense of moral responsibility which for a long time felt their self-sufficiency without the need of postulating per-

---

[1] *Kritik d. praktischen Vernunft*, part i. Bk. 2, 4, p. 147 in Reclam.
[2] *The Belief in Immortality and the Worship of the Dead,* vol. i. 1913 ; vol. ii. 1922.

sonal immortality. Without doubt ethical considerations did bring eventually this doctrine to birth in Javhism, but it was the very strength of Israel's religious and ethical teaching, built up upon the supposition of a this-worldly requital of good and evil, which provided a theological barrier difficult to overcome and which held back speculation on a future existence. Even although the sufferings of the righteous and the misfortunes of Israel, who at least was no worse than the nations who triumphed over her, did bring travail of soul to faithful believers and inspire doubt even within them, yet the moral law of a this-worldly recompense as taught by the prophets in respect of the nation, and by both the teacher of wisdom and the Deuteronomist in respect of the individual, could not be modified without seeming to impeach Jahve's world-government and that interpretation of history which was the heart of Israel's religion. The very form of the belief in an after-life which Israel at length chose, namely, a resurrection or revivification of the physical body to a life on earth, represents a concession to her this-worldly ethic.

The resistance which the Deuteronomist doctrine of reward and retribution offered to the idea of immortality may be observed from three successive stages of this doctrine's history. So far back as half a millennium before the *belief* in a resurrection found lodgment in the Book of Daniel, and from that time in the faith and theology of Judaism, Ezekiel (*c.* 37) is acquainted with the *notion* of a resurrection. Since in the Book of Ezekiel there is indubitable evidence of a transformation of elements of Babylonian mythology [1] to the uses of Hebrew religious thought, an adaptation entirely intelligible from the circumstances of place and time in which the author wrote, we cannot reject the possibility that in the famous vision of the valley of dry bones, where the dry bones are called to life, clothed with flesh and rise an exceeding great army, we have a similar adaptation,

---

[1] Chap. 1[4f.], 9[2f.], 26[20], etc. See *Das Alte Testament im Lichte d. Alten Orients*, p. 617 f., A. Jeremias.

so far as Hebrew thought and feeling then permitted, of the Iranian teaching [1] of a resurrection to an after-life.   The teaching

[1] Hölscher in his *Geschichte der israelitischen und jüdischen Religion*, p. 137, says of the vision in Ezekiel *c.* 37 : " The resurrection is here only a picture, but perhaps the picture was inspired by the Iranian resurrection belief." If, as Hölscher (*Hesekiel, der Dichter und das Buch*, 1924, p. 174 f.) believes, chap. 37 is post-exilic and is the work of a redactor of the Persian period, Iranian influence is much more probable. Postulating this influence for the period when Ezekiel wrote (592–570 B.C.), that is about half a century before the Persian ascendancy, is more difficult. But, as C. T. Harley Walker points out, (" Persian Influence on the Development of Biblical Religion," *Interpreter*, April 1914, p. 313 f.), if there were not many Persians in Palestine there were Jews in Babylon who had opportunity to learn about Persian religion. It was in Babylonia Ezekiel wrote. Borrowing, subtle and partly unconscious, took place. The mention in Ezek. 8[17] of those who " hold a branch to their nose " cannot be explained away as a textual corruption, even though the LXX (" behold how they sneer [at me] ") perhaps rightly interprets the intention of the passage. Undoubtedly (see Haug, *Religion of the Parsis*, p. 4, cf. Walker, *op. cit.* p. 319) the reference is to the Persian ritual of holding out the *Barsom* twigs at time of prayer. Conservative opinion as represented by Moulton (" Hibbert Lectures," 1913, on Early Zoroastrianism) and Pettazzoni (*La Religione di Zarathustra*, Bologna, 1920) believes that it was Iranian religion which borrowed from Judaism. The latter admits only that Persian dualism influenced Jewish conceptions. Söderblom (*La vie future d'après le Mazdéisme*) stresses the differences in Jewish and Iranian eschatology and argues from these differences for Jewish independence, but fails to assess adequately points of agreement, in particular agreement in apparent inconsistencies of thought (cf. Bousset, *op. cit.* p. 509 f.) which reveal contact with Iranian religion. In the Book of Daniel and in the Apocalyptic writings which follow, the Iranian influence becomes manifest. See Eduard Meyer *Ursprung und Anfänge des Christentums*, 1925, vol. ii. pp. 174–199 ; Reitzenstein, *Das iranische Erlösungsmysterium*, 1921, p. 122 ; and *Die hellenistisch. Mysterienreligionen*, 1927, p. 292. When J. Baillie (*And the Life Everlasting*, 1934, p. 150) speaking of the resurrection and other eschatological elements, says : " The best opinion seems, however, to be more and more pointing to an independent origin of these doctrines among the Jews themselves," this statement in neither of its branches is to be taken as altogether correct. No one is likely to borrow an idea unless there is something already in his own mentality responsive to the idea. The Hebrews were quite aware long before the time of Ezekiel of the belief in dying and rising gods. Indeed Jeremias (*op. cit.* p. 304, cf. Sellin, *Intro. to O.T.*, p. 221) thinks that the Tammuz (Adonis) myth is the source of the Biblical resurrection-belief. But the Jewish-Persian idea of resurrection as a revivification of the physical body to a life here upon earth is different from the concept of a life beyond as held by the nature-religions (see above, pp. 145, 181, note 1 and 3). Except for Job 19[25] Humbert (*op. cit.* p. 185)

of a resurrection of the dead is rooted in Persian eschatology.
Bold as is the imagery that characterizes Ezekiel's writings, the
amplitude of the picture presented in the thirty-seventh chapter
does not suggest that the ideas here are simply woven out of
his own inner consciousness and still less that he is evaluating
any thought culled from Hebrew prophecies of the past. But
whatever be the origin of the idea, it is significant that in the
same book and at the same time in which the idea of resurrection
now emerges only to be transmuted into a powerful metaphor
of a revival of national power and fortune, the Deuteronomist
teaching of reward and retribution is felt to be in urgent need of
amendment in the interest of a more sharply stressed individualism. Ezekiel substitutes for the belief that guilt and the consequence of guilt are transferred from fathers to children, his
doctrine of personal responsibility. That Ezekiel knew of no
other context of the idea of resurrection than that which he
himself gives it in his vision is incredible. Yet in this period,
when early contact with Iranian thought was possible, and
doubtless took place, no recourse is made to this nor any aid
accepted from it in lightening the burden of the Deuteronomist
theory of divine recompense. The dogma of reward becomes,
through Ezekiel, less elastic, and the this-worldly religious and
moral outlook upon man, his conduct and his relationship to
God, becomes more doctrinaire and theologically more firmly
established.

A second phase of the inner religious struggle may be regarded as beginning with the composition of the Book of Job
(c. 450 B.C.), though possibly the problem of the sufferings of the
righteous had become acute much earlier. The author of the
Book of Job is the outstanding representative of those who gave
voice to questioning and doubt as to the scope of the Deuteronomist doctrine. If Job does not desert the ground of the *general*

thinks that the ideas of Egypt on the other world had no influence on Israel.
Fichtner (*op. cit.* p. 126) expresses the same view as Humbert in regard to
the idea of the Judgment of the dead.

validity of that doctrine, nevertheless the actual effect of the poem (*c.* 3–31) and still more so of the divine speeches (*c.* 38 f.) is to call into question the right of man to ascribe every individual case of suffering to the law of recompense. But, however great is the merit of the Book of Job as a literary masterpiece and as an attempt of deep religious piety to show that the orthodox teaching which explained misfortune by moral desert was not universally true, there is ample indication that the orthodox position sustained every attack, whether implicit or explicit, with success. Within the limits of that position the author of Ps. 73 remains ; although, by spiritualizing the chiefest good of life, ordinarily conceived of as consisting in material values, through the thought that for him this was the consciousness of the nearness of God, the writer projects a conception capable of far-reaching consequence.

There is no subject in the whole of the Old Testament upon which the fire of intellect and criticism is seen to beat so persistently as upon the topic of reward in relation to conduct and life.[1] If the Deuteronomist doctrine, now the dogma of the Jewish Church, had fallen, then there would have seemed to collapse with it the whole structure of the temporal interpretation of history that had been in course of erection since the days of the prophets. The religious interpretation of history according to which God's anger and favour had descended on nation and kings in proportion to their backsliding or obedience was the support on which rested the faith in God's revelation of Himself to the race. The application of the theory of reward and retribution to the life of every single Israelite certainly invoked doubt

---

[1] If, besides the Elihu speeches in the Book of Job and the hymn on wisdom (*c.* 28) generally acknowledged to be additions, the poem (*c.* 3–31), the divine speeches and the Folk-tale (Prologue and Epilogue) be all regarded as from different hands, then this literary industry would provide even more striking testimony of the intellectual interest in the great topic of the age. If even the poem (3–31) has been expanded from an original nucleus (cf. Baumgärtel, *Der Hiobdialog*, 1933 ; Norbert Peters, *Das Buch Hiob.*, 1928) this industry and interest appear all the greater.

and difficulties, but this theory was deeply involved in the Prophetic theology and in the political-religious scheme of thought that had grown out of it. Thus the significance of the Book of Job is not merely that it states a moral problem of personal religion, but that the deductions to be drawn from the personal problem spelled the dissolution of prophecy.[1] The prophetic theme was subjected to doubt. If there be no personal retribution there can be no punishment of peoples. The plan of revelation and redemption was obscured.

The two parties which emerge within Judaism under the description of "the righteous" and "the wicked" (or "scoffers"), reflect, if they did not arise directly out of, the inner religious conflict that centred in the acceptance or denial of the Deuteronomist doctrine. Possibly these two factions existed even earlier, as Bousset[2] thinks, than the days of Ezra and Nehemiah, but we may hold with certainty that it was the founding of the Jewish "Church" under these religious leaders which accentuated the opposition. The formulation of orthodox opinion and teaching under the ægis of an institution separates those within from those without, the strict from the lax. But from the psalms, the Book of Enoch (cf. 102[6f.], 105[5f.]) and the Wisdom of Solomon (chap. 2) we perceive that there was an intellectual basis of the antagonism. The so-called "wicked" doubted the belief in a world-judgment and the glorious manifestation of God in the End-Time. The judgment of Israel and the nations at a certain point of time in the future might concern those alive at that time but, as life was short, such a judgment had no meaning for those living at present. They scoffed at God's providence—at least as "the righteous" understood it ; and evidently employed the *argumentum ad hominem* by pointing to the misfortunes of "the righteous" as bearing the manifest disproof of the whole reward-theology. The description of "the

---

[1] Cf. Gressmann, *Israel's Spruchweisheit*, p. 57. Job signifies the end of prophecy not only in the sense of its consummation but also of its dissolution.

[2] *Rel. d. Jud.*, p. 183.

wicked," as it has come to us, is that given by the orthodox party and we cannot tell how far the charge of actual wickedness is justified. "The good" and "the bad" of the two parties of Greek political life of whom Theognis of Megara speaks, represented no real *ethical* distinction. But religious orthodoxy has often in good faith associated heresy with immorality. When, however, we find that in the Hellenistic age many of "the wicked" or liberal Jews adopted Hellenism and were ready to die for their new faith, we perceive that they were not simply irreligious.[1] They were the *disjecta membra* of orthodox Judaism. In the conflict with them Judaism consolidated with greater determination and faith the simple belief that God's justice and world-government would be impeached if it were admitted that man could leave the world-stage without experiencing requital for good and evil. Yet we cannot doubt that many of "the wicked" went no farther than did Qoheleth, who taught that it was useless for man to try to penetrate to the things that shall be and that the law of retribution found no justification in fact. For the author of the Wisdom of Solomon who has either Qoheleth or his disciples in view, such teaching represents the height of wickedness.

In the process of the development of thought we discern that the pessimistic elements of the Book of Job (*c.* 28) its emphasis upon God's transcendence and inscrutable purpose had done their work. But the main stream of Judaism continued in the channels of thought that had been shaped out for it by the past—the faith once delivered to prophets and teachers. The Chronicler had more faithfully than ever recorded Israel's history in light of the traditional doctrine and after "the wicked" had liberally expressed themselves, the piety of the age, as represented by Jesus Sirach, still stoutly upheld the Deuteronomist teaching and its this-worldly requital. In Sirach there may even be traced a conscious disparagement of the whole spirit of the Book of Job. He extols (49[9]) Job, but it is not the

[1] Cf. 1 Macc. 7[5f.], 14[14.36], Megillath Taanith vi.

Job of the book to whom he refers but the Job of tradition mentioned by Ezekiel (14$^{14.}$ ^{20}), that is, the uncomplaining Job of the Folk-tale. Sirach evidently did not regard the Book of Job as having anything to do with history, for in behalf of orthodox thought upon reward he directs the attention of his readers to the generations of old, the heroes of Scripture (2^{10}), and exclaims : " Look to the generations of old and see ; Whoever trusted in the Lord and was put to shame ? Or who did abide in His fear and was forsaken ? " The *summum bonum* remains the familiar one : gladness, joy, and length of days (1$^{12f.}$). He makes much of the semi-mystical thought that at a man's "latter-end," on the day of death, God may reveal the full content of requital and recompense (cf. 7^{36}). Thus, if we regard Sirach as representing the end of an epoch, the time immediately before the Maccabean revolt begins, we see that in spite of the fact that in this period Qoheleth knows of those who cherish the hope of an other-worldly existence, and though the this-worldly theory of recompense has largely broken down, orthodox Judaism maintains the Deuteronomist dogma absolutely un-impaired. In reality the abandonment of this teaching in its purely temporal aspect had been long overdue. The plea which Sirach brings forth, rather lamely, on behalf of an ideal im-mortality, that is, that a man may live for ever in the memory of coming generations, shows that he was aware of a weakness in the traditional theory, and conscious of the necessity of provid-ing a substitute for other theological belief concerning man's destiny.

Under the persecution which caused the Maccabean rising and without doubt forcefully aided by the martyrdom of those who suffered death in the struggle against the government of Antiochus IV., another phase of the religious conflict within Judaism itself is reached. Messianic hopes that ever had shown a tendency to be dormant in time of peace were now awake. The day of the consummation of Israel's history and redemption was now at hand. In the apocalypse of Daniel the belief in a resurrection appears, a recalling to life, in the End-Time that is soon to arrive, of many of the particularly pious and of others who were particularly impious. At last Jahvism which had been acquainted for centuries with the idea of an after-life was presented with a form for that idea that was suitable to its genius. In the literature of the succeeding years we sense the embarrassment that comes with sudden wealth and can trace the efforts made to relate the new conception to the old notions of Sheol, the Day of Judgment, the blessings of the new age and to other features of the prophetic eschatologies (*e.g.* cf. 1 Enoch 45[4.5] with Isa. 65[17], 66[22]). At first as in the older sections of the Book of Enoch there is no clear picture presented of the final events.[1] But gradually belief assumes definite forms. It is held in the parables of Enoch (51[1-3], cf. 45[1-3], 61[5]) and in 4 Ezra 7[32f.] that all the dead will rise. In the Hellenic circles of Judaism, in the Fourth Book of Maccabees, The Wisdom of Solomon, and Philo, the new thought makes way for the quite different idea of an immediate immortality after death.[2] What appears to be the position of the Second Book of Maccabees, that the righteous alone have part in the resurrection, becomes the more general view of Judaism (Pharisaism) as a whole. But one thing the new dogma of the new " righteous " is unable to do. It does not abolish the old Deuteronomist doctrine. As we have seen [3] this still persists, even in the crudest form, in the Second Book of Maccabees (9[5f.], etc.) and in the Wisdom of Solomon 3[10. 16f.] and in early Christian thought. Even to-day the effects of this doctrine are not negligible and are often covered by the expression, " the rough justice of life." Only forty years ago Mr. C. G. Montefiore pointed to the necessity of purifying the Jewish liturgy from the many traces of the central idea of this teaching, the *lex talionis*, the law of measure for measure.

---

[1] Cf. Bousset, *op. cit.* p. 270 f.

[2] The poem of Pseudo-Phokylides (103, 104) seeks to combine both the Hellenic and the Jewish teaching.

[3] Cf. chs. iii. and iv. and E. Balla,—" Das Problem des Leides," etc., in *Eucharisterion*, 1923, p. 255.

Although the belief in a future life provided a convenient place where man could store his dreams, his expectations and his hopes of redress, religious faith rooted in an age-long inheritance of thought was still prone to hold that God's justice was completely vindicated in the present world. When we read in the Jewish liturgy of to-day in the prayer of the morning-service : " He bestoweth loving-kindness upon a man according to his work ; He giveth to the wicked evil according to his wickedness " [1] we have the body and substance of the teaching of those teachers of Wisdom who, as Gressmann rightly thinks,[2] influenced even the earliest of the prophets in respect of the doctrine of reward. The doctrine received its worst blows in the Wisdom-school, in the Book of Job, and in Qoheleth. But it is significant that in the darkest days, it is Sirach, perhaps the most representative of that school, who champions the orthodox view most fully and impressively.

The three phases through which the Deuteronomist doctrine passes from the time of Ezekiel to that of the writer of Second Maccabees—namely, perception of its weakness in respect of the idea of hereditary guilt and its consequent improvement, its emergence from attack as the accepted belief of " the righteous " or orthodox Church-party, its persistence even when overcome in theory alongside the new thought—demonstrate that the urge which the idea of immortality received from the necessity of vindicating the justice of God as a God of requital met with no force so counteractive and obstructive as the traditional teaching of reward and retribution. Since Israel rejected the belief in immortality known to it as associated with natural religion the only opening for such a belief was that of rational religious inference. That the *idea of resurrection* emerged only through inference without aid from elsewhere or simply as " a result of the great war," the Maccabean revolt, is unbelievable. But there had held the field a very potent rational

[1] Page 3, *Authorised Daily Prayer Book*, Singer, 1925.
[2] *Op. cit.* p. 56.

religious inference which through the Deuteronomist school had been the instrument of interpreting the people's history and upon which had been built up a high ethic and useful pedagogic. It was this inference, and the high moral and religious standard it produced, which postponed the fruition of the belief in immortality.

CHAPTER IX

The Figure of Wisdom

1

WITH the appearance of a definite monotheism in Israel, that is, from the time of the Exile onwards, the deity becomes more and more conceived of as a transcendent Being. Already in the Book of Ezekiel we see this process begun. Jahve, it is true, converses with the prophet, addressing him as " son of Adam " ; in trance or vision, but nevertheless regarded as constituting an actual experience, Jahve appears to Ezekiel, grasps him by the hair of the head (8³), leads him forth (8⁷ᶠ·), and brings him to Jerusalem (40²). But on other occasions the divine purposes are carried out by intermediate beings, a spirit (*Ruach*) as quickening (2²) or compelling power (3¹⁴, 8³, 11¹) or by an angel (40³ᶠ·). In the vision of the destruction of Jerusalem (8, 9, 10), six angels of slaughter, accompanied by another in linen dress with a writer's inkhorn at his side—a recording angel—are charged with the execution of Jahve's fierce judgment. The seven angels, without doubt, represent the seven planetary divinities of Babylonian religion (Gunkel, *Arch. f. Religionswiss*, i. p. 294 f.), who are transformed by Ezekiel into assistants of Jahve and become in later belief (Tobit 12¹⁵ ; Ap. John 4⁵, 8²) the seven archangels. The recording angel reveals unmistakably the features of the Babylonian deity, Nabu (Nebo). Since the time of second Isaiah the idea of Jahve as Creator is emphasized, and the supra-natural concept of deity is indicated in the Priestly Code by the position given to the word of God as a creative power (Gen. 1 ; cf. Ps. 33⁶), and by the care with which anthropomorphic descriptions of the divine activity are avoided. The deity is now felt to be more fittingly described as " the Highest " ; He is surrounded, after the manner of an earthly monarch by His court, by His serving angels, "the holy ones" (Ps. 89$^{6.8}$; Job 5^1, etc.), who are intermediaries between the "Almighty" (so LXX for El Shaddai) and the world. These intermediary angels perform the most varied of functions ; there are angels of punishment or misfortune (Ps. 35$^{5f.}$; Prov. 17^{11}), angels of death who visit the dying (Job 33^{22}), protective angels (Ps. 34^8, 91$^{11f.}$), angels who carry the prayers of the pious to God (Tobit 3^{16}, 12$^{12.15}$). The angels are even praised together with God (Tobit 11^{13}), and we learn from the Book of Job that man could turn to the angels to intercede for him (5^1, cf. 33^{23}). In the Hellenistic age, in the Book of Tobit (Raphael) and especially in the Apocalyptic literature (e.g. in Dan.—Gabriel, Michael), we meet with particular names of angels. This development of religious thought had no doubt within Israel itself that which may be regarded as fostering it, namely, the conception of the "Angel of Jahve," the *Mal'ak Jahve*, or representative in Palestine of the God of Sinai at the various cult-places. But, as Meyer (*Israeliten und ihre Nachbarstämme*, p. 216), says, this Angel of Jahve had remained a mere "theological formula," "a lifeless shadow." That which gave impetus to the assumption of angel intermediaries between God and man was the growth of the idea of the transcendency of Jahve and the conversion, largely consequent upon that idea, of non-Israelite deities into servants or agents of Jahve. But even the idea of a transcendent Creator God cannot have developed in Hebrew thought without influence from without which ripened it, not only in its earlier but in its later stages.

Under the necessity of connecting the world of men with the God, who in majesty and nature was so far above this world, there were two courses which Judaism could take and which it took. It transformed the deities of foreign worship into angels, who, representing the functions of the Supreme Being, were more or less the equivalent of abstract ideas or divine attributes, and on the other hand it turned such abstract ideas as the *spirit* of God (as world creating power, Job 33^4 ; Jud. 16^{15} ; Apoc.

Bar. 23[5]; as filling all things, *Sap. Sol.* 1[7]; as ruling in history, Isa. 63[10]) and the *word* of God (Ps. 107[20], 119[50]) into what may be called hypostases or personifications of the divine activity and power. *Wisdom*, which we perceive to be personified in the latest collection of the Book of Proverbs, namely, chaps. 1–9 (400–300 B.C.), in Job 28, in Sirach 24[3-6], in *Sap. Sol.* (6[18], 7[7f.], 8[3f. 13. 17], 9[4.9]), the Book of Baruch (3[9]–4[4]), and in the First (42[1-2]) and Second (30[8]A) Books of Enoch, receives in the speculations of earlier Judaism a more important place than do the Spirit and the Word. Both the words hypostasis and personification have difficulties of definition attached to them when they are applied to the Word, the Spirit, and Wisdom, but it is sufficiently evident in the literature concerned that Wisdom is regarded as a Being dependent on God but in some sense separate from Him. When we meet with Wisdom as a personification it is something more than such poetical personifications[1] as, "the Arm of Jahve," "the Countenance of Jahve," the "Righteousness which goes before Jahve" (Ps. 85[14]), which attain to some degree of independence. As the angelology of Judaism cannot be explained by the figure of the Mal'ak Jahve alone, neither can the origin and development of that other type of intermediary, Wisdom, be satisfactorily explained by the supposition that its parent was poetic thought, and that this parent continued to supply its offspring's clothing.

A study of the origin of personified Wisdom is of importance, not only for the history of the religion of Judaism, but for the religious history of Christianity. It is generally assumed that in the prologue of the Gospel of St. John the doctrine of the *Logos* or *Word*—the *Word was God* ; *the Word became flesh*—has descended from the Jewish speculation regarding Wisdom. The question therefore arises : Why did the Evangelist substitute " the Word " for " Wisdom " ? That he desired to begin his

---

[1] Cf. the long list of such personifications in Schencke (p. 86), *Die Chokma (Sophia) in der jüdischen Hypostasenspekulation* (Kristiania, 1913).

Gospel with an introduction which would be a counterpart to the opening of the Book of Genesis is possible. But in Gen. 1 the " Word " is only referred to indirectly. The answer usually given, and which seems to carry most probability with it, is that the writer of the prologue applied the Logos speculation of Alexandrian Judaism, perhaps indeed that of Philo. Bultmann, in his study of " the religious historical background of the prologue of the gospel according to St. John " [1] argues, that while Stoic teaching which influenced Hellenistic Jewish writers was able to do ample justice to the idea of the Logos as a cosmic power, and while in the Wisdom literature of Judaism there is the idea of Wisdom as an immanent power of understanding and knowledge, there is reason to search for the idea of the Logos or Word *as the deity of revelation, as the divine Bearer of revelation*, in sources of religious belief of a much earlier date than that of Hellenistic Judaism. In seeking for this source Bultmann draws attention to the Mandæan doctrine of the cosmic, or heavenly Man, Enosh-Uthra, who is described as " a (or, the) Word, a son of words." This means that, since Mandæan sources reflect Iranian religious thought, Persian mythology is probably the ultimate source of the concept of the Word as divinity of revelation. Following upon Bultmann's inquiry into the origin of the chief conception in St. John's prologue, Schraeder [2] comes to three groups of conclusions, namely, that the prologue of the fourth Gospel is a reconstruction and Christianizing of a Gnostic Aramaic hymn in which the term translated by the Greek " *Logos* " was the Aramaic " *Memra* " [3]; that this late Jewish Gnostic hymn extolled the identity (Einheit) of the divine Messenger who should come into the world—that is, the cosmic or heavenly Man, Enosh—and the Light of the Divine Word, or Memra ; that, further, the Enosh tradition as preserved in

[1] " Der religionsgeschtl. Hintergrund des Prologs zum Joh-Evang., in *Eucharisterion* (1923). See p. 14 f., 23.

[2] R. Reitzenstein and H. H. Schraeder, *Studien zum antiken Synkretismus aus Iran und Griechenland*, 1926. Cf. pp. 306, 330, 350.

[3] Cf. C. F. Burney, *The Aramaic Origin of the Fourth Gospel*, 1922.

Mandæan sources has its counterpart in the account of the
heavenly Man (Aramaic : *son of Man*) in the seventh chapter
of the Book of Daniel.   In regard to the origin of the conception of the cosmic Man (*Urmensch*), Schraeder indicates this
when he says that the idea connects with " the only religious
speculation of ancient Oriental religion which had fully
developed the idea and had given it a central position in its
teaching, namely, the religious speculation of Iran " (*op.
cit.* 307).

The aspect of Schraeder's conclusions which is of immediate
interest to our inquiry into the character of Wisdom and its
origin is his view that the Word (Memra) which he takes to be
substantially the same (p. 330) as the personified Wisdom of the
Wisdom literature was united by Jewish Gnosticism with the
heavenly Man.   That we do not know how early this union or
equation which the Gnostic hymn extols, was made, does not
greatly affect the question with which we are concerned.   But it
is of great significance that one side of the equation, namely,
the conception of the heavenly, pre-existent Man, which was of
such consequence for Jewish Apocalyptic [1] (cf. 1 Enoch 46 ;
4 Ezra 13) and Christian thought, is, if Schraeder is right, derived
from Persian religion.   For, if the other side of the equation, the
figure of Wisdom, cannot be regarded as an independent growth
within Judaism itself, there is, under the circumstances, special
reason for looking for its origin in that place where its companion
in the Gnostic hymn belonged, particularly if it is known that
here conceptions similar to that of Wisdom were current.
Indeed it is in Iranian religion in the form this took under the
reformer Zoroaster [2] that Bousset and others think that Wisdom
arose.

[1] Cf. Bousset, *Rel. d. Jud.*, p. 267, 3rd ed.
[2] E. Meyer, *Ursprung*, etc., Bd. ii. p. 58, gives date of Zoroaster as at
latest *circa* 1000 B.C.   J. Hertel (*Die Zeit Zarathustras*, 1924) who identifies
the patron of Z. with the father of Darius places Z. in sixth century B.C.
In which case we must distinguish between *old* Iranian religion and that of
Zoroaster.

2

Eduard Meyer in his work *The Origin and Beginnings of Christianity* (vol. ii. p. 105 f.) states his opinion that in Jewish theology the personifications of the holy Spirit and Wisdom did not grow into independent figures as in Iranian religion, or as did in Judaism itself the devil and angels, but remained half theological, half poetical conceptions. Meyer admits that there is a parallel between the archangels of Zoroastrian religion and the figure of Wisdom, but thinks that there is no occasion to speak of influence from this direction and that the speculation regarding Wisdom in Judaism is a plant that grew on Jewish soil without its having even been ripened by contact with Iranian beliefs. This opinion of Meyer is the more notable and worthy of weighing, because he traces most conclusively the influence of Iranian religion in the growth of dualistic thought in Judaism (cf. Test. xii.) and upon Jewish eschatology. He has no hesitation, for example, in taking the description of the " Ancient of Days," who appears in the book of Daniel along with the " Man " in the great world-judgment, to be a trans-ference to Judaism of the picture of the Persian supreme deity Ahura Mazda. " The ancient Deity, a person stricken in years, with a majestic head of snow-white hair ' pure as wool,' clad in dazzling white raiment—when," asks Meyer, " had a Jew from his own store of notions of the deity ever pictured Jahve thus ? " [1] The fiery stream wherewith world-judgment is executed, Meyer points out, is the same means which effects the process of world-judgment in Persian belief. Moreover, neither here nor in Daniel is the fire a mere metaphor, indicating as hitherto, in prophetic poetic language, the cleansing purpose of God. But the per-sonification of Wisdom, he concludes, though it has its analogies in Zoroastrianism is a natural and independent product of Jewish thought. Heinisch also in his treatise on *The Personal Wisdom of the Old Testament*, although he has no indecision in speaking

[1] E. Meyer, *Ursprung*, etc., Bd. ii. p. 199. In early Phœnician religion (*RS. Tablets*, p. 13, Jack) El is called " Father of Years."

of the Old Testament Wisdom as an hypostasis and real personification, ends his study of the subject by saying : " In cautious weighing of all the circumstances, the conclusion is forced upon us that in Israel the idea of the divine Wisdom developed quite independently, without any influence from outside. An attribute of Jahve has grown into an hypostasis through the urge of poetic speech to describe divine attributes as persons, a process in which supernatural guidance was not wanting." [1]

The view of such an impartial scholar of the quality of Meyer and the painstaking analysis which Heinisch gives of conceptions similar to that of personified Wisdom, at least in Babylonia and Egypt, might cause us to pause before rejecting the opinion that the urge of poetic expression was a sufficient cause of the phenomenon under our consideration. But irrespective of the fact that divine guidance may most appropriately be conceived as manifesting itself in fructifying minds through minds in contact, sympathy, or opposition, there is one feature which distinguishes the appearance of the Jewish speculation on Wisdom even from the emergence of the doctrine of the resurrection which was no product either of logic or of poetry and upon which we cannot believe that external influence had no effect. This feature is the suddenness with which the estimate of wisdom as a means of securing happiness and individual welfare and all mundane goods and blessings is all at once converted into the mystical concept of Wisdom as a personal divine Being in some way instrumental in creation. Bousset (*op. cit.* p. 520) rightly remarks that this personified Wisdom " emerges so suddenly in Jewish literature and so mysteriously, that we may at once conclude that it is of alien origin." The personified Wisdom is quite different, in light of the unexpectedness of its appearance and of the particular character with which it is endowed, from those examples of personified attributes of Jahve in which

---

[1] *Die persönliche Weisheit des A.T. in religionsgesch. Beleuchtung,* Münster, 1933. p. 60.

Hebrew poetry is sufficiently rich. These examples make the
contrast with Wisdom all the more profound and striking. " So
much seems in any case clear from the investigations of Bousset
and Reitzenstein," says Bultmann (*op. cit.* p. 19), " that in the
background of all the utterances and thoughts which they have
sifted there is a much older mythological speculation, the origin
of which is indeed not completely clear. Only it is above all
question that the Wisdom-speculation is not of Jewish origin.
The figure (of Wisdom) and its *mythos* cannot be explained from
Israelitish-Jewish premisses."

Another consideration of a more general kind may here be
brought to bear against the theory that neither in its speculation
regarding Wisdom nor elsewhere, for example in its eschatology,
did Judaism admit or transform foreign elements. Since the
discoveries of papyri at Elephantiné in Egypt have revealed
that a Jewish colony there in the fifth century B.C.,[1] worshipped
besides Jahve two other divinities, Anath-bethel and Ashem-
bethel, we are made aware not simply of a decline into poly-
theism on the part of these Jews, who had apparently brought
this type of worship with them from Palestine,[2] but of that
urge which may be regarded as partly responsible for the figure
of Wisdom or rather which the conception of Wisdom met and
purified, namely to provide Jahve with consorts of associates
($\pi\alpha\rho\acute{\epsilon}\delta\rho\omicron\iota$). Anath-bethel and Ashem-bethel are the wives of
Jahve.[3] Wisdom appears in Prov. 1–9 described in terms that
depict her as Jahve's darling daughter. Hempel is without
doubt right in his judgment, that Ezekiel, whose writing is at
its freshest and best when he is fashioning mythological conceptions or foreign religious ideas into the clothing of his thought
and teaching, has in view in his picture of the two sisters Ohola

[1] Mercenary soldiers perhaps already settled in Egypt under Psammetuh I
(664–609) or in the time of Ezekiel under Psammetich II. (594–88). Cf. Meinhold, *Einführung in das A.T.*, p. 168.

[2] See *Myth and Ritual*, p. 185.

[3] See Hempel, *Altheb. Lit.*, p. 168. Hölscher, *Gesch d. isr. und jüd. Rel.*,
p. 115.

and Oholiba (chap. 23), who represent for him the people of Israel and Judah whom Jahve has betrothed,[1] those very forms of popular religion which Anath-bethel and Ashem-bethel allow us to perceive. Personified Wisdom, raised to be an associate with Jahve, may well be viewed in this aspect as a spiritual substitute and sublimate of the well-attested grosser expression of popular religious belief and worship. The witness of Elephantiné is the best guide not only to the understanding of the spirit of Ezek. 23 but to the appreciation of its religious historical background. That this type of religion entailed in cultic practice, and as a consequence in social life, sensuality (cf. Ezek. 23[36f.]) is clear and explains how " harlotry," " adultery," " whoring after other gods " became metaphors for unfaithfulness to Jahve. The Jewish worship at Elephantiné, the prophecy of Ezekiel upon the two sister brides of Jahve, the splendidly drawn description of the adulteress and her lover in Prov. 1–9 (cf. 7[6f.]), the warnings against adultery from which wisdom will save the youth, appear each to give portions of the same historical picture in its religious and social aspects. In this regard it is interesting to note the character of the language of Sirach a century or more later than Prov. 1–9. In exhorting the youth to meditate upon Wisdom he says :

> [Blessed is he] that peereth into her window,
> And hearkeneth at her doors, . . .
> She will meet him as a mother,
> And as a youthful wife will she receive him (14[23], 15[2]).

Here in Sirach's language there may be nothing more than the natural imagery of poetry ; the advice to embrace Wisdom. His language is mainly traditional, and largely based upon Prov. 1–9. But a glance backwards into Israel's history is sufficient to show that if the complexion of Sirach's language is now purely poetical, it is also the afterglow of conflicts that were concerned with sterner realities. The poetic faculty may never be disregarded as an element of any human conception of

[1] Read chap. 23 in Moffatt's translation.

religious value, but it is otherwise quite certain that behind the traditional langauge of Sirach and behind the personification of Wisdom there were conditions that had extremely little to do with poetry. The figure of Wisdom, representing the spiritualizing and moralizing of religion, is thus one of the finest accomplishments of Judaism, and it is significant that it appears as a product of the ethical-religious teaching of the Wisdom-school.

3

The difficulty with which we are confronted in a search for the mythological background of the figure of Wisdom or for the religious conceptions of non-Israelite origin which gave rise to Wisdom does not spring from a paucity of similar ideas and speculations among the peoples with whom Israel had contact but rather from a wealth of similar ideas. Among these peoples there are deities who are reported to have been, as Wisdom is described, active in creation or who appear as personifications of a divine attribute, principle, or force.

In the Babylonian religion the goddess or god (?) Mummu who plays a rôle in the Creation Epic *Enuma elis* (I. 4) is generally regarded as signifying " form " or " the principle of formation." The Babylonian theologians explain the name of this deity by a term *rigmu* which is taken to mean " Word." [1] Damascius (*de princ.* 125) hands down the tradition of Eudemos of Rhodes that Mummu was " the only begotten son " of Tiamat (the salt-water ocean, the " principle " of Chaos) and Apsu (the fresh water) and represents " the intelligible world." According to Böhl [2] Mummu is the hypostatic divine Word and it is important to note that the Babylonian *bit mummi* is interpreted as meaning " house of wisdom " or school.[3] The Babylonian Ea (God of the waters) is described as " Mummu who forms all " and Marduk,

---

[1] Cf. Gressmann, *Altorient. Texte*, p. 109.
[2] *Orient. Literaturzeitung* 19 (1916), 265 f.
[3] Cf. Gressmann, *op. cit.*

Ea's son, appears in a hymn as "son of Mummu," and also is called "Mummu who created." The character of Mummu as a personified principle or power is seen from the fact that Marduk's son, Nebo, the scribe-god, also in turn is named in similar terms "the Wisdom of Mummu, the begetter of the sons (of the gods)." Ea, Marduk, and Nebo are all wisdom-deities ; Ea is "the wise one of the gods who knows all" (Cod. Ham. xxvi, R 101), "who knows all wisdom" "who embraces all in spirit, cunning, and wise" (*Enuma elis* I. 18 ; I. 60 ; II. 127). Though Marduk is the vanquisher of Chaos (Tiamat), Ea represents the principle of all creative formation, and is contrasted with Mummu who, Hehn thinks, is the symbol of the blind creative forces of the chaotic masses.[1] Further, as the originator of the world Ea is also thought of as he to whom mankind owes its origin, its cult of the gods, its culture, the knowledge of all implements, arts, and crafts. Ea is "the father of the gods, the Lord of the inscrutable wisdom." The creation of the world which is ascribed to Ea and to Marduk ("the first born son of Ea" Cod. Ham. I.9) is occasionally also ascribed to Nebo. Nebo's functions concern the government of the world. He is "the Overseer of the whole of heaven and earth" "the wise, clever, under-standing one who holds the bond of heaven and earth," that is, he sees to the preservation of the world ; he is the "Orderer of the whole," he without whom "no decree of council is fixed in heaven." He is the giver and protector of life and also "Lord of works of art and skill." Moreover, Nebo is a religious teacher and the trainer of mankind ; his spouse is "Tashmet" a name which signifies "Hearing" or "Revealing" ; he "holds the totality of the commandments" and is "perfect in instructions"[2] The sufferer prays to Nebo to be enabled "to walk uprightly before thee, thereby may I satisfy myself," "Put truth in my mouth, let (good) thoughts be in my heart."[3]

---

[1] Hehn, *Sünde und Erlösung nach bibl. und bab. Anschauung*, p. 6.

[2] See Heinisch, *Die persönliche Weisheit*, p. 24 f.

[3] J. Pinckert, *Hymnen und Gebete an Nebo*, n. 11, 14.

In view of the impression which the Babylonian Creation myth made upon the account of creation in Genesis, it is quite conceivable that the Babylonian theological ideas attaching to Mummu as word or principle of formation influenced Judaism when, with the growth of the conception of the transcendence of Jahve, intermediaries between him and the world were postulated. Schraeder lodges the objection that Mummu in the Creation myth is one of the three divinities who oppose the realization of world order as effected by Marduk and that the description of Mummu as " intelligible world (cosmos) " is probably not so early as Eudemos but is an interpretation offered by the Neoplatonist Damascius, Eudemos' reporter.[1] But even so, we may have to reckon with the possibility of the character of this divinity having changed under later theological reflection or cosmological speculation prior to the appearance of the Jewish Wisdom. Of the other deities of the Babylonian pantheon who may seem to have, beside Mummu, most claim to be regarded as possible prototypes of personified Wisdom are the two children of Shamash, the sun-god ; Kettu the " Right " or the " Truth " and Mesharu " Probity " or " Rectitude " who have their equivalents in Phœnician cosmology (Saduk and Misor).[2] These appear as pure personifications of divine attributes. Also Meissner mentions the divine Word *amatu* as having been hypostatized by Babylonian speculation.[3] That Nabu, whom we see in Ezekiel's vision of the destruction of Jerusalem converted into the recording angel of Jahve, continued to exercise considerable influence[4] upon the Jewish imagination may make us more open to believe that Judaism was capable of assimilating and transforming also some of the subtler elements of Babylonian theology.

Egyptian religion provides striking parallels to the Jewish

---

[1] J. Pinckert, *Hymnen und Gebete an Nebo*, p. 319.   [2] Schencke, p. 88.
[3] *Babylonien und Assyrien*, ii. pp. 47 ; cf. p. 124.

[4] Cf. Jub. 4²³ ; 1 Enoch 12³ᵗ·, 15¹, 89⁷⁰ᵗ· ; 4 Ezra 14⁵⁰ in Kautzsch, *Pseudep.* p. 348 ; Gunkel, *Archiv. für Religionswiss.*, 1898, p. 299 f., *Der Schreibergott Nabu im A.T., und im Judentum* ; Bousset, *op. cit.* p. 353 f.

figure of Wisdom. The goddess Maat, the deity of Truth and Justice seems to be little more than the personification of an abstract idea. In the picture of the judgment of the dead where in the scales of justice the heart of the dead is weighed against the truth symbolized by a feather, the feather is the symbol of Maat. But with the Jewish conception of Wisdom an even closer analogy is presented by Egyptian theological thought in respect of the God Ptah who is not only the god of artists and all handworkers but who installs the king as ruler and gives him wisdom, health, fame, and long life (cf. *Sap. Sol.* 9). Moreover, he is the Creator of the world from whom a " word " went forth and by this " word " the deities were brought into existence.[1] These different deities, again, were regarded as if they were but attributes of Ptah whose various aspects they revealed, while being identical with him.

In consideration of the influence which Egyptian wisdom-writings had upon Israel's wisdom-writers, it might seem that for the idea of Wisdom as a divine person, the patron God of the Egyptian wise, the god Thoth, had had some significance. Thoth was a moon-god, god of the art of accurate accounting, of science and wisdom. He is a deity of revelation : " the beginning of speech, the bearer of knowledge, the opener of the concealed." He is praised as the " God of the first beginnings of time," as the " King of eternity," the " oldest God." As the deity of the scribes he is the initiator of culture ; as deity of wisdom, the god of handworkers, builders, and artists ; as the giver of the principles of order, he is also the Creator and Governor of the world.[2]

Reitzenstein points to the attraction which the Egyptian conception of Thoth had already at an early date for the Greeks.[3] Plato mentions this deity twice (Phaidr. 274c ; Phileb. 18B).

---

[1] See Schencke, *op. cit.* p. 88.

[2] Heinisch, *op. cit.* p. 31. Cf. also Erman, *Lit. d. Aegypter*, p. 186 on Thoth as " Leader of men."

[3] *Zwei religionsgeschichtliche Fragen*, p. 88 f.

Before the time of Herodotus progress had been made in equating Greek and Egyptian deities. Thoth suggested, in his character as interpreter or revealer, the Greek Hermes (ἑρμηνεύς).
Reitzenstein further stresses the fact that in the early Hellenistic period the places of Re the sun-god and Thoth the moon-
god and their relationship to each other were taken over by
Osiris and the goddess Isis.[1] Isis appears now as " the wisest
of all the gods," as the law-giver and teacher of agriculture
(Ptolemaic Stele, *Diodor.* I. 27). On a votive-offering she has the
name " Isis Righteousness " (115–114 B.C.). The Greeks derived
her name εἶσις (Eisis) from εἰδέναι (eidenai) meaning " to know."
She is called Sophia (Wisdom) and Gnosis (Knowledge), the
Beginning or Beginner (Genesis) from whom spring the genetic
principles (γεννητικαὶ ἀρχαί) of creation and life (Plut. *c.* 43). She
is the " Bestower of life " (*Ti-anch*) and Life itself (*Anchit*) ;
she is Providence (*pronoia*) and Understanding (*phronesis*).
Reitzenstein (*op. cit.* p. 108) shows that " Isis-Wisdom (Sophia)
in Hellenistic songs and traditions could interchange and was
interchanged with Hermes-Word (Logos)."

On comparison of Babylonian and Egyptian thought it must
seem that Egyptian theology as represented by the speculations
regarding Isis (which no doubt were partly developed from older
reflections upon Ptah and Thoth) offers something that appears
to be the most complete counterpart to the figure of Wisdom in
Judaism. In the opinion of Reitzenstein the Jewish personified
Wisdom is a product of Egyptian and Iranian thought. The
Egyptian conception of Isis, he thinks (*Poimandres*, p. 249, note 1)
exercised its influence upon Persian religion and is responsible
for the Iranian figure *Armaiti* who presents a very close analogy
to Wisdom. Hölscher expresses himself in similar terms regarding the origin of Wisdom as " partly due to speculation in
regard to Isis-Sophia and perhaps partly to Iranian-Babylonian
thought." [2] But at this stage it may be enough to remark that
while the Isis speculation of Egypt which seems only to appear

---

[1] *Op. cit.* p. 104 f., 106 f.   [2] *Op. cit.* p. 185. f.

in the Hellenistic age may be considered to have influenced
the Wisdom literature of this age and thus to account for some
of the features which Wisdom acquired in development, we are
not entitled to regard Prov. 1–9, where personified Wisdom first
most clearly appears, as a work of Hellenistic Judaism. These
chapters, even if dated as late as 300 B.C., and they cannot safely
be placed later,[1] appear too early in the Ptolemaic period, when
the Isis-Sophia speculation itself arose, to have been influenced
by this.

4

Before we consider the question of Persian (Zoroastrian)
influence in shaping the mystical figure of Wisdom in Judaism
we must here take account of the view of Wilhelm Schencke
(*Wisdom—Chokma in the Jewish Hypostasis-speculation, op. cit.*
above), that the conception of personified wisdom arose in
Judaism itself and grew out of Hebrew mythology. Little
original as later Judaism was and syncretic in character, he says,
we do not need to suppose an alien mythology. The old
Israelite religion could not be described as monotheistic. The
various *numina* who were subordinated to Jahve had nevertheless stood beside Him. Judaism had had a polytheistic folk-
religion as its background and under the progress of monotheistic thought, resulting in the transcendentalism of which
we have spoken, the idea of Wisdom as an hypostasis may have
arisen as naturally as did the poetic personifications of other
divine attributes. According to Schencke it is probable that
the form of myth from which the figure of Wisdom was later
drawn was a Paradise-myth. The tree of knowledge with its
wonderful fruit, which was the food of the gods and imparted
to them the gift of wisdom, had been under the custody of a
particular goddess. This goddess was regarded later as the wife

---

[1] Sellin, *Intro. Prov.*, 1–9, " About the fourth century," p. 208. Cf. p. 267.
Gressmann, *Z.A.W.*, 1924, p. 286, " Die neugefundene Lehre des Amen-em-
ope " places Prov. 1–9 definitely in the Persian period.

or daughter or beloved associate (πάρεδρος) of Jahve. Later still when monotheistic thought challenged and modified the older traditions, the two deities, the goddess and Jahve, coalesce and Jahve appears as the sole possessor of wisdom, supremely wise. Finally as Jahve becomes more and more remote from the world and doings of men, the old prototype of wisdom again emerges to play a rôle as intermediary but in such a manner that all traces of the original Being who was independent of Jahve are, so far as possible, removed to the background, though they still here and there continue to be perceptible.

With this paradise myth of which we have a version in the Jahvistic story in Genesis (2[4f.]), Schencke (so also Gunkel, " Genesis," *S.A.T.*, p. 67) connects the oracle in Ezek. 28[11f.], where Ezekiel, in prophecying the fall of the king of Tyre, clearly refers to a myth which told of the expulsion from the mountain of God in paradise of a being who dwelt among the Cherubim, possessed wisdom and glory but who through iniquity and pride forfeited his rank and dignity. ' Bousset and others think that this being was the cosmic Man.[1] " Not improbably," says Schencke, " a myth was current that wisdom (Hokma) had once been stolen from God against His will. At that time wisdom was ' in the council of Eloah (God).' Into this council some one— most probably the primeval (cosmic) Man—had gained entrance by stealth and taken (the) wisdom away." [2] That a myth of this type, which has its parallel in the story of Prometheus' theft of the divine fire, was known to the Hebrews, Schencke submits, is discernible in the words of Eliphaz to Job (Job 15[7f.]) :

> Wert thou the first man to be born ?
> And wert thou brought into being before the hills ?
> Didst thou listen in the council of Eloah (God)
> And didst thou snatch [3] wisdom to thee ?

---

[1] *Rel. d. Jud.*, 3, p. 352. The myth, however, seems to be due to a mingling of the Adam myth (Eden) with that of the cosmic Man (Mountain of God).

[2] *Op. cit.* p. 74. · Cf. pp. 9 f., 12.

[3] Heb. gara'=*to cut off*. Peake (*Century Bible*) gives the meaning as *draw*, Schencke (cf. Kautsch " rissest(du).").

Here the reference is certainly to the pre-existent Man. It is not so clear that the verb in the last line means " to snatch " or " seize " but it may have this meaning and may intend taking away with violence or stealth. We may, however, admit that Schencke is right when he says that wisdom here is spoken of as something that can be " separated from God," " something tangible . . . almost a quantitative entity."

When we reflect upon the myth which Schencke postulates we must recognize its value as a much desiderated attempt to define the way in which it might be supposed Hebrew thought arrived unassisted at the idea of Wisdom as a personal Being. But its value is really even greater in that when we examine his conclusions they show how inadequate this supposed myth is to explain the character of personified Wisdom as this appears in Prov. 1–9 or Job 28.

A paradise myth was doubtless at a very early date a common possession of the peoples of Canaan, and in Genesis (2^{46}–3^{24}) we have the form of it as this was fashioned by Hebrew religion. A Babylonian element in the myth is indicted by the mention of the rivers of Mesopotamia, Hiddekel (Tigris) and Euphrates, by the appearance of Cherubim and of religious motives which are present in the stories of Adapa and Gilgamesh. It is very generally agreed that in the older tradition of the myth the serpent represented a god who disturbed the plans of the Creator-god.[1] Hebrew thought has modified this trait to suit its conception of Jahve.[2] Possibly this other god who is the only other divinity, besides Jahve, interested in the tree of knowledge was the guardian of the tree and the prototype of the goddess who in Schencke's account is given custody of the tree ; or possibly again, due to the place and prominence given to the serpent in the Hebrew form of the myth, the figure of the goddess custodian has dropped from the original picture. But the form in which the paradise myth first appears in Hebrew mythology, with the only active divine associate of Jahve

[1] Cf. Stade, *Bib. Theol.*, p. 242.   [2] Cf. Stade, *op. cit.* ; Gunkel, *op. cit.*

mentioned as interested in the tree of knowledge being, or having
been converted into, Jahve's opponent, does not offer a good
beginning for such a development of the myth as Schencke
describes.   Neither does the connection of wisdom in Job 15⁷ᵗ·
with the cosmic Man, who in no wise can be regarded as of
Israelite origin,[1] speak for a purely Israelite mythology having
developed the conception of personified Wisdom as beloved
associate of Jahve.   We can perceive that after the Exile the
older loans from Babylonian mythology were supplemented by
an even larger income from that source and from elsewhere.
In face of this it is rather difficult for us to imagine Hebrew
thought threading its way unassisted through the different stages
of a paradise myth such as Schencke constructs.

By the verses of the fifteenth chapter of Job as interpreted
by Schencke, and we believe interpreted rightly, we are brought
no nearer the idea of Wisdom as a person, but wisdom is here, as
he says, regarded as " a tangible thing," " a quantitative mass."
The conversion of a quality into a tangible thing, as something
belonging to God but yet separable from Him, represents rather
a lapse backward into primitive thought than an advance towards
the real personification of an attribute.   That the Hebrew
mind was prepared for the speculation regarding Wisdom need
not be denied.   No mind will receive impressions which it is
not susceptible to taking.   Only antecedent preparatory conditions normally conduce to borrowing.   That primitive Oriental
thought might regard wisdom as a substance, or as a quality
that might be obtained by eating a substance ; that poetry
could personify an attribute of God ; that the idea of the
transcendence of Jahve in the course of the development of
monotheistic thought explains the need for intermediaries—all
these factors were preparatory.   When Bousset and Reitzenstein, however, speak of the suddenness with which personified
Wisdom appears in Judaism, they mean by this that the appearance of this mystical turn of thought and the *actual character*,

---

[1] Cf. Schraeder, *op. cit.* above and Bousset, *op. cit.* p. 265 f.

functions, and features of Wisdom are startlingly new. These new
funds of thought which Judaism now displays call for explanation. Further, from Job 28 and Prov. 1–9, where we first meet
with personified Wisdom, we observe that where we must look
for the origin of this figure is not in a paradise myth, however
inseparable this type of myth may be from it, but in a creation
myth, and that of a kind purer and subtler than the Babylonian.
Schencke finally himself seems to see that something more than
the process of thought he describes is necessary to account for
the Jewish wisdom speculation, and says that the assumption
of influence through Parsism (p. 92)—possibly with Babylonian
elements (p. 86)—is " extraordinarily apposite." But if Iranian
influence is appealed to at all it is impossible for us not to make
it responsible for those features of Wisdom which in Judaism
appear new but which in Iranian sources are characteristic.

5

In the twenty-eighth chapter of Job Wisdom is a personality.
The theme of the chapter is that man cannot find the way to
Wisdom. Only God knows where Wisdom dwells.

> God knows the way to her
> And He has knowledge of her abode.   (v. 23)
> When He fixed the weight of the wind
> And decreed for the waters their measure,   (v. 25)
> When He made rules for the rain,
> And paths for the lightning flash,   (v. 26)
> He saw her then and studied her :
> He established [1] her and proved her.   (v. 27)

That these verses were more than a poetic description of
God's power and wisdom we would not be justified in concluding,
if they stood alone and unrelated in the literature of Judaism.
It is when they are read in the light of the descriptions of
Wisdom (Prov. 1–9), which appear at no distant date [2] from

---

[1] Set her up (exalted ?)

[2] Chap. 28 is later than the dialogue of Job, *i.e.* later than 450 B.C. On
question of relationship of Prov. 1–9 to Job, see Cornill's *Intro. to O.T.*

Job 28, that we may judge that there was a common background
of mythological conceptions upon which these verses already
drew. In the statement that God " studied " Wisdom and
" proved " her (searched out, or tested her knowledge) is the
suggestion that Wisdom provided the plan and laws of Creation
which God adopted and found to be good.

Since we must regard Proverbs, chaps. 1–9, as belonging to
the Persian Period of Israel's history, or at least as having been
composed before the syncretic influences of the Hellenistic
Period became acute, it is essential for an inquiry into the
original source of Wisdom that we examine the description
of Wisdom given in these chapters carefully and in some
detail.

Wisdom declares her relationship to Jahve, to the world, and
to men, 8[22f.] :

Jahve begat [1] me at the beginning of His ways,
The first of His works, of old (*He begat me*). (22)
I was installed [2] from everlasting, from the beginning.
Or ever the earth was. (23)
When there were no depths (*tehomoth*) I was born :
When there were no fountains abounding with water. (24)
Before (the bases of) the mountains were sunk,
Before the hills was I brought forth : (25)
While as yet He had not made the earth nor open places,
" Nor the green " (*we-desheh*) of the soil of the world. (26)

When He prepared the heavens I was there :
When He drew the vault (circle) upon the surface of the deep (*tehom*), (27)
When He made the skies firm overhead,
When he fixed firmly the fountains of the deep (*tehom*), (28)
When He set the sea its bound,
That the waters should not transgress His commandment ;
When He " made strong " [3] the foundations of the earth, (29)

---

[1] Cf. Oesterley, *Comm. on Proverbs, ad loc.* Burney, *J.T.S.*, xxvii. (1926),
pp. 160–177. For discussion on the word, see Schencke.
[2] Sense is " installed," or appointed as a king is. Cf. Ps. 2[6]. There is no
need to change the Hebrew text to " I was founded."
[3] With LXX.

Then I was by Him as master-workman.[1]
And I was His delight day by day;
Rejoicing [2] before Him continually,   (30)
Rejoicing in the world [3] of His earth,
And my delight was with the sons of man.   (31)

This pre-existent Wisdom has a revelation to give to man and
her invitation and message are thus described 8[4f.] :

Unto you, O men, do I call,
And my voice is unto the sons of man.   (4)
And the opening of my lips shall be right things,   (6b)
For my mouth utters truth (*Emeth*),
And lips of wickedness are an abomination unto me (LXX).   (7)
In righteousness (*Zedek*) are all the words of my mouth,   (8a)
They are all plain to him that understands,
And right to those who find knowledge (*Da'ath*).   (9)
I walk in the path of righteousness (*Zedakah*)
In the midst of the ways of judgment (justice, *Mishpat*)   (20)
For whoso finds me finds life,   (35a)
All who hate me love death.   (36b)

Wisdom is contrasted in a striking manner with her opponent
Folly, who competes with her for the love and obedience of
men, 9[1f.]:

Wisdom has built her house,
She has hewn [4] out her seven pillars.   (1)
She has sent her maidens out to cry
On the high places of the city :   (3)
"Come, eat my bread
And drink of the wine that I have mingled."   (5)
Folly is clamorous . . .   (13)
She sits at the door of her house,
On a seat in the high places of the city,   (14)

---

[1] *Amon*=workmaster (cf. Sap. Sol. Gr. *technitis*), so Smend (*Alttest. Religionsgesch*, p. 490), in accord with the weight of the evidence. Vul.=*opifex*.

[2] Lit. *sporting*.

[3] Volz translates Erdkreis=circle, or round of the earth. LXX=completion (perhaps " perfection of His earth ").

[4] " Hewn," as more difficult reading is perhaps to be preferred to LXX," has set up."

To call to them that pass by :   (15a)
" Stolen waters are sweet
And bread in secret is delicious."   (17)
But he (who is without understanding) knows not that the dead [1]
    are there ;
In the depths of Sheol are her guests.   (18)

The chief features of personified Wisdom which Prov. 1–9 permits us to observe are : (1) that Wisdom was begotten of God before the world was created ; (2) that She was installed or appointed by God either to rule or to be an associate with Him in His rule ; (3) that Wisdom was a master of works or artificer whose plans for the creation were evidently studied and approved by Jahve (cf. Job 28), Jahve Himself being the Creator ; (4) Wisdom is an associate of Jahve in whom He has constant delight ; (5) Wisdom's message and functions are particularly concerned with mankind : She reveals the way of life and righteousness ; (6) Wisdom's dwelling or house has seven pillars ; (7) She is contrasted with Folly (or " woman " of foolishness), and what She bestows is compared with what Folly offers : the ways of Folly are Death ; (8) the character of Wisdom's message is a proclamation of Truth (*Emeth*), Righteousness (*Zedek*), Knowledge (*Da'ath*), and Judgment, Justice, or Law (*Mishpat*).

Viewing the characteristics of Wisdom, Bousset (*op. cit.* p. 520) came to the conclusion that the figure of Wisdom in Judaism derived from Persian religious belief, according to which the supreme God of light and of truth, Ahura Mazda (the Lord of Wisdom) had created six divine beings to be His intermediaries between Himself and the world. Of these six " holy immortal ones," or Amesha Spentas, created by Ahura Mazda before the phenomenal world existed, Bousset considered one, *Armaiti*, whom Plutarch (*De Is. et Os.* 47) called Sophia or Wisdom, to be the prototype of the Jewish figure. In equating Sophia with Armaiti, Plutarch was probably drawing

[1] The " shades."

from early Greek authors, possibly from Hermippus (*c.* 250 B.C.), who had a competent knowledge of Iranian religion,[1] or from Theopompos, who lived in the fourth century (*c.* 320). In the Gathas, the genuine utterances of Zoroaster, which are thus, even at the lowest date assigned to him, considerably earlier than the earliest appearance of personified Wisdom in Judaism, the six heavenly intermediaries have the same character as the Jewish Wisdom in that they appear sometimes as personal Beings and at other times as abstract ideas. They are " the embodiment of the powers on which the God-willed world-order depends." [2]

Both Andreas and Schraeder [3] are of the opinion that in the time before Zoroaster the Amesha Spentas represented to the adherents of the old Iranian religion deities of the elements (fire, water, wind, etc.), and that the Reformer converted them into purely spiritual Bearers of the creative functions of Ahura Mazda. Meyer strongly protests against this idea, and thinks that originally they were abstractions. Volz [4] and Geiger [5] also express the view that the intermediaries of Zoroastrianism are not deposed deities of the elements, but arose out of abstract ideas and then were personified as patron divinities. The question does not seem to be of much importance for us here, although it is difficult to believe that all of these beings— particularly one in whom we are especially interested (Asha)— arose out of mere abstract notions. It is sufficient for us to note their general character. " They are not," as Volz aptly puts it, " as in the Babylonian and Egyptian religions, separated from the supreme God, so that each represents something outside of Him, as, for example, the Sun in contrast with the Moon, the Waters (*e.g.* Ea) in contrast with the Heavens, but

---

[1] See Haug (West), *Essays on the Religion of the Parsis*, p. 9.

[2] Meyer, *op. cit.* p. 62. Cf. n. 2.

[3] *Op. cit.* p. 279.

[4] " Der heilige Geist in den Gathas des Sarathuschtra, *Eucharasiterion*, i. 1923, p. 326.

[5] *Sitz. Ber. d. Akad. d. Wiss. Wien Phil.-Hist.*, Kl. 176, 7 Abh.

they and Ahura Mazda form one concept ; they are, as it were, the features of His face ; they cannot even be called angels or archangels, even though in prayers and poetical speech they appear as definite personal beings, and are invoked as such " (p. 326 *op. cit.*).

The Amesha Spentas, who in the Gathas are the personified elements of the perfect kingdom of God which is the aim of the divine Will, are, in the order in which Geldner [1] ranges them : *Asha*, " the right Law " ; *Vohu mano*, " the good Disposition " ; *Khshathra*, " the Kingdom (of God) " ; *Armaiti*, " Devotion (Piety) " ; *Haurvatāt*, " Perfection " ; *Ameretāt*, " Immortality." Of these six hypostases, two of them, Vohu mano and Armaiti, have been singled out by those who assume that the Jewish Wisdom is a product of the contact of Judaism and Persian thought, and each has been given preference as the Prototype of Wisdom. Bousset's preference for Armaiti is somewhat adversely affected by the fact that although Plutarch certainly translates Armaiti as *Sophia*, Armaiti represents the bountiful earth [2] as the patron of agriculture, and as the instructress in this art is the declarer of the divine wisdom. But at the same time she is also Piety, and it has been suggested that the truth that Piety is the beginning of wisdom and the Hebrew maxim that " the Fear of the Lord is the beginning of wisdom " bring Armaiti and the Hebrew Wisdom into close relationship. Perhaps more can be said for Vohu mano. Darmesteter pointed to the similarity of Vohu mano and the Logos (Word) of Philo, and Schencke tentatively expresses the view that Vohu mano's character has contributed to the conception of Wisdom. Vohu mano appears as intermediary in the work of creation (Jasna 31[11]) as mediator and content of the eschatological consummation (Jasna 45[5. 8], 46[7], 48[8]) and as content of the religious and moral

---

[1] " Die Zoroastrische Religion " (*Das Avesta*), 1926, p. 2.

[2] In Prov. 8[22], the earth and the waters that fructify it are given very prominent mention among the created things. The " deeps " (Tehomoth) are an echo of Babylonian mythology.

life (34² cf. 33⁶).¹ Ahura Mazda consults with Vohu mano in regard to the creation of all things (47³). He is placed first in Plutarch's list of the Persian intermediaries with the name εὔνοια or " good Will "; he represents the good religious sense.

Now, it may seem that, although Armaiti is patron of the earth, and although the character of Vohu mano as " Good Disposition " is not particularly distinctive of the Jewish Wisdom, their functions otherwise as intermediaries, especially those of Vohu mano, make it probable that Judaism was dependent on Iranian thought in view of the singular appearance of Wisdom in Judaism. Such loans as Judaism made were certainly not textual borrowings. It is unlikely that any particular one of the Persian intermediaries contributed all to the Jewish concept of Wisdom. We may take it that Haurvātāt (" Perfection ") and Ameretāt (" Immortality ") contributed little or nothing. It is rather their general character which, therefore, must be considered as having made impression on Judaism. As Geldner states, the intermediaries " retain in the Gathas the double character of persons and abstract qualities and express the different variations of a common fundamental idea." ² This continues also to be their characteristic ; they and Ahura Mazda, the Lord of Wisdom, have all " the same thought " and " the same action." ³ But while this is true, and while Vohu mano and Armaiti may each have influenced the conception of Wisdom, it must appear from a study of the Zoroastrian intermediaries in the Gathas that the Amesha Spenta, who seems to approximate most to the Jewish Wisdom, has received singularly little attention. We mean the figure of *Asha vahishta*, " the right Law," whom Plutarch calls " Truth," ⁴ who represents " Purity " and all the religious and moral duties of man; Asha is the representative of Religion

---

¹ Cf. Volz. *op. cit.* p. 341.   ² *Op. cit.* p. 2.
³ See Stave, *Über den Einfluss des Parsismus auf das Judentum*, p. 205.
Cf. Yasht, 19⁶, 13⁸³.
⁴ ἀλήθεια.

or Belief, who watches over the divine law and is " the embodiment of the world-order " (*astvat ashem*). Asha is the genius
of righteousness and the judge in the final judgment.[1] The
three holy immortal ones who are, most frequently mentioned
in association with Ahura Mazda are Asha, Vohu mano, and
Armaiti, [2] and in placing Asha next to Ahura Mazda, Geldner
would seem to have taken into account the frequency with which
this position is accorded to Asha in the texts.

With the different features of divine personified Wisdom
which we have traced in Prov. 1–9 we must now, therefore,
compare what the Gathas have to say about Asha. In Prov. 8[22]
it is said that Wisdom is begotten of Jahve. In the 44th Jasna
v.[3]) Ahura Mazda is described as " the first Begetter (Geldner
—' Erzeuger ') of Asha (the Law)." Not only Asha, but also
all the other intermediaries are the teachers of men, but Ahura
Mazda says to Zoroaster, " Thou shalt see my Asha when I
call it together with Armaiti to come into my Presence. . . .
Thou shalt come to be instructed in the law (Asha) " (Jas. 43[10. 12]).
Asha is more than the other intermediary Beings associated
with teaching and revealing. The prophet beseeches Ahura
Mazda, the Lord of Wisdom, and Asha for new revelations of
their will : " O Wise One and Asha, I entreat you to say what
according to the mind of your wisdom is to be done rightly
to distinguish how we should teach Religion " (Jas. 49[6]).
In the Gathas, as in Proverbs, Religion (in Hebrew the " Fear
of the Lord ") is predominantly morality, " cultivation of
' Asha ' (the Right) a pure life according to the commandments
of God, deeds, prayer, knowledge, acknowledgment of God ;
offerings and cultus take quite a secondary place." [3] In

---

[1] Cf. Pfleiderer, *Early Christian Conception of Christ*, p. 142.

[2] Armaiti, like Wisdom in Proverbs, is feminine. The gender of Vohu mano
and Asha appears as masculine but they are neither male nor female. Cf.
Schencke, p. 85, note 6 ; and see Bultmann, *op. cit.* p. 22. " In the different
sources the male and female figures of the Bearers of Revelation change or
appear combined."

[3] Volz, p. 328.

Prov. 8[4f. 20] the message of Wisdom is concerned with truth (Emeth), righteousness (Zedek), knowledge (Da'ath), judgment (Mishpat). Asha is the special personification of all these. Asha is " the Right " (cf. Prov. 8[6b. 9]). The interest of Asha in the world of men is markedly clear in the question : " When, O Wise One, will the mornings of the days break when the living world holds fast to Asha (the Law) ? (When) will the right knowledge (come) through the exalted words of the future saviours ? " (Jas. 46[3]). We have something here reminiscent of the call of Wisdom in the first chapter of Proverbs : " Wisdom calls aloud in the streets. . . . O heedless ones, how long will you choose to be heedless ? " (1[20f.]). " So long as I have power," says the prophet, " so long will I preach that men strive after Asha (the Law) " (Jas. 28[4]). In the Gathas there is the same contrast between falsehood and truth, life and death (Jas. 30[3f.]), righteousness and wickedness, as is so marked in the appeals of Wisdom in Prov. 1–9. Wisdom invites men to choose wisdom. In the great decision or choice between good and evil, of which the thirtieth Jasna speaks, the Holy Spirit gave the whole world an example by choosing the Right, that is, by choosing Asha. Those who do evil are those " who turn from the Good Disposition, who fall away from the wise Lord and from Asha (Law) " (Jas. 32[4]). Here again we notice the very close relationship between the supreme Lord and Asha. " The paths of the good teaching " (Jas. 46[4] ; cf. Prov. 8[9. 20]) are the paths of Asha. " Lips of wickedness are an abomination unto me," states Wisdom (Prov. 8[8]) ; the opponent of Asha is the lie (Druj) (30[8]).

The dualistic form of thought which is characteristic of Iranian religion might be expected in Prov. 1–9 where Wisdom is opposed to Folly, wickedness to truth, life to death. But it must, however, be remarked that this dualism is present, and that both in Prov. 1–9 and in the Gathas this opposition of principles is depicted in the same way : Wisdom offers her guests good food, bread and wine ; Folly entices with " stolen waters " and " bread in secret," that is, with death-dealing food (9[10]).   According to Jasna 51[1], " there flows sweet refreshment therein, O Asha, for him who, according to his deeds, O wise one, receives the best as reward."   This sweet refreshment (cf. Jas. 49[10]) has as its opposite " the evil foods " (49[11]) which is the final reward of those who do and speak wickedly, that is, those who are opposed to Asha, who is the truth and the true Belief (49[3]).   Besides this, as in Prov. 1–9, the house of Wisdom and the house of Folly are contrasted, so, too, in the Gathas mention is made (48[11]) of " the beautiful dwelling-place " which is the future reward of the good and of " the dwelling of the Lie " (Geldner—" the female Satan ") where the wicked who have a false belief and false religion are " the proper house-mates " (49[11]).

We interpret Prov. 8[23] as meaning that Wisdom, before ever the earth was, was appointed to her task or rule.   Her function, like that of Asha, is that of instruction and, in creation, of devising the plans which God adopts.   Though Vohu mano is described (see above) as being the adviser of Ahura Mazda in the work of creation, Asha, whose emblem and element is fire, is also regarded in that light.   Asha is " the holiest fire, the source of all good in creation " (Haug, op. cit. p. 155 on Jas. 43[12]) and is supposed to be spread everywhere as the cause of all life.   As being both Law and fire, Asha performs the task of exercising judgment and justice upon men.[1]   Ahura Mazda, " with Asha, his skilled adviser, distinguishes between the righteous and the unrighteous " (Jas. 46[17]).   In the phrase, " skilled adviser," we have something approaching the description of Wisdom as technician, or master of works (Amon). Fire, in the religion of Zoroaster, is the means of destruction and purification in the eschatological judgment.   In references to this judgment Fire is connected with the Holy Spirit (cf. St. Matt. 3[11]),[2] but it is an element that goes out from Asha

---

[1] Cf. Jas. 31[9].
[2] Cf. Volz, p. 342 ; Jas. 31[3], 47[6], etc.

(the Law) or is Asha. " Of thy fire, O Ahura (Mazda) which has its strength through Asha . . . we wish that it obtain for the faithful man visible comfort " (Jas. 34[4] ; cf. 32[7], 51[9]). A passage (Jas. 36[2]) which Geldner states reaches back to the time of the Gathas, and which indeed must reflect the reverence for fire in the Iranian religion previous to Zoroaster, calls Fire the " son of the Wise Lord " (Ahura Mazda). Translators differ as to whether in this passage Fire is called " the Joy of Mazda Ahura," or not,[1] but enough has been adduced to show that the character of Asha as Instructor, as Truth, as " skilled Adviser " of God, as " son of the Wise Lord," approaches exceedingly closely to that of Wisdom as Instructress, as master-workman,[2] and as Jahve's delight. Asha provides a much closer analogy to Wisdom than does either Vohu mano or Armaiti. Armaiti has traditionally (cf. Plutarch, above) the name Sophia and is of feminine gender (see note, p. 247), but as Bultmann states : " The name Wisdom for the divinity of Revelation is as unessential as is the feminine gender." [3] This is evident from the fact that in the Fourth Gospel it is the masculine Logos or Word upon whom the functions of Wisdom devolve.

In other passages of Prov. 1–9, besides those we have cited above as referring to personified Wisdom, there are what might appear to be traces of contact between Judaism and Iranian thought. We choose one in particular, as it bears out what has been said regarding the nature of Asha as Law and Fire. In Prov. 6[23] it is said : " For the commandment is a lamp (nēr) and the Law (Torah) is light ('or)." That here we have possibly more than the application of a metaphor, metaphor though it remains, is seen from the fact that this type of comparison in Judaism (cf. Ps. 119) becomes increasingly common

---

[1] Cf. Volz, p. 342, " Die Freude des Maz. Ahura "; and Geldner, op. cit. p. 15.

[2] In the description of creation in the Gathas (Jas. 44[3-5]) Ahura Mazda is twice called the Artist (Künstler). As in Prov. Jahve, so in the Gathas, Ahura Mazda is the Creator.

[3] Op. cit. p. 22.

as the Law is more hypostatically conceived.[1]   The full development of the notion is reached in the Fourth Book of Ezra (13[39]),
where it is said the Son of Man will destroy in the judgment
the godless nations " without labour by the Law which is
compared unto Fire." This is an example of the " theology
of light," as Reitzenstein calls it (*Die Hellenist. Mysterien-
religionen*, p. 292), which we see emerging in Judaism and which
he seems to be right in saying springs at least in its later and
more developed form from Persian thought.   There, in Iranian
religion, Ahura Mazda is the God of Light, Fire is His son, and
Fire (Asha) is the means of Judgment.   Already in Prov. 6[23],
though this possibly (see Oesterley's *Commentary*) is a later
addition to the collection of maxims in chapters 1–9, we are
justified in seeing a deposit of that ever-increasing mystic
thought which gave in Judaism to the Law and to Wisdom,
and later in Gnosticism to Gnosis, the property of enlightening
and which has its origin in the Iranian contrast of darkness
and light (σκότος and φῶς).[2]   In the Gathas (Jas. 50[10]) the
light is the element of Ahura Mazda and of Asha, His Law—
" The star-lights, the sun, the rising day-star, all redound to
Thy praise, O Asha, O wise Lord."

Of the chief features of Wisdom there is only one which
has not a counterpart in the description of Asha.   Wisdom is
spoken of as having built her house and " hewn out her seven
pillars."   A mythical trait of this sort is not found in Iranian
sources, but, as Reitzenstein has shown, leads us to Babylonia,
which appears indeed to have been the direction from which
Judaism received Iranian influence.   Chaldean and Iranian
thought in the time of Prov. 1–9 had largely coalesced.   In
his commentary Oesterley thinks that the picture of the seven
pillars of Wisdom is a description of an ordinary well-to-do
house ; three pillars on either side of the quadrangle and one
at the end farthest from the entrance.   " The end where the

---

[1] See Briggs, *I.C.C.* Psalms.
[2] On the Law, Wisdom, and Light, see *Origins of Hanukkah*, p. 178 f.

entrance was would have no pillar in order to leave the space
at the entry free." Reitzenstein (*Iranische Erlösungsmysterium*,
p. 208), remarking that it is an adventitious idea of exegetes
to explain the seven pillars in this way, says that Oriental
houses have four or nine pillars, but that even if a house with
seven pillars could be found, this would not satisfy the conception that the house rests on them. Reitzenstein would
appear to be perfectly right—and Gressmann and Bultmann
agree with his view—in seeing behind the picture of the seven
pillars the impression made on the world of the time by the
great temple of Babylon, the House of the foundation of the
heaven and the earth, which Herodotus (I. 181) describes.
Seven immense towers, one above the other, reached mountain-
like to the skies and supported the House of Life, the House
of the Mountain, the room in which was the nightly couch of
the God and of a priestess, who obviously represented a
consort goddess. From this reference to the House of Life,
the House which was the bond between heaven and earth,
we may interpret the picture of the Foolish woman who, also
like Wisdom, sits at the door of her House, but whose guests
are as the shades of Sheol in the land of Death.

Our examination of the figure of Wisdom in Prov. 1–9 thus
leads to the conclusion that Wisdom in Judaism owes its origin
to Iranian thought upon the Amesha Spentas, in particular to
the conception of Asha. That Iranian religion as mediated to
Judaism was interwoven with Babylonian elements is indicated
by the description of the House of Wisdom and later (p. 259 f)
we shall observe that this Babylonian element in the description
of Wisdom in Prov. 1–9 reveals more than a mythological
ornamentation. Doubtless the Gathas, both in form and in
religious beliefs, display quite a different world of thought from
that which appears in the first section of the Book of Proverbs.
There is no borrowing *en bloc* on the part of the latter, nor,
indeed, would we expect this. Heinisch, who rejects the
supposition that Jewish Wisdom speculation received any

influence from Iran, points to differences between the Zoroastrian hypostases and the Jewish Wisdom. " It is striking," he says, " that the heavenly beings [of Persian thought] have so much significance for the great judgment after death . . . while these after-life notions play no rôle in the Book of Proverbs nor in Jesus Sirach." [1] In the Gathas there is not that emphatic warning against adultery from which Wisdom shields and protects. Also, Heinisch stresses that while in Judaism Wisdom is a personified attribute of God, in Zoroastrianism the divine beings represent nature-deities who have been reformed into personified abstract ideas. But these divergencies are not such as can be regarded as ruling out the probability of contact. We cannot hope to find all the features of Iranian belief concerning the Amesha Spentas in Judaism. We have already seen how, although the wisdom-writers cannot but have been aware of the Egyptian belief in an after-life and judgment, they did not in their loans from the Egyptian wisdom-writings assimilate the Egyptian teaching of a future world. The same attitude Judaism preserved so long as possible in regard to Iranian belief in the resurrection of the dead. The large part which warnings against adultery play in the latest collection of Jewish maxims may well be an independent characteristic due to the didactic purpose of the book and the social conditions of the age, but the need for such moral instruction may not be dissociated from the background of religious practices and thought, where Jahve Himself was conceived of as having a female consort.[2] The contrast in the Gathas is between Asha and the Druj, that is, between Belief (Truth) and Falsehood, between Good and Evil, Knowledge and Ignorance, Light and Darkness, Life and Death (cf. Jasna 30[4-6]); in Prov. 1–9 the contrast between Wisdom and Foolishness is essentially the same.[3] To point out such differences as Heinisch

---

[1] Op. cit. p. 45.   [2] Cf. above, p. 229 f. and below p. 295 f.
[3] On these contrasts (Persian dualism) in Test. xii. Cf. Meyer, op. cit. Bd. ii. p. 106. Reitzenstein (Studien zum antiken Synkretismus, p. 19), says

indicates between the Jewish and the Persian speculation is
not sufficient for a proof of Jewish independence. What
Judaism did take over was in accordance with its own needs,
was interpreted by its own spirit and was not a slavish borrowing.
What is astonishing is how many of the features of personified
Wisdom as divine Intermediary closely correspond to the older
Iranian picture of Asha and Asha's functions. In this connection it is of interest to note the observation which Hölscher
has made (*op. cit.* p. 185, note 3) in regard to the frequent poetic
personifications of " Goodness and Truth " in the later literature
of Judaism (Ps. 89³. ¹⁵, 57⁴, 61⁸, 40¹² ; cf. Prov. 20²⁸, 3³, 14²² ;
Ps. 85¹¹ᶠ. ; Isa. 16⁵). "These evidently correspond," he says,
" to Vohu mano and Asha of the Gathas." [1]

6

The figure of Wisdom, who, in Prov. 1–9, is represented as
begotten of God and in some sense as His assistant in creation,
is further developed in the Hellenistic age. Some of the most
prominent of the new features are : Wisdom " came forth from
the mouth of the Most High " (Sir. 24³) ; Her throne " was
in the pillar of cloud " (v.⁴) ; She compassed the heavens and
walked in the chaotic depths (v.⁵) ; Wisdom held sway over
every people and nation, and sought a resting-place among
them, but the Creator persuaded her to make her dwelling-
place in Israel. Wisdom took up her abode in Jerusalem
(vv.⁶⁻¹¹) and there exercised her authority. According to

(with reference to Jas. 30⁴⁻⁶): "These Oriental fundamental ideas must be
fully appreciated if we would understand only that single sentence in the
great prologue of St. John: 'In Him was Life and the Life was the Light of
men and the Light shines in the Darkness,' etc.; indeed if we would understand the whole of that great hymn."

[1] Schraeder, *op. cit.* p. 324, note 1, objects that LXX translates Hebrew
ḥesed we-emeth " grace (goodness) and truth " by ἔλεος καὶ ἀλήθεια, while
Vohu mano is rendered by Plutarch as εὔνοια not ἔλεος. But this techni-
cality of translation hardly prejudices Hölscher's supposition. The Hebrew
Ḥesed provides an excellent translation or equivalent for Vohu mano.

1 Enoch 42[1. 2], Wisdom found no place where she might dwell among the children of men, so returned to heaven and took her seat among the angels (cf. 1 Enoch 84[3], 94[5]). Finally, in Sirach (24[23]), Wisdom is equated with " the book of the Covenant of the Most High, the law which Moses commanded." With this we must connect the statement (Sir. 1[14]) that, " To fear the Lord is the beginning of Wisdom and with the faithful was she [Wisdom] created in the womb." Upon this follows a verse which Smend conjectures read in the original Hebrew : " With men of truth hath she been established for ever " (1[15]). In the Wisdom of Solomon, where Wisdom is described as the Artificer of all things (7[22]), Wisdom is " an effluence of the glory of the Almighty," " more mobile than any motion," " a breath of the power of God," " an effulgence from everlasting light and an unspotted mirror of the working of God and an image of His goodness " (7[24-26]). She " passes into holy souls " (v.[27]), and " being compared with light, she is found to be before it " (v.[29]). She shares with God the heavenly throne (9[4]) and is the beloved of the Sovereign Lord (8[3]). She is " initiated into the knowledge of God and chooses out for Him His works " (8[4]). Wisdom is the saviour of men (9[18]). The youth takes her for his bride (8[2]) and because of her obtains immortality (8[13]). She is the revelation of God, sent from the heavenly throne to man (9[10]). In 2 Enoch (30[8A]) it is said that Wisdom received from God the commission to create man.

In this characteristization of Wisdom in the Hellenistic period there is a considerable advance in speculative thought, particularly in respect of the identification in Sirach (cf. 1 Bar. 4[1]) of Wisdom, with the Law and the idea that Wisdom is created in the faithful in the mother's womb. Both of these conceptions support and substantiate that which we have observed in the earlier Wisdom passages in regard to the connection of the hypostases Wisdom and Asha. As Asha (Belief, Truth, Religion) is the Law, the identification of Wisdom with the Law, " the book of the covenant of the Most High,

the commands of Moses " only represents a closer approximation
of the Iranian and Jewish figures. In the Hellenistic period
Iranian influence upon Jewish thought had become more acute.
The later idea that the Law was " the precious instrument
wherewith the world was created " (Sayings of the Fathers 3[19])
is doubtless rather a carrying out to its logical consequence
of the thought already initiated by the equation of the Law
and Wisdom than due to a further leaning up~n Persian conceptions ; but, with this, the process, started by contact with
Zoroastrian religion, reached completion. Also the altogether
new notion that Wisdom—or the Law as the same as Wisdom
—enters into the soul of the faithful at birth or is created
together with the soul, brings us to the same source from which
the figure of Wisdom originally sprung. In *Test*. xii., a book
which, as Meyer shows, is particularly inspired by Persian
dualistic thought, we meet with the conception of the Law
as enlightening every man. There (Lev. 14[4]) Levi says : " Yea,
ye shall bring a curse upon your race, because the light of
the Law which was given to lighten every man, this ye seek
to destroy by teaching commandments contrary to the ordinances
of God." We recognize the same phrase and idea when, in
the prologue of the Fourth Gospel, it is said of the Logos, " in
him was Life and the Life was the Light of men." In Sirach,
Wisdom has a wider and a narrower application. In the first,
she is poured over all God's works and all flesh has something
of her (1[9f.]) ; in the narrower aspect, she attaches herself to the
faithful or pious ($\pi\iota\sigma\tau o\acute{\iota}$), *a parte potiori* the members of Sirach's
own race, in the mother's womb. Now in what appears to be
an understudy of Asha, namely, the *Daēna*, another personification of Religion or Belief, Iranian religion specified the better
" I " or " Self," [1] considering it (or her) as the reflection or
double of the soul. Like Wisdom in Sirach, she appears to be

---

[1] See my *Origins of the Festival of Hanukkah*, p. 180, note 1, on the Daēna.
Also Reitzenstein, *Die hellenist. Mysterienrelig.*, p. 168. Cf. Gatha Ahuna-
vaiti (Jas. 30[11]) and Haug's (*op. cit.* p. 152), note on *daena*.

joined to the soul of man.   When the pious man dies his Daēna
comes to meet him.   She is described exactly as Wisdom is
in Sirach and the Wisdom of Solomon, as a beautiful and radiant
maiden.   The pious man, we are told in *Yasht*, xxii. 1–36,
asks who she is.   She answers : " I am thy Daēna, O youth,
thou that thinkest good, speakest and doest and art of good
belief."   She reveals to him that it is his earthly piety that
has made her beautiful.   She has an evil counterpart corresponding to Folly in Prov. chap. 9.   Gressmann,[1] indeed for this
reason, among others, regarded the Daēna as the prototype
of the Jewish Wisdom.   But while the character and functions
of the Daēna are too slight to account for the origin of Wisdom
in Judaism there is great probability that later, as being essentially an understudy of Asha, she did contribute to the psychological conception, in Sirach, of Wisdom as the companion of
the soul of the pious.   How fruitful the idea of the Daēna was
is seen from the fact that in Manichæism, which represents
the last stage of Iranian religion in the third and fourth centuries
A.D., we have also an account of this " virgin who is like to the
soul of this perfect(ed) one," appearing to the perfect one after
his death, to save him and guide his soul to heaven.[2]   She is
the " virgin of light," whom Augustine (*contra Faustum*, xx. 6)
mentions as the male-female being, Wisdom, of the Manichæan
doctrine.   In Mandæism, in which the same stream of Iranian
thought runs, the place of this virgin is taken by Manda d'Haije,
that is, by "knowledge of life " (γνῶσις ζωῆς) or by " knowledge of God " (γνῶσις θεοῦ) who is called the image or reflection
of the soul.[3]   The language of Sirach and the Wisdom of
Solomon may be viewed as having received not a little of its
content from this Iranian conception of the higher " Self."
In Sirach 14[20f.], 51[13f.]   Wisdom is a noble and tender woman

---

[1] *Zeitsch. für Kirchengesch.* xli. 1922 " Das religionsgesch. Problem usw,"
p. 174.
   [2] See Reitzenstein, *Iran. Erlös-Mysterium*, p. 28.
   [3] Cf. Reitzenstein, *op. cit.* p. 33 f. Cf. pp. 173 f., 178.

whom he who is desirous of her seeks to know and possess. When he has found her (Wisdom-Law), " she will meet him as a mother and as a youthful wife she will receive him " (15²). She is " beheld of them that love her " (Sap. 6¹²). She is fairer than the sun and surpasses the stars in light (Sap. 7²⁹). Immortality is the gift of living with her and of kinship with her (Sap. 8¹⁶ᶠ·).

From the account which we have given of the origin of the figure of Wisdom in Judaism, tracing the prototype of this figure to the Asha of the Gathas, the earliest documents of Zoroastrianism, it is evident that no room is left, *so far as the origin of Wisdom is concerned,* for such influence as Reitzenstein supposed to proceed from the Isis-Sophia theology (cf. p. 235 above). In view of the great missionary activity of the Isis-cult, it is not unlikely that in the Hellenistic period this theology was known, not only to Alexandrian Judaism, but also, as Schencke thinks (p. 81), in Palestine. But whatever influence this teaching had upon the Jewish Wisdom speculation, it could only be in the development of such features of Wisdom as are not accounted for in the older Persian sources. The case which Reitzenstein makes out for Egyptian influence upon Jewish Wisdom speculation is strongest in respect of the Wisdom of Solomon (*circa* 30 B.C.), and here in this book Egyptian influence, he admits, is mingled with that of Stoic and Platonic ideas.[1] Similarly, we must also reckon with Greek thought as having inspired certain of the later characteristics of Wisdom. When Wisdom, according to 1 Enoch 42² (105–64 B.C.), after seeking a place among the children of men, retires to heaven and there takes up her abode, whence she will return to the world in the Messianic times (5⁸, 48¹, 49¹ᶠ·, 91¹⁰· cf. 2 Bar. 44¹⁴ ; 4 Ezra 8⁵²) [2] we have quite certainly an echo of the legend of Dikē (Δίκη, Aratus, *Phain.* 96 f.). Dikē, in

---

[1] *Zwei religionsgesch. Fragen,* p. 109 f. Cf. Poimandres, p. 44 f. See Schencke's criticism of Reitzenstein, *op. cit.* p. 81.

[2] See Charles, *Apoc.,* vol. ii., note on 1 Enoch 42².

the golden age when Kronos ruled, had her abode with men, remained yet with them in the age of silver, though wandering to the mountains, but, when the age of iron came, took flight to the heavens and shines there as "the virgin" among the constellations.[1] Later the Pesikta of Rab Kahana,[2] which reflects very old Midrashic tradition, renders more faithfully than 1 Enoch the Dikē legend applying it to the Shekinah (the Glory or Presence of God), a kindred figure to Wisdom.

7

In the foregoing pages we have examined the features of personified Wisdom as divine intermediary and have traced these in the main to the influence of Persian thought. We had occasion to surmise (see above, p. 230) that the Jewish conception of Wisdom arose through opposition to the sensual cults of surrounding peoples to which Israel was drawn. It now remains to place this surmise in the light of greater certainty, and to do this we must now return to fuller consideration of that element of Babylonian mythology which we saw revealed in the picture of the seven pillars of Wisdom, and, further, pay particular regard to the "woman of folly" (*ēšeth kesīluth*, Prov. 9[13]), with whom Wisdom is there contrasted. It is possible that from this contrast Wisdom herself has absorbed certain features of Babylonian (Chaldean) origin.

Gustav Boström (*Proverbiastudien*, Lund, 1935), in a highly valuable critical study of Prov. 1–9, under the title of "Wisdom and the Strange Woman," [3] shows that the *strange* woman

---

[1] See Thalheim (article "Dikē-Justice") in Pauly-Wissowa's *Ency.* Aratus applies to Dike Hesiod's legend (see *Works and Days*, line 197 f.) of Aidos and Nemesis. In the Hellenistic period Iranian-Babylonian Aion-mysticism (teaching regarding world-periods) had united with Hellenic mythology of the golden age. See Norden, *Geburt des Kindes*, p. 29 f.; E. Meyer, *op. cit.* Bd. ii. 189 f.; Wernicke, Αἰων, in Pauly-Wissowa; G. Beer (Kautzsch, *Pseudep.*, Bd. ii. p. 261) on 1 Enoch 42, note k.

[2] On the Pesikta of R. K., see *Origins of Hanukkah*, p. 228.

[3] "Die Weisheit und das fremde Weib."

(*iššah zarah*; *nokriyyah*; 2^{16}, $5^{3f.}$, 6^{24}, 7^5) whom the youth,
exhorted to turn to Wisdom, is warned to avoid and shun, does
not signify, as commentators have commonly believed, simply
the unmarried prostitute or simply the woman who is an
adulteress, the wife of "*another*," but is a *foreign* woman, a
woman of another race. The Hebrew word *zarah* (strange),
especially when explained by the parallel epithet *nokriyyah*,
can bear only the literal sense of *foreign*. The strange woman,
who is none other than the "woman of folly," is a foreigner in
Israel, who invites the young Israelite to be her partner in the
fertility cult which has its well-known prototype in the worship
of Ishtar or Astarte. In Prov. 7 the strange or foreign woman
is a married woman. That her invitation to the youth is to no
ordinary act of adultery appears in her assurance (7^{14}) : " Sacrifices of peace-offerings are upon me (that is, are obligatory or
due from me) ; to-day I have paid my vows." The youth
partakes with her in the sacrificial meal and with the cult-feast
is associated the sexual act. " The vow of the strange woman
is aphroditic and the offering of her body in service of the deity
is a consequence of the vow " (Boström, *op. cit.* p. 108). Ordinary adultery is certainly mentioned in ch. 6^{29}, but the phrase-
ology and thought in the passages dealing with the strange
woman are quite different from those that refer to mere adultery
in ch. $6^{29f.}$. If the strange woman was simply " the wife of the
neighbour " (cf. v.^{29}), why, asks Boström,[1] does this latter phrase
occur not a single time in the by no means rare or brief sections
which speak of the strange woman ? This query is all the more
significant if, as Oesterley [2] thinks, the verses $^{29-31}$ in ch. 6 are
an interruption of the thought of the chapter, and betray the
hand of a later wisdom-writer.

The practical and religious motive of the foreign fertility
cult was the blessing of obtaining children.[3] Vows were paid to

---

[1] *Op. cit.* p. 144.   [2] Commentary, *ad. loc.*
[3] *Johannesbuch der Mandäer*, 80, 4–7, and Boström, *op. cit.* p. 108 f., on
this and other motives of sacred prostitution.

the goddess of fecundity and the rites were in her honour. To
such vows, Boström conjectures, the legal decisions of Num.
30⁴⁻¹⁷ *originally* stood in close relationship. These legal decisions
place the vows of women under the control of father or husband
should he come to hear of the vow. In Num. 30 much is made of
this proviso. In Prov. 7¹⁹ the married woman fulfils her religious
vow without the knowledge of her husband. The form of the
laws in Num. 30⁴ᶠ· may reflect Canaanite practice. Ezekiel
(16³) recognizes that the " abominations " which he condemns in the Jerusalem cultus are of Canaanite heritage.
He appears to refer to the rites of religious prostitution
(cf. Hos. 4¹³ᶠ·).

It is not necessary to weigh in detail the evidence which
Boström (p. 129 f.) adduces to prove that a special mark of the
fertility cults was sexual intercourse *between people of different
races.* See Herodotus. I. 199 (ἀνδρὶ ξείνῳ), Lucian's *De Syria
dea,* § 6, and Socrates' *Historia Ecclesiastica,* I. 18. Nor need
we inquire into the significance of the custom. Presumably
the original primitive notion was that union of this kind brought
new powers of fecundity to the tribe. It is sufficient if we
appreciate that in the eyes of a strict Jahvism such cults were
per se foreign and that in practice the danger to Jahvism would
spring from the numerous foreign residents (traders) in the towns
of Palestine, particularly in Jerusalem.

When now we seek to answer the question what particular
fertility cult the passages in Prov. 1–9 concerning the strange
woman have in view, we are led at once to the Babylonian worship of Ishtar. In the description of the house of Wisdom as
a house of seven pillars (Prov. 9¹), Reitzenstein, as we have
mentioned, saw a direct reference (p. 252 above) to the seven
étages or pillars of the temple (the tower) of Babel. In opposition to the false House of Life, but after the same plan, Wisdom
raised her House. But this observation of Reitzenstein only
touches upon a wider field of mythological conceptions, according to which the seven planets were represented as the seven

pillars of the cosmos. Boström (p. 5 f.) proves clearly, particularly from Pausanias (III. xx. 9), that the idea of the seven planets as pillars of the world structure is ancient tradition, and that the notion of the seven pillars in Prov. 9[1] is by no means specifically Jewish, but was taken over by Judaism. He argues that the description of the house of Wisdom has not in view the temple of Babylon, but flows directly from the Babylonian astral mythology. This is possibly true. This mythology appears to have been responsible for the plan of the temple at Babel itself and for this plan's cosmological significance.[1] Nevertheless, we may well accept the view of Reitzenstein that the great temple at Babylon did supply the immediate prototype of the house of Wisdom. That temple evidently made tremendous impression on surrounding peoples. And, as the cuneiform inscriptions show (Jensen, *Kosmologie*, p. 99 f. ; cf. Anz, *op. cit.* p. 84), the local name for that temple was the *Tower of the Seven Planets*. The building would most certainly be the most lively reminder of the mythological conceptions it embodied. It is, however, what may be deduced from this mythology that is of greater moment. In Gnostic writings Wisdom (Sophia) is said to be the " Mother " of the seven planets, and there we also meet with the idea that the planets are the creators of the world.[2] If we seek to trace these thoughts to the Babylonian source to which such conceptions point, the mother of the seven planets can only be represented by Ishtar, " the Queen of heaven," who bears the name " Ishtar of the stars." [3] And if this be so, that is if Ishtar is intimately connected with that mythology, which leaves its deposit in the description of the house of Wisdom, in Prov. 9[1], we must also

---

[1] Cf. Anz, *Zur Frage nach dem Ursprung des Gnostizismus*, p. 83 f. and note 5, p. 141 above. Also J. Berger, *Elementary Education in the Talmud*, p. 16, *re* the early astronomical belief that the planets corrected the false ambulation of the zodiacal signs.

[2] Bousset, *Hauptprobleme der Gnosis*, cap. i.

[3] J. Plessis, *Étude sur les textes concernant Ištar-Aštarté*, Paris, 1921, pp. 77, 79, 83, 204. Cf. Jer. 7[18], 44[17t].

identify this same Ishtar-Astarte, the goddess of love, as the
deity of the cult referred to in the descriptive passage (Prov. 7)
concerning the *foreign* woman. Thus Boström is led, and, as
it seems, rightly, to the conclusion that the Jewish figure of
Wisdom is " a compensation for the dethroned Astarte," who
from the point of view of Judaism might be said to be " the
Woman of Folly " herself.

But may we reach the conclusion that Wisdom owes her
origin to the contrast with Ishtar ? Or, to put the question in
a better form, does this contrast supply the content of the figure
of Wisdom ? Boström (p. 174) wisely suggests no more than
that this contrast provides us with one of the roots (*mit einer
der Wurzeln*) of the Jewish conception of Wisdom. The practical religious issues of the time in which Prov. 1–9 were composed, the need of opposition to the type of foreign cult which
attracted women in the days of Jeremiah (44[17f.]) and left its
mark upon the religion of the Jewish diasporate in Elephantiné,
may be held to be an important factor in the emergence and
development of Wisdom. Such features of Wisdom as are disclosed in her being compared with a " mother " and " bride,"
whom the youth is urged " to love " and " embrace " may
perhaps best be explained by opposition to the prevalent and
seductive Ishtar, Astarte, and Anath cults. But here we must
distinguish between the more outward and the more fundamental characteristics of Wisdom. Wisdom is, after all, a cold
substitute for Ishtar. The conception of Wisdom is a *theological*
product of the wisdom-schools, intensely practical in the main
though the wisdom-writers are.

Much could be advanced in support of the view that Wisdom
is no other than Ishtar purified and converted to Judaism.
Boström's opinion is that there once existed a myth to the effect
that Ishtar created the cosmos with the help of the seven planets,
who were conceived of as assistant divine beings (*op. cit.* p. 12 f.).
She is called " creator of wisdom," " counsellor of the gods "
(cf. Heinisch, *op. cit.* p. 25).   Gula, who appears to be a form of

Ishtar, is said to " be the preparer of the heaven and the earth." [1]
Another form of Ishtar, Siduri Sabitu, is called the " goddess of
wisdom, the guardian-spirit of life " (Surpu, II. 172).   But
wisdom is not the chief or most prominent characteristic of
Ishtar.   Other Babylonian deities are more suitable as counterparts to Wisdom both in respect of the attribute of wisdom
itself and of being world-creative forces or principles (cf. *Mummu*,
amatu, above).   Above all, the opposition seen in Prov. 1–9
itself between the Supreme God, concerning whom it is said
that the strange woman " forgets the covenant of her God "
(2^{17}),[2] and the deity of the fertility cult in whose honour the
woman offers herself, displays that trait of polytheistic religion
to which Volz refers (see p. 244 above) when he remarks in
regard to the Iranian intermediary powers that these are not,
as are the divine agents in the Babylonian and Egyptian religions, separated from the supreme God, but are, as it were, the
features of His face.

When we consider the character of Wisdom as intermediary
Being active in creation, her relationship to Jahve not as a mere
associate deity but, as begotten of Him, an " effluence " of His
glory, an " effulgence from everlasting light," a subtle power,
" more mobile than any motion " (Sap. Sol. $7^{22f.}$), her identification with the Law, with Religion or Belief, we may perceive
that she owes her origin not solely or chiefly to Jewish conflict
with Babylonian Ishtar worship, but rather to Jewish contact
with that Chaldean-Iranian syncretic religion in which the more
speculative, ethical, and spiritual element is Iranian.

[1] Hehn, *Die biblische und die babyl. Gottesidee*, 1913, p. 48 f.

[2] For exegesis of Prov. 2^{17}, see Boström, *op. cit.* pp. 18 f., 33 f., 136 ; " her
God " is the *foreign* (*supreme*) God of the strange woman.

INDEX

INDEX

THE KERR LECTURESHIP.

THE " KERR LECTURESHIP " was founded by the TRUSTEES of the late Miss JOAN KERR of Sanquhar, under her Deed of Settlement, and formally adopted by the United Presbyterian Synod in May 1886. In the following year, May 1887, the provisions and conditions of the Lectureship, as finally adjusted, were adopted by the Synod, and embodied in a Memorandum, printed in the Appendix to the Synod Minutes, p. 489.

On the union of the United Presbyterian Church with the Free Church of Scotland in October 1900, the necessary changes were made in the designation of the object of the Lectureship and the persons eligible for appointment to it, so as to suit the altered circumstances. And at the General Assembly of 1901 it was agreed that the Lectureship should in future be connected with the Glasgow College of the United Free Church. From the Memorandum, as thus amended, the following excerpts are here given :—

II. The amount to be invested shall be £3000.

III. The object of the Lectureship is the promotion of the Study of Scientific Theology in the United Free Church of Scotland.

The Lectures shall be upon some such subjects as the following, viz. :—

A. Historic Theology—

(1) Biblical Theology, (2) History of Doctrine, (3) Patristics, with special reference to the significance and authority of the first three centuries.

B. Systematic Theology—

    (1) Christian Doctrine—(*a*) Philosophy of Religion, (*b*) Comparative Theology, (*c*) Anthropology, (*d*) Christology, (*e*) Soteriology, (*f*) Eschatology.

    (2) Christian Ethics—(*a*) Doctrine of Sin, (*b*) Individual and Social Ethics, (*c*) The Sacraments, (*d*) The Place of Art in Religious Life and Worship.

Further, the Committee of Selection shall, from time to time, as they think fit, appoint as the subject of the Lectures any important Phases of Modern Religious Thought or Scientific Theories in their bearing upon Evangelical Theology. The Committee may also appoint a subject connected with the practical work of the Ministry as subject of Lecture, but in no case shall this be admissible more than once in every five appointments.

IV. The appointments to this Lectureship shall be made in the first instance from among the Licentiates or Ministers of the United Free Church of Scotland, of whom no one shall be eligible who, when the appointment falls to be made, shall have been licensed for more than twenty-five years, and who is not a graduate of a British University, preferential regard being had to those who have for some time been connected with a Continental University.

V. Appointments to this Lectureship not subject to the conditions in Section IV. may also from time to time, at the discretion of the Committee, be made from among eminent members of the Ministry of any of the Nonconformist Churches of Great Britain and Ireland, America, and the Colonies, or of the Protestant Evangelical Churches of the Continent.

VI. The Lecturer shall hold the appointment for three years.

VII. The number of Lectures to be delivered shall be left to the discretion of the Lecturer, except thus far, that in no case shall there be more than twelve or less than eight.

VIII. The Lectures shall be published at the Lecturer's own expense within one year after their delivery.

IX. The Lectures shall be delivered to the students of the Glasgow College of the United Free Church of Scotland.

XII. The Public shall be admitted to the Lectures.